WEIGHT TRAINING

Steps to Success

Thomas R. Baechle, EdD
Creighton University
Omaha, Nebraska

Barney R. Groves, PhD
Virginia Commonwealth University
Richmond, Virginia

Leisure Press
Champaign, Illinois

Library of Congress Cataloging-in-Publication Data

Baechle, Thomas R., 1943-
    Weight training : steps to success / Thomas R. Baechle, Barney R.
  Groves.
           p. cm. -- (Steps to success activity series)
    Includes bibliographical references (p.).
    ISBN 0-88011-451-7
    1. Weight training. I. Groves, Barney R., 1936- . II. Title
  III. Series.
  GV546.3.B34 1992
  613.7'13--dc20   91-25316
                                      CIP

ISBN: 0-88011-451-7

Acquisitions Editor: Brian Holding
Developmental Editor: Judy Patterson Wright, PhD
Assistant Editors: Valerie Hall, Moyra Knight, Dawn Levy, and Kari Nelson
Copyeditor: Wendy Nelson
Proofreader: Laurie McGee
Production Director: Ernie Noa
Typesetter: Kathy Boudreau-Fuoss
Text Design: Keith Blomberg
Text Layout: Denise Lowry, Tara Welsch, Kimberlie Henris
Cover Design: Jack Davis
Cover Photo: Wilmer Zehr
Line Drawings: Keith Blomberg
Chart Diagrams: Kathy Boudreau-Fuoss
Printer: United Graphics

Instructional Designer for the Steps to Success Activity Series: Joan N. Vickers, EdD, University of Calgary, Calgary, Alberta, Canada

Leisure Press books are available at special discounts for bulk purchase for sales promotions, premiums, fund-raising, or educational use. Special editions or book excerpts can also be created to specification. For details, contact the Special Sales Manager at Leisure Press.

Printed in the United States of America

10   9   8   7   6   5   4   3   2

Leisure Press
A Division of Human Kinetics Publishers, Inc.
Box 5076, Champaign, IL 61825-5076
1-800-747-4457

Canada Office:
Human Kinetics Publishers, Inc.
P.O. Box 2503, Windsor, ON N8Y 4S2
1-800-465-7301 (in Canada only)

Europe Office:
Human Kinetics Publishers (Europe) Ltd.
P.O. Box IW14
Leeds LS16 6TR
England
0532-781708

Contents

Series Preface   v
Preface   vii
The Steps to Success Staircase   ix
The Renaissance in Weight Training   1
Physiological Considerations   4
Nutritional Considerations   13
Women in Weight Training   16
Preparing Your Body to Train   18

Safety and Technique Fundamentals

Step 1   Using Equipment Safely   20
Step 2   Lifting and Spotting Fundamentals   29

Practice Procedures

Step 3   Identifying Practice Procedures   40

Selecting Exercises for the Basic Program

Step 4   Selecting a Chest Exercise   45
Step 5   Selecting a Back Exercise   59
Step 6   Selecting a Shoulder Exercise   70
Step 7   Selecting a Bicep (Arm) Exercise   83
Step 8   Selecting a Tricep (Arm) Exercise   94
Step 9   Selecting a Leg Exercise   106
Step 10   Selecting an Abdominal Exercise   115

Charting Workouts

Step 11   Completing Your First Workout Chart   124
Step 12   Making Needed Workout Changes   128

Program Design Variables

Step 13   How to Select and Arrange Exercises   133
Step 14   How to Manipulate Training Loads, Reps, Sets, and Rest Periods   141
Step 15   How to Determine Training Frequency and Program Variation   152
Step 16   How to Tailor a Program to Your Needs   163

Rating Your Total Progress   172

Appendixes

A: Alternate Exercises   174
B: Muscles of the Body   188
C: Weight Training Workout Chart   189
Glossary   192
References   196
About the Authors   197

Series Preface

The Steps to Success Activity Series is a breakthrough in skill instruction through the development of complete learning progressions—the *steps to success*. These *steps* help individuals quickly perform basic skills successfully and prepare them to acquire advanced skills readily. At each step, you are encouraged to learn at your own pace and to integrate your new skills into the total action of the activity.

The unique features of the Steps to Success Activity Series are the result of comprehensive development—through analyzing existing activity books, incorporating the latest research from the sport sciences and consulting with students, instructors, teacher educators, and administrators. This groundwork pointed up the need for three different types of books—for participants, instructors, and teacher educators—which we have created and together comprise the Steps to Success Activity Series.

This participant's book, *Weight Training: Steps to Success*, is a self-paced, step-by-step guide that you can use as an instructional tool. The unique features of this participant's book include

- sequential illustrations that clearly show proper technique,
- helpful suggestions for detecting and correcting errors,
- excellent practice progressions with accompanying *Success Goals* for measuring performance, and
- checklists for rating your technique.

A comprehensive instructor's guide, *Teaching Weight Training: Steps to Success* (in press) will accompany this participant's book. It will emphasize how to individualize instruction. Each *step* of the instructor's guide will promote successful teaching and learning with

- teaching cues (*Keys to Success*) that emphasize fluidity, rhythm, and wholeness,
- criterion-referenced rating charts for evaluating a participant's initial skill level,
- suggestions for observing and correcting typical errors,
- tips for group management and safety,

- ideas for modifying the difficulty level,
- quantitative evaluations for all drills (*Success Goals*), and
- a complete test bank of written questions.

The series textbook, *Instructional Design for Teaching Physical Activities* (Vickers, 1990), explains the *steps to success* model, which is the basis for the Steps to Success Activity Series. Teacher educators can use this text in their professional preparation classes to help future teachers and coaches learn how to design effective physical activity programs in school, recreation, or community teaching and coaching settings.

After identifying the need for various texts, we refined the *steps to success* instructional design model and developed prototypes. Once these prototypes were fine-tuned, we carefully selected authors for the activities who were not only thoroughly familiar with their sports but also had years of experience in teaching them. Each author had to be known as a gifted instructor who understands the teaching of sport so thoroughly that he or she could readily apply the *steps to success* model.

Next, all of the manuscripts were carefully developed to meet the guidelines of the *steps to success* model. Then our production team, along with outstanding artists, created a highly visual, user-friendly series of books.

The result: The Steps to Success Activity Series is the premier sports instructional series available today.

This series would not have been possible without the contributions of the following:

- Dr. Rainer Martens, Publisher,
- Dr. Joan Vickers, instructional design expert,
- the staff of Human Kinetics Publishers, and
- the *many* students, teachers, coaches, consultants, teacher educators, specialists, and administrators who shared their ideas—and dreams.

Judy Patterson Wright
Series Editor

Preface

Weight training has become a very popular activity among students in our schools and colleges and among older adults interested in fitness and appearance. The reason for this popularity is quite simple. The results dramatically contribute to improved strength, muscle tone, and body reproportioning. Unfortunately, there aren't very many books on the subject that the inexperienced person can use with confidence. Often terminology is confusing, explanations are not clear, and readers are expected to assimilate too much information at one time. The approach taken in this book does not assume that one explanation or illustration is sufficient for becoming skilled at and knowledgeable about weight training. Instead, carefully developed procedures and drills accompany each step (chapter), providing ample practice and self-testing opportunities.

One focus of the book is on learning weight training exercises and developing the knowledge needed to design weight training programs. The exercise techniques that need to be learned progress from the simple to the complex, and the training loads progress from light to heavy—light while you are learning the exercises, heavier later to bring about exciting results! Organizing exercises and loads in this manner also offers the best opportunity to learn exercises quickly and without fear of injury.

You will find that the use of practice procedures, drills, and self-testing activities is certainly unique. It is unfortunate that it has taken so long to approach teaching the content and skills of weight training in this very effective way.

There are several people who directly or indirectly have influenced the development and completion of this book, whom we would like to thank. Of special note are our colleagues Drs. William Kraemer, Steven Fleck, John Garhammer, and Michael Stone, whose research contributions have added much to our knowledge of weight training. It is also appropriate to acknowledge the information sharing that has occurred through the educational activities of the National Strength and Conditioning Association. We would like to acknowledge Roger Earle, whose contributions to the content of this text were substantial, and Todd Bivins, who assisted with the illustrations. Critically important were the support and direction provided by Dr. Judy Patterson Wright, our developmental editor. Last, we want to thank Stacy Wepfer and Buddy LaBrenz, whose assistance in typing made the completion of this book a reality.

Thomas R. Baechle
Barney R. Groves

The Steps to Success Staircase

Get ready to climb a staircase—one that will lead you to become stronger, more fit, and knowledgeable about weight training. You cannot leap to the top; you get there by climbing one step at a time.

Each of the 16 steps you will take is an easy transition from the one before it. The first few steps of the staircase provide a foundation— a solid foundation of basic skills and concepts. As you progress further, you will be able to perform workouts in a safe and time-efficient manner, and you will know when and how to make needed changes in program intensity. As you near the top of the staircase, the climb eases, and you'll find that you have developed a sense of confidence in your weight training skills and knowledge, and you will be pleased with how your body is changing.

To understand how to build your training around the steps, familiarize yourself with the directions presented at the end of this section. The "Renaissance of Weight Training" section that follows will help you gain insights into and a better appreciation for weight training's tremendous popularity today. Also familiarize yourself with the "Physiological Considerations" and "Nutritional Considerations" sections to gain understanding of and appreciation for how your body reacts and adapts to training, and the importance of proper nutrition. Taking time to read the "Women in Weight Training" section will provide you with an understanding of special issues of importance. The section "Preparing Your Body to Train" properly prepares you to begin each workout.

Follow the same sequence each step (chapter) of the way:

1. Read the explanations of what is covered in the step, why the step is important, and how to execute or perform the step's focus, which may be a basic skill, concept, or approach, or a combination of them.
2. Follow the Keys to Success illustrations showing exactly how to position your body to execute each exercise correctly. There are three general parts to each exercise. One is a preparation phase where the techniques of getting into position are performed. The other two are execution phases, usually involving the performance of the upward and downward movements of an exercise. For each large muscle group exercise in the basic program, you may select one exercise from three choices: a free weight exercise and two machine exercises.
3. Look over the common errors that may occur and the recommendations for how to correct them.
4. The practice procedures and drills help you improve your skills through repetition and purposeful practice. Read the directions and the Success Goals for each drill. Practice accordingly and record your score. Compare your score with the Success Goal for the drill. You need to meet the Success Goal of each drill before moving on to practice the next one because the drills progress from easy to difficult. This sequence is designed specifically to help you achieve continual success.
5. As soon as you select all exercises in the basic program, you are ready to complete your first workout chart, make needed workout changes, and follow the basic program for 6 weeks (minimum). This is the time to evaluate your technique against the Keys to Success Checklists.
6. Steps 13 through 16 prepare you to design (instead of simply follow) a program, one especially for you. There are many helpful instructions, examples, and self-testing opportunities (with answers included) that will prepare you for the challenge. For example, formulas are provided to assist you in the difficult task of determining initial training loads and also for making needed adjustments to them.

7. Use the information in the appendixes to either add or replace alternate exercises within the basic program (see Appendix A), to locate specific muscles (see Appendix B), and to chart your workout progress (see Appendix C).

Good luck on your step-by-step journey of developing a strong, healthy, attractive body—a journey that will be confidence building, rich in successes, and fun!

The Renaissance in Weight Training

Demonstrations of strength have captured the interest and imagination of people as far back as ancient times, but the merits of activities designed to develop strength have not always been well understood or appreciated. For many years it was believed that training with weights provided few if any benefits and, in fact, would result in poor levels of flexibility and impair neuromuscular coordination. A special concern was that training with weights would result in tremendous increases in muscular size. This was a primary concern among women, many of whom had been led to believe that having a strong-looking physique, or being strong, was unfeminine. These myths kept many from enjoying the benefits of weight training. It was not until the 1930s, when two physical therapists, DeLorme and Wadkins, reported successful results using weight training in the rehabilitation of arm and leg injuries of soldiers, that the "renaissance" in attitudes about weight training began. The term *weight training* as used here pertains to the use of barbells, dumbbells, machines, and other equipment (weighted vests, bats, elastic tubing, and so on) for the purpose of improving fitness levels and appearance. *Strength training*, on the other hand, refers to the use of such equipment for the express purpose of improving athletic performance.

As weight training became more popular, it prompted researchers to study its effects, resulting in the discovery that the myths associated with weight training (e.g., that it reduces speed and causes "muscle-boundness") were unfounded. As the concerns about muscle hypertrophy (muscle size increase) and losses in speed, flexibility, and coordination dwindled, the benefits of increased strength (the ability to exert maximum force in a single effort), muscular endurance (the ability of a muscle to contract for an extended period of time without undue fatigue), and improved fitness became more apparent. Today we see people in all walks of life engaging in weight training—nonathletes as well as athletes in many sports, such as swimming, wrestling, baseball, softball, gymnastics, volleyball, tennis, and golf. Recently, training for endurance events, such as the marathon and triathalon, has begun to include strength training.

Simultaneous with the dispelling of myths and a more universal use of weights among athletes and the general public was the growth in companies producing weight training equipment. One in particular made a dramatic impact: Nautilus. The Nautilus equipment design and marketing strategy created a different image of weight training. The attractive and sophisticated machines placed in clean, well-lighted surroundings were a far cry from the rusty barbells and dumbbells typically found in the less-than-aesthetic surroundings of traditional weight rooms. These changes, along with others by competing equipment companies, made weight training not only an acceptable activity, but a trend-setting one among well-respected businesspeople.

Impetus has also come from competitive lifters—those who compete in weight lifting and power lifting. Competitive weight lifting includes "quick lifts" (snatch, and clean and jerk), whereas power lifting includes slower moving lifts (squat, bench press, dead lift). The lifts contested in power lifting require less skill, and the training typically produces greater muscularity, which explains some of the reasons for its growing popularity over weight lifting. Perhaps more popular, especially among women, is competitive bodybuilding, where contestants are judged on muscular size, symmetry (muscular balance), general impression (appearance, mannerisms, etc.), and posing skill.

WEIGHT TRAINING TODAY

Many colleges and professional sport teams have full-time strength and conditioning

1

coaches. Health clubs are filled with weight training enthusiasts, and high schools, colleges, and universities are offering weight training courses to thousands of students. In addition, weight training programs are also gaining in popularity among older populations, including individuals with osteoporosis and patients in cardiac rehabilitation programs.

Today, there are 1 million people weight training on a regular basis who probably do so for one or more of the following reasons: to improve their health status, to reproportion or sculpture their bodies for appearance's sake, for competitive purposes (Olympic-style weight lifting, power lifting, or body building), and athletic performance.

There is little doubt that weight training has gained universal acceptance as an expedient method of accomplishing these outcomes. The Dark Ages for weight training, marked by myths, have given way to scientific evidence encouraging its use and an enlightened understanding of its benefits. The educational organization best recognized throughout the world as the clearinghouse for accurate and up-to-date weight and strength training information is the National Strength and Conditioning Association (NSCA). The NSCA hosts state clinics and national and international conferences, publishes several types of journals, funds research and scholarships, and has its own certification program. For information about the NSCA, call 402-472-3000 or write to NSCA, P.O. Box 81410, Lincoln, NE 68501.

ESSENTIALS OF PRODUCTIVE TRAINING

As you begin your training, there are some suggestions that will make training more fun, safer, and more effective. The essentials to productive training presented here are described in more detail later.

Training on a Regular Basis

The adage ''Use it or lose it'' is, unfortunately, true regarding the body and its cardiovascular efficiency, strength, muscular endurance, flexibility, and lean muscle mass. The body is unlike any machine yet to be developed. The body's efficiency improves with use, and it deteriorates with disuse. This is in total contrast to machines. As researchers undertake studies involving older populations, it becomes apparent that individuals who follow regular exercise programs maintain their fitness levels. Herbert De Vries, a well-respected researcher, contends that the losses in strength typically observed in older individuals are more a function of sedentary living than of the natural aging process.

Gradual Increases in Training Intensity

The body adapts to the stresses of weight training when training occurs on a regular basis, and when the intensity of training sessions is progressively increased over a reasonable period of time. Conversely, when the intensity of training is haphazard, the body's ability to adapt and become stronger and more enduring is seriously compromised. The dramatic improvements typically observed in response to training do not happen under these conditions, and the excitement that prompts you to continue training is no longer present. As excitement dwindles, attendance at training sessions becomes more and more difficult, and improvements become nonexistent. Muscle soreness does not go away, which discourages further training.

Regular Attendance at Training Sessions

Sporadic training has often been the demise of many with good intentions. All too often, cessation of a regular training program begins with an innocent day of missing a workout and ends with missing many more. With each training session missed, the goal of improved fitness, strength, and appearance moves farther out of reach. It is important not to miss that first workout, because decreases in training status begin to occur after 72 hours of no training.

Attitude and Perseverance

To maximize the time spent in training, you must learn to push yourself to the uncomfortable point of muscle failure during many of your sets. You must be willing to persevere through the discomfort (not pain) that accompanies reaching this point. Believing that weight training can make dramatic changes in your health and physique—which it definitely can—is essential to making the commitment to train hard and regularly. Typically, you will feel the difference in muscle tone (firmness) immediately, and strength and endurance changes become somewhat noticeable after the 2nd or 3rd week. Be prepared, however, for variations in performance during the early stages of training, and do not become discouraged if one workout does not produce the outcomes of a previous one.

Your brain is going through a learning curve, too, as it tries to figure out which muscles to "recruit" (call into action) for which movement in each exercise. Thus, it is a time in which your neuromuscular system (your brain, nerves, and muscles) is learning to adapt to the stimulus of training. Be patient! This period is soon followed by significant gains in muscle tone and strength and the disappearance of muscle soreness. This is truly an exciting time in your program! At this point your attitude dictates the magnitude of the future gains you will experience.

Sound Nutrition

Nutrition is also a key factor. It makes no sense to train hard if you are not also eating nutritionally sound meals. Poor nutrition in itself can reduce strength, muscular endurance, and muscle hypertrophy. Because training puts great demands on your body, your body needs nutrients to encourage adaptation and promote gains. To neglect this aspect of your training program is definitely an oversight if you are serious about improving.

Although many who train are convinced that protein supplementation is vital to making gains, there is little research to support this belief. More information on nutrition and the issue of protein supplementation is included in the "Nutritional Considerations" section.

Adequate Rest

The intervening days of rest in your training program are really important to gains in strength, muscular endurance, and size. To train on consecutive days, without the rest that allows the body to adapt, may result in injury, a plateauing in gains, or a drop in performance.

Quality of Exercise Execution

Many people seem to believe that more repetitions in an exercise is synonymous with improvement, regardless of the technique used during execution. The speed with which repetitions (reps) are performed is a very important factor in your ability to execute quality repetitions. In exercise programs designed to develop power, explosive exercise movements are required. However, in a beginning program, slow, controlled movements are desired. Consider "slow" to mean that approximately 2 seconds are used to complete the upward and downward phases of an exercise. It is especially important that exercises be performed at a rate slow enough to permit full extension and flexion at a joint (e.g., in the bicep curl, the elbow is fully extended and then fully flexed). Jerking, slinging, and using momentum are not recommended ways to complete a repetition. Remember that *the quality of the performed exercise should be viewed as being more important than simply the number of repetitions performed*, especially when the goal is improved flexibility. Other recommendations concerning proper exercise execution are provided in Steps 4 through 10 and Appendix A.

Medical Clearance

A history of presence of certain conditions, such as joint (e.g., arthritis, surgery), respiratory (e.g., asthma), or cardiovascular (e.g., hypertension, arrhythmias, murmurs) problems, may or may not make weight training exercises an inappropriate activity to undertake; however, the implications of such conditions must be addressed before developing an exercise program, and certainly before exercise actually begins. Be sure to consult a physician if you have any of these conditions.

Physiological Considerations

When weight training occurs on a regular basis and is accompanied by wise eating habits, various systems of the body change in positive ways. Muscles become stronger, assume greater work loads, and show less fatigue with each additional session of training. The neuromuscular system works in better harmony, as the brain learns to selectively recruit specific muscle fibers that possess the needed characteristics to handle the various loads, speeds of movement, and movement patterns required in different exercises. Some changes in the cardiovascular system also occur, although they are minimal. These adaptive responses to training are described in this section. Gaining a good understanding of how your body changes in response to training will increase your interest in and appreciation for training. A brief discussion of steroids is also presented here.

MUSCLE STRUCTURE

On the basis of structure and function, muscle tissue is categorized into three types: smooth, striated, and cardiac. In an activity such as weight training, the development of striated muscles is of paramount importance. As shown in Figure F.1, striated muscles, sometimes referred to as skeletal muscles, are attached to the bone via tendon. Skeletal muscles respond to voluntary stimulation (from the brain).

Although skeletal muscles (of which there are about 400) are grouped together, they can function separately or in concert with others. Which, and how many, skeletal muscles become involved in a workout depends upon which exercises are selected and the techniques (e.g., width of grip or stance, angle at which the bar is pushed or pulled) used during their execution. Throughout this text are illustrations and explanations of the muscle groups that are worked when performing many different exercises.

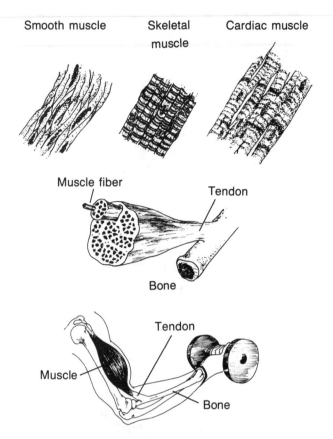

Figure F.1 Tendons attach skeletal muscles (one of the three types of muscle tissue) to the bones.

TYPES OF MUSCLE CONTRACTION

There are three different types of muscle contractions that can occur while weight training: static, concentric, and eccentric.

Static Contractions

A contraction is *static* when tension develops in a muscle but no observable shortening or lengthening is observed. Sometimes during the execution of a repetition, a sticking point is reached, and there is a momentary pause in movement. The muscle, at this point, would be described as being in a static contraction. Perhaps a more understandable example would be of a person attempting to push a bar off his or her chest (as in the bench press) when the load is too great to allow *any* upward movement.

Concentric Contractions

A concentric muscle contraction is when tension develops in a muscle and the muscle shortens. This type of contraction occurs, for example, in the bicep muscles as the dumbbell is moved upward toward the shoulders as shown in Figure F.2a. Another example of a concentric contraction is when the chest muscles contract, pulling the upper arms upward during the early phase of the bench press exercise. When tension develops in a muscle and a concentric contraction occurs, "positive work" is being performed.

Eccentric Contractions

An eccentric contraction is when tension develops in a muscle but the muscle lengthens. Using the bicep curl as an example again, once the dumbbell is at the shoulders and the lowering phase begins, the bicep muscle, as shown in Figure F.2b, is eccentrically contracting to control the descent of the dumbbell. There still is tension in the bicep muscle; the difference (as compared to the concentric contraction) is that the muscle fibers slowly lengthen to control the rate of lowering of the dumbbell. Using the example of the bench press described earlier, the controlled lowering of the dumbbell to the chest is accomplished by the eccentric contraction of the chest muscles (and the triceps). This is referred to as "negative work," because it is being performed in the direction opposite to that of the concentric (positive) muscle contraction. Eccentric (lengthening) contractions are largely responsible for the muscle soreness associated with weight training.

FACTORS AFFECTING STRENGTH GAINS

The strength that you may develop is influenced by neural changes that occur through the process of learning exercises, increases in muscle mass that occur in response to training, and your fiber type composition.

Strength Defined

The term *strength* refers to the ability to exert maximum force during a single effort. It can be measured by determining a one-repetition maximum effort, referred to as a "1RM," in one or more exercises. For example, if you loaded a bar to 100 pounds and were able to complete only one rep, your 1RM equals 100 pounds. Strength is specific to a muscle or muscle area (this is the specificity concept).

Neural Changes

Two reasons have been proposed for strength increases that occur in response to weight training. One is associated with neural changes and the other involves increases in muscle mass. The term *neural* relates to the contribution of the nervous system working with the muscular system to increase strength. In doing so, the nerves that are attached to specific muscles are "taught" when to "transmit." Thus, an improvement in technique occurs that permits handling poundages more efficiently (with less effort).

Furthermore, through repetition one's body becomes able to recruit more fibers. Thus, there is a learning factor that contributes to strength changes, some of which may be quite dramatic. It is generally well accepted that it

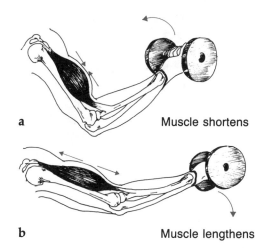

a Muscle shortens

b Muscle lengthens

Figure F.2 Concentric contraction (a) and eccentric contraction (b).

is this neural-learning factor that accounts for the strength improvements realized during the very early weeks of weight training.

Related to Muscle Mass

Although the neural-learning factor will continue to play a role, continued gains in strength are mostly associated with increases in muscle mass. As the cross-sectional area of the muscle becomes greater (because the individual fibers become thicker and stronger), so does the muscle's ability to exert force. Therefore, the neural factor accounts for the early increases in strength, whereas muscle mass increases are responsible for the changes seen later.

STRENGTH INCREASES— WHAT TO EXPECT

Depending on training habits and level of strength at the time of initial testing, the muscle group being evaluated, the intensity of the training program, the length of the training program (weeks, months, years), and genetic potential, strength increases due to training typically reported range from 8 percent to 50 percent. The greatest improvements are seen among those who have not weight-trained before and in programs involving large-muscle exercises, heavier loads, multiple sets, and more training sessions. Unique characteristics, such as the lengths of muscles and the angles at which their tendons insert into the bone, provide mechanical advantages and disadvantages and are factors that also increase or limit one's strength potential. The effects of steroid use on strength and muscle mass is discussed later.

In regard to comparisons between men and women, it is well established that the quality of muscle tissue and its ability to produce force is identical in both sexes. Therefore, it should be no surprise to find out that when comparisons are made of women and men who have followed similar weight training programs, the women and men are found to respond similarly. Since a typical woman possesses less muscle mass than a typical man, her absolute strength may not be as great; but her poten-

tial for improvement (percentage-wise) is. These issues and their implications are discussed in more detail in the next section.

WHEN TO EXPECT STRENGTH CHANGES

The strength improvements that do occur are not typically noticeable until the 2nd or 3rd week of training. The 1st week is usually characterized by losses in strength, perhaps due somewhat to muscle soreness. Fatigue may also be a contributing factor. Decreases in strength performance are especially apparent during the final training session of the 1st week. So do not be surprised if you feel weaker toward the end of the 1st week. Of course in the weeks ahead you will be impressed and excited about the substantial strength improvements, which sometimes will be as great as 4 percent to 6 percent per week. The actual reasons for these strength changes are discussed next.

WHAT ACCOUNTS FOR THE INCREASE IN MUSCLE SIZE?

Exactly what accounts for muscle-size increases is not fully understood; however, factors that are often discussed are hypertrophy, hyperplasia, and genetic potential.

Hypertrophy

Muscle-size increases are most often attributed to an enlargement of existing fibers, the same fibers that are present at birth. Very thin protein myofibrils (actin and myosin) within the fiber increase, creating a larger fiber. The collective effect of increases within many individual fibers is responsible for the overall muscle-size changes observed. This increase in existing fibers is referred to as *hypertrophy* (Figure F.3).

Hyperplasia

Although hypertrophy is the most commonly accepted explanation of why a muscle becomes larger, there are studies suggesting that fibers split lengthwise and form separate fibers. The splitting is thought to contribute

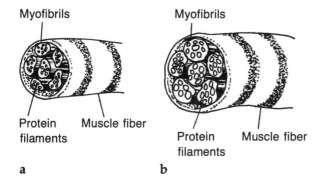

Figure F.3 Muscle hypertrophy—the muscle before training (a) and after training (b). Note the changes in the diameters of the protein filaments that make up the myofibrils.

to an increase in the size of the muscle. This theory of longitudinal fiber splitting is referred to as *hyperplasia*. (Remember that hypertrophy, not hyperplasia, is the most common explanation for increase in muscle size.)

Genetic Potential

If one accepts hypertrophy as the process whereby existing fibers increase in size, then one must also accept the idea that there are (genetic) limitations regarding the extent to which muscle will increase in size. This is because increases are due to the thickening of fibers that already exist. Just as we know that some people are born with muscle-tendon attachments favoring force development, the same is true in regard to the number of muscle fibers. Some people are born with a greater number of muscle fibers than others, and therefore their genetic potential for muscle-size growth is greater. Regardless of your genetic inheritance, your challenge is to design an effective program of training and to train diligently so that you develop to your full potential.

NEUROMUSCULAR SYSTEM

The neuromuscular (nerve-muscle) system is responsible for coordinating the interplay of signals sent from the brain to the muscles and received by the brain from the muscles. Your muscle fiber type composition may influence

your success in weight training and in other activities.

Fiber Type

The striated muscle tissue mentioned earlier can be categorized into two basic types, each with similar signal transmission capabilities but unique characteristics. *Fast-twitch* muscle tissue has the capacity to produce a great deal of force but fatigues quickly. Typically it will also gain in size more rapidly. Fast-twitch fibers, because of their high force capability, are recruited during weight training exercises and in athletic events requiring high levels of explosive strength (e.g., shot put, discus, javelin, football). *Slow-twitch* fiber is not able to exert as much force but is more enduring—that is, it can continue contracting for longer periods of time before fatigue occurs. Slow-twitch fibers are recruited for aerobic-oriented events (e.g., distance running, swimming, biking) that have lower strength but greater endurance requirements.

Fiber Type and Genetic Potential

Not everyone possesses the same proportions of fast-twitch and slow-twitch fibers. Individuals who possess a greater number of fast-twitch fibers have a greater genetic potential to be stronger and, therefore, to be more successful in certain ''strength-dependent'' sports or in an activity like weight training. Conversely, individuals with a high percentage of slow-twitch fibers have greater genetic potential to be successful in events requiring lower levels of strength and greater levels of endurance, such as long-distance swimming or marathoning events.

MUSCULAR ENDURANCE

Muscular endurance is the ability to perform repeated muscle contractions (using moderate loads) for a given period of time, or the ability to extend the period of time before muscular fatigue occurs. In this it is different from strength, the measure of a single, all-out effort. But it is similar to strength in that endurance is specific to the muscle or muscles involved.

For instance, as a result of regularly performing a high number of reps in the bicep curl, muscles in the upper arm (anterior) will improve in their endurance. But this training will not improve muscular endurance in the leg muscles.

Weight training appears to bring about muscular endurance improvements in two ways: by increasing anaerobic qualities in the muscle, and by reducing the number of muscle fibers involved during earlier periods of an activity, thereby leaving some in reserve should the activity continue. The reduction in the number of fibers involved is related to strength improvements that permit a task to be undertaken using a lower percentage of effort. For example, if you had to perform a 25-pound bicep curl and had 50 pounds of strength in your biceps, this exercise would require 50 percent of your strength. If, however, your bicep strength increased to 100 pounds, the task would now require only 25 percent of your strength and, thus, a lower percentage of effort.

CARDIOVASCULAR SYSTEM

The effects of weight training on cardiovascular fitness, typically expressed as changes in oxygen uptake (the ability to transport and utilize oxygen by the muscles), have been studied by numerous researchers. It appears safe to say that weight training programs involving heavy loads (i.e., weight) with few repetitions and long rest periods between sets have only a minimal effect on cardiovascular fitness. However, when weight training programs include light to moderate loads, a higher number of reps (12 to 20+), and very short rest periods between sets, moderate (5 percent) improvements in oxygen uptake may be expected. The extent of such changes is also influenced by the intensity and length of the overall training period (weeks, months, years) as well as fitness and strength levels at the start of a training program. It would be an oversight to disregard these considerations when evaluating the merits of reported cardiovascular fitness improvements attributed to weight training programs.

THE TRADE-OFF

In programs where the program design variables of load, number of reps, and length of rest periods between sets are manipulated to produce changes in oxygen uptake, typical increases in strength are not experienced. Similarly, programs designed to produce high levels of strength result in minimal or no improvement in cardiovascular fitness (refers to the specificity concept). Thus, there is a trade-off; weight training programs designed to produce cardiovascular fitness will negatively affect potential strength gains, and programs designed for strength will have a negative effect on cardiovascular fitness improvements.

The most effective way to develop cardiovascular fitness is to engage in aerobic training activities such as walking, running, swimming, cycling, or cross-country skiing. Such activities involve continuous, rhythmic movements and are sustained for a longer duration than anaerobic activities such as weight training. Guidelines that will help you develop an aerobic exercise program can be found in the texts by Corbin and Lindsey (1988) and Hoeger (1989) listed in the References section. A well-designed fitness program will include both weight training and aerobic activities.

MUSCULAR COORDINATION

Some people still believe that weight training will somehow negatively affect muscular coordination. The heaviness in the arms and legs, and the numb feeling (loss of ''touch'') that occurs immediately after a set of reps, are only temporary and will not reduce coordination levels. Weight training sessions most likely will have the opposite effect. Handling and moving bars from the floor to overhead, balancing the bar on your back (back squat), and evenly pressing dumbbells (dumbbell flys) all contribute to improving muscular coordination.

FLEXIBILITY

Weight training exercises performed using good technique and in a controlled manner can improve strength throughout all ranges of joint motion. Exercises performed in this way will improve flexibility as well as provide a better stimulus for strength development, and they may reduce the likelihood of injury. There is no reliable evidence to support the contention that properly performed weight training exercises reduce flexibility or motor coordination.

MUSCLE SORENESS— THEORIES AND EXPLANATIONS

You should not be surprised or discouraged to find that the first week or two of weight training is accompanied by extreme muscle soreness. It is natural to feel as if 300 of your approximately 400 muscles have been stung rather than exercised. Muscle soreness, in varying degrees, is experienced by virtually all who weight train. There is no definitive explanation of why we experience delayed muscle soreness, but the following theories are most often presented:

- Micro (minute) tears of muscle and connective tissue cause muscle soreness.
- Ischemia (lack of oxygen to muscle tissue), which occurs as a natural consequence of intense work and may be due to muscle spasms, causes muscle soreness.

Although there is not a consensus of opinion as to why we experience muscle soreness, it is known that the eccentric (or ''negative'') phase of exercise movements is a major cause. As an example, the lowering (eccentric) phases of the bicep curl and bench press result in muscle soreness, but the upward (concentric) phases do not. Usually the discomfort of muscle soreness subsides after 3 days, especially if you stretch before and after training. Surprisingly, the very thing that stimulates the soreness (i.e., exercise) helps to alleviate it. Light exercise combined with stretching activities is ideal for speeding the recovery from muscle soreness.

OVERTRAINING

Overtraining is a condition in which there is a plateau or drop in performance over a period of time. This occurs when your body does not have time to adequately recuperate from training before the next workout. Often the overtrained state is a result of overlooking recovery needs, working out too aggressively (especially too soon after illness), or not following recommended program guidelines presented in this text.

The physical warning signs of overtraining are

1. extreme muscular soreness and stiffness the day after a training session;
2. a gradual increase in muscular soreness from one training session to the next;
3. a decrease in body weight (especially when no effort to decrease body weight is being made);
4. an inability to complete a training session that, based upon your present physical condition, is reasonable;
5. a sudden or gradual increase of 8 to 10 beats per minute in resting heart rate (taken at the same time and under the same conditions every day);
6. a lowered general physical resistance to illness as evidenced by persistent colds, headaches, and so on;
7. a loss of appetite;
8. a swelling of the lymph nodes in the neck, groin, or armpits;
9. constipation or diarrhea; and
10. an unexplained drop in physical performance during competitive or recreational activities.

If you develop two or more of the above symptoms, you should reduce the intensity, frequency, and/or duration of training until these warning signs abate.

It is more desirable to prevent overtraining than to try to recover from it. To help prevent overtraining,

- increase training intensity gradually;
- alternate aggressive with less aggressive training weeks—allowing for sufficient recovery between training sessions (variation in training);
- get adequate amounts of sleep;
- eat properly;

- monitor your physical vital signs (blood pressure, resting heart rate, and so on) and note significant changes; and
- make adjustments in training intensity as needed.

BODY COMPOSITION

Body composition considers the amount of fat weight and fat-free (muscle, bone, organ) weight that makes up your physique. This is in contrast to judging your physical makeup solely on what the weight scale registers as your body weight. Thus, body composition is a more effective way to determine your health and fitness status. Two factors that have a profound effect on body composition are dieting and exercise.

The Diet Dilemma and Weight Loss

Approximately 65 million people are on some type of diet at any given time in America. Millions more are going on diets every day. Some are losing weight, but many are gaining it back. All hope to somehow find the answer. The truth is that diets designed to create a fast weight loss typically are not effective in helping people stay healthy and trim; in fact, many of those diets are actually harmful.

Metabolic Rate Fluctuations

There are good reasons why diets typically don't work and better reasons why wise food selection plus regular exercise will work. Crash diets, in particular, are not effective because the body quickly adapts to a lower food intake by reducing its metabolic rate (i.e., the rate at which food is burned for energy). This compensatory action by the body resists the burning of fat. When there is a dietary restriction resulting in a loss of 10 pounds, for example, the body adjusts to the restricted diet. Later, when an increase in food intake occurs, even though daily consumption is still less than it was before dieting, the body treats the increase as an excess and stores it as fat.

Fluctuations Due to Water Loss

You should realize that the weight loss experienced during the early part of a strict diet program is usually loss of water, not of fat. Many diets restrict carbohydrate intake. This reduces the water content of the body because much of the water stored in our bodies is accumulated in the process of storing carbohydrates. This weight loss due to the reduction of water stores is only temporary. Once the fluid balance is restored, the weight scale does not reflect the loss of body fat that was assumed to have occurred.

Muscle Tissue Loss

Also, if the dieter consumes less than about 1,200 kilocalories a day (for a female) or 1,500 kilocalories a day (for a male), muscle tissue is usually lost as well as fat. The farther the caloric intake dips below this amount, the more muscle tissue is lost compared to fat. So even though the dieter loses weight, he or she is actually fatter expressed as a percentage of body weight than before dieting, because the ratio of fat weight to lean body weight increases. *The goal of a sound diet should be to reduce total body weight without losing muscle tissue.* People who are on the roller coaster of dieting, gaining weight, and dieting again may be weakening their body every time they diet. This ''yo-yo'' approach is the wrong way to lose weight; it has a negative effect on the body, and it is ineffective for permanently losing body fat.

Body Size Considerations

It appears that many overweight people justify their overeating to themselves by thinking that because their bodies are heavy, they need more food to nourish them. Actually, the opposite is true in many cases. Too much of their body weight is fat, which, unlike muscle, is not metabolically active tissue. In other words, fat does not contribute to burning off fat. Exercising muscles burn calories; the more muscle there is, the greater is the energy expenditure and the faster is the reduction of stored fat. An example of this is to compare two individuals who are the same height, one of whom weighs more and is in worse physical condition than the other. The lighter person has more muscle and less stored fat due to a good fitness level and will require a greater caloric intake than the less active, heavier, fatter, and less muscular person.

VALUES OF WEIGHT TRAINING AND AEROBIC EXERCISE

For many, the only effective way to decrease excess body fat is to moderately reduce caloric intake while participating in an aerobic and weight training program at the same time. These exercise programs will burn calories and maintain or build muscle tissue, which encourages an improvement in the fat-to-muscle ratio. In 40 minutes of aerobic exercise, the average individual burns approximately 480 kilocalories. Keep in mind that aerobic activities involve the large muscles in continuous movement, as in cycling, swimming, walking, jogging, cross-country skiing, and rope skipping. These activities promote the greatest caloric expenditure. Golf, on the other hand, is not a continuous and rhythmic activity and burns only half the calories that swimming the backstroke does for individuals of the same body weight.

Weight training does not expend as many calories as aerobic exercise, but it does maintain or increase muscle mass. This is important because not only does muscle tissue expend calories, but the body will recognize that it needs the muscle tissue exercised during weight training and will burn up fat instead. A woman typically does not become as muscular as a man, so it is unlikely that a woman will significantly gain body weight in response to weight training, unless she makes an effort to do so (by increasing food intake and following a program designed to develop hypertrophy).

LOSING FAT WEIGHT

If you want to lose body fat, attempt to lose it at a maximum rate of 1 to 2 pounds per week. Losses greater than this result in losses of muscle tissue. A pound of fat has approximately 3,500 kilocalories, so a daily dietary reduction of 250 to 500 kilocalories will total about 3,500 to 7,000 kilocalories a week. This will promote the recommended loss of 1 to 2 pounds of fat per week. The following charts provide two examples of fat reduction programs designed to lose 2 and 1 pounds, respectively, per week. The weight training programs are assumed to include 8 or more large-muscle exercises and 3+ sets of 6 or more reps.

Sample Fat Reduction Program 1

Type of activity	Kcal expenditure		Total kcals
Dietary reduction	500 fewer kcals/day × 7 days	=	3,500
Jogging	40 minutes @ 480 kcals/day × 4 days	=	1,920
Weight training	60 minutes @ 540 kcals/day × 3 days	=	1,620
			7,040

7,000 kcals/week = 2-pound weight loss/week

Sample Fat Reduction Program 2

Type of activity	Kcal expenditure		Total kcals
Dietary reduction	250 fewer kcals/day × 7 days	=	1,750
Jogging	20 min @ 240 kcals/day × 3 days	=	720
Weight training	40 minutes @ 360 kcals/day × 3 days	=	1,080
			3,550

3,500 kcals/week = 1-pound weight loss/week

The above programs are presented merely as guidelines; actual weight loss will differ from person to person, depending on the type and intensity of the exercise. For more information on caloric considerations as they relate to weight training, see Stone and O'Bryant (1987). Also realize that the body's metabolic rate is increased for several hours after exercise, which further increases the caloric expenditure of this activity. In addition, as the amount of muscle mass increases (even if only slightly), the body expends more calories performing any type of activity.

GAINING FAT-FREE WEIGHT

Most people who exercise have no interest in gaining body weight; however, there are some who participate in weight training programs specifically to gain muscle. To accomplish this, one has to increase caloric consumption while weight training. The weight training will stimulate muscle growth, and thus body weight increases. The consumption of additional calories (beyond one's daily needs) provides the basis for the increase in muscle tissue. The addition of 1 pound of muscle requires 2,500 kilocalories more than normal metabolic needs. An equal increase in proteins and carbohydrates (with a special emphasis on complex carbohydrates) and a maintenance of fat intake should help promote lean tissue growth (and an increase in muscle size).

Protein Needs and Supplements

Although protein, mineral, and vitamin supplementation is strongly endorsed by many, little, if any, research has been presented that substantiates claims of improved muscular endurance, hypertrophy, or strength. Again and again, dieticians, exercise physiologists, and sports medicine physicians conclude that a normal diet will meet protein dietary needs of the typical person. The exception may be that an increase in carbohydrate intake is required of those who participate in aggressive weight training programs, to provide enough calories (energy) to be able to maintain a high training intensity.

STEROID USE CONSIDERATIONS

To shape your body to make it stronger, more attractive, and healthier, you must eat well-balanced meals, train hard, and allow time for sufficient recovery between workouts. It is human nature to look for shortcuts, but there really aren't any. There is a lot of interest in steroids because they are seen as a shortcut; however, they have their drawbacks, the most significant of which relates to your health.

Types of Steroids

There are two forms of steroids: oral, or pill, form; and water- or oil-based liquid that is injected using a hypodermic needle. These two forms are gauged for potency by comparing the anabolic effects (muscle-building and strength-inducing) versus the androgenic effects (increased male or female secondary sex characteristics such as increased body hair length or density, voice lowering, and breast enlargement). This ratio is termed the *therapeutic index*.

Adverse Side Effects

Studies included in position papers by the National Strength and Conditioning Association (Wright & Stone, 1985) and American College of Sports Medicine (1987) on steroid use have cited increases in muscle size and strength, but not all outcomes from their use are that positive. The health consequences of steroid use can include chronic illness such as heart disease, liver trouble, urinary tract abnormalities, and sexual dysfunction. A shortened life may be a consequence. There are also immediate short-term effects, including increased blood pressure, acne, testicular atrophy, gynecomastia (male breast enlargement), sore nipples, decreased sperm count, prostatic enlargement, and increased aggression. Other side effects that have been reported include hair loss, fever, nausea, diarrhea, nosebleeds, lymph node swelling, increased appetite, and a burning sensation during urination. The major psychological symptoms include paranoia, delusions of grandeur, and auditory hallucinations.

When steroid use is discontinued after short-term use, most side effects disappear. However, females who take steroids may have permanent deepening of the voice, facial hair, baldness, clitoral enlargement, and decrease in breast size.

The most serious effect of taking anabolic steroids is the increased probability of developing coronary artery disease. Users often have high levels of (total) cholesterol, low levels of the high density lipoprotein (HDL) component, and elevated blood pressure, all of which are significant heart disease risk factors.

Nutritional Considerations

Nutrition is basically the study of how carbohydrates, proteins, fats, vitamins, minerals, and water provide the energy and substances required for maintaining bodily functions during rest and exercise conditions. When a sound nutrition program is combined with regularly attended training sessions, success is a natural outcome. The discussion that follows defines and identifies the different food groups, nutrients, and vitamins and their sources.

CARBOHYDRATES

The primary and most efficient source of energy for the body is carbohydrates. These are categorized as either simple or complex. The simple carbohydrates (sugars) are divided into monosaccharides (e.g., fruit sugar, honey, and milk) and disaccharides (e.g., sugar from purified sugar beets and sugar cane). Complex carbohydrates (polysaccharides) are found in vegetables, cereals, grains, and pasta. Carbohydrates provide 4 kilocalories per gram. For those who train intensely, an increased intake of complex carbohydrates is very important.

Carbohydrate Sources

Preferred sources include cereals, breads, flours, grains, fruits, pasta, and vegetables. Other sources are syrups, jellies, cakes, crackers, and honey.

PROTEINS

Proteins are the building blocks of all body cells. They are responsible for the repair, rebuilding, and replacement of cells as well as for regulating bodily processes involved in fighting infection. If the supply of carbohydrates and fats is insufficient and the responsibility of repairing, rebuilding, and regulating metabolic functions has been met, protein is used as a source of energy.

The basic units of protein are the amino acids. Of the 20 amino acids, 8 (or 9, depending what reference is consulted) are termed *essential* amino acids and must be supplied through the diet. The other 12 (or 11) can be produced by the body; these are the nonessential amino acids. Proteins provide 4 kilocalories per gram.

Protein Sources

Foods that contain all eight of the essential amino acids are called complete proteins. Meat, fish, poultry, eggs, milk, and cheese are ideal sources of complete proteins. Incomplete sources of protein include breads, cereals, nuts, dried peas, and beans.

FATS

Fats provide a concentrated form of energy (9 kilocalories per gram)—more than twice that of carbohydrates or proteins. Fats are involved in the maintenance of healthy skin, insulating against heat and cold, and cushioning vital organs, and they are the major storage form of energy.

Fat Sources

Fats can be found in both plant and animal sources. Sources include the fats in meats, such as beef, lamb, chicken, and pork, and egg yolks. Other sources are dairy products, such as cream, milk, cheese, and butter.

VITAMINS

Vitamins are essential nutrients needed for many body processes. They are divided into two types, fat soluble and water soluble. Regardless of the type, vitamins do *not* contain energy or calories, and extra vitamin supplementation will not provide more energy. The types of vitamins, their functions, and the food sources that contain them are listed in Table F.1

MINERALS

Minerals function in the body as builders, activators, regulators, transmitters, and controllers of the body's metabolic processes. Table F.2 is a short list of three of the most important minerals and their functions and food sources.

Table F.1 Vitamin Functions and Sources

Vitamin*	Functions	Food sources
A (fat soluble)	Growth, healthy skin, bone and teeth development, proper night vision, and infection resistance.	Liver, kidney, egg yolk, dark green leafy vegetables, cantaloupe, peaches, apricots, pumpkin, tomatoes, whole milk, and cheese.
D (fat soluble)	Needed to absorb and utilize minerals (calcium and phosphorus), and for the maintenance of healthy bones and teeth.	Fortified milk, fish liver oils, liver, fish (herring, sardines, tuna, salmon), and egg yolk.
C (water soluble)	Necessary for building and maintaining cells, healthy teeth, gums, and blood vessels. Improves iron absorption, aids in resisting infection, healing wounds, and synthesizing hormones that regulate bodily functions.	Citrus fruits and juices, strawberries, cantaloupe, tomatoes, broccoli, raw green vegetables, cabbage, potatoes, and tomato juice.
Thiamine (B-1) (water soluble)	Needed to utilize carbohydrates for energy and helps to maintain the nervous system.	Whole grain products or enriched breads and cereals, meats (especially pork), poultry, fish, liver, dry beans and peas, soybeans, peanuts, and egg yolk.

(Cont.)

Table F.1 (Continued)

Vitamin*	Functions	Food sources
Riboflavin (B-2) (water soluble)	Needed to utilize proteins and carbohydrates for energy in the body. Maintains healthy skin, especially around the mouth, nose, and eyes.	Milk, cheese, liver, kidney, heart, animal meats, eggs, green leafy vegetables, enriched breads, and cereals.
Niacin (water soluble)	Necessary for a functional nervous system, healthy skin, and normal digestion. Aids the cells in using oxygen to release energy.	Poultry, meats, fish, organ meats, Brewer's yeast, peanuts, peanut butter, legumes, dark leafy vegetables, potatoes, whole grain or enriched breads, and cereals.

*The above list is not complete, but the cited vitamins are among those important for exercise metabolism.

WATER

While not really a provider of energy for activity, water provides the medium for, and is one of, the end products of activity. Water makes up about 72 percent of the weight of muscle and represents 40 to 60 percent of an individual's total body weight. Through the regulation of thirst and urine output, primarily, the body is able to keep a delicate water balance. When an appropriate balance is not maintained, the body's ability to function normally is compromised.

SUMMARY

The typical guidelines for a healthy diet—55 percent, 30 percent, and 15 percent of carbohydrates, fats, and proteins, respectively—are

Table F.2 Mineral Functions and Sources

Mineral	Functions	Food sources
Calcium	Needed for structure of bones and teeth, healthy nerves, and muscle activity. Necessary in healing wounds and broken bones.	Milk, yogurt, hard cheeses, salmon and sardines with tiny bones, turnip greens, collard greens, mustard greens, ice cream, and cottage cheese (although it has less calcium than hard cheeses).
Phosphorus	Needed in combination with calcium for bones and teeth. Required for enzymes used in energy metabolism. Regulates the balance between acids and bases in the body.	Milk, cheese, ice cream, meat, poultry, fish, whole grains, cereals, nuts, and legumes.
Iron	Needed to form hemoglobin, which carries oxygen from the lungs to the body cells.	Liver, other organ meats, lean meats, poultry, shellfish, egg yolk, green leafy vegetables, whole grain and enriched cereals and breads, legumes, and raisins.

appropriate for those who are weight training. However, you may want to slightly increase (by 5 percent) the amount of carbohydrates and decrease (by 5 percent) the amount of fats. Try to select complex, instead of simple, carbohydrates and unsaturated, instead of saturated, fats. A diet that includes appropriate amounts of fluids (6 to 8 glasses) and is selected with these diet guidelines in mind will provide the necessary energy and nutrients to promote positive changes in your strength, endurance, and muscularity.

Women in Weight Training

Women's decisions to participate in weight training have all too often been negatively influenced by misinformation. This brief section highlights the areas of most concern to women and the benefits of weight training for women.

VALUE OF WEIGHT TRAINING

The value of weight training is well documented, yet there remains a reluctance among women to follow these programs. The primary reason appears to be a fear that weight training will produce massive bulk or losses in flexibility and muscle coordination. Some also believe that women are not capable of tolerating or adapting to the rigors of weight training programs, and that their potential for improvement is not comparable to men's. Intertwined with these concerns are social and cultural influences that convey to women the message that weight training is somehow an inappropriate activity, that being strong is unfeminine.

Women's Strength and Potential for Strength Compared to Men's

Perhaps the structural differences between women and men have led us to believe that women do not have the same capacity as men to gain in strength. Granted, a typical female has a lighter skeleton, narrower shoulders, and wider hips relative to total body size, weighs 30 to 40 pounds less, and carries approximately 8 percent more body fat than a male of the same age. However, the *quality of muscle tissue is identical*. It follows, then, that there should not be any differences in the muscle tissue's ability to exert or resist force. As a result, the higher strength levels typically observed in males is attributed to the *quantity* of muscle tissue, not to qualitative differences in muscle tissue.

The quantitative muscle differences favoring men are quite large. In the typical male, for example, muscle mass accounts for approximately 40 percent of the total body weight, whereas in the typical female it represents only 23 percent. This advantage, combined with

better exposure to well-conceived weight training and sport programs, has enabled males to exhibit higher strength levels. Such differences help to explain why women have been found to be 43 percent to 63 percent weaker in upper body strength, and 25 percent to 30 percent weaker in lower body strength.

To conclude from this that women do not have the same potential as men to gain strength is entirely incorrect, however. A female can develop strength relative to her own potential, but it will not be at the absolute strength levels achieved by males of similar body weights. Depending on the muscle group being evaluated, the intensity of the program, and the length of training (weeks, months, or years), the strength increases typically reported in women range from 12 percent to 38 percent. Improvements in strength approaching 38 percent and greater are more common in programs that have involved large muscle group exercises, heavier loads, fewer repetitions, multiple sets, and longer training periods.

Comparisons of men and women following similar weight training programs reveal not only that women respond with significant increases in strength, but that their rates of strength improvement may exceed those of men. This large and relatively fast strength gain is indicative of individuals who are farther from their potential. Thus, when women begin weight training, their improvements are often more dramatic than the gains made by males. Of interest is the fact that when strength in the leg and hip areas is related to body weight (a measure called relative strength), especially to lean-muscle weight rather than to total body weight, women's ratios are found to be similar to men's.

The Benefits and Effects on Body Composition

Until women understand that they can experience significant improvements in muscle tone without equal gains in muscle hypertrophy, the reluctance to pursue intensive weight training programs will continue. Studies have made it quite clear that the acquisition of excessive muscle hypertrophy is not a natural outcome of weight training in women. Testosterone, an anabolic hormone that plays an important role in muscle building (but is not the sole determinant), is at much lower levels in women than in men: about 10 times less than of men. At the same time, it is incorrect to say that there will not be *any* changes in muscle hypertrophy in women in response to weight training. The typical female may experience slight increases in muscle size, especially in the upper arm and shoulder. Typically, however, a reduction in intramuscular adipose (fat) tissue accompanies this, yielding a small change in overall girth. Total body weight remains about the same for most women as these alterations in body composition occur. There may be a 30 percent increase in muscle size without a noticeable increase in limb girth. This explains why most women in weight training programs experience increases in lean muscle mass and strength without necessarily acquiring visible muscle hypertrophy. The body composition alterations cited here result in a better ratio of lean muscle tissue to adipose tissue, which provides women with a more attractive body appearance. An excellent in-depth discussion of the issues surrounding women's responses to weight training is presented in a paper by Holloway and Baechle (1990) and the position paper published by the National Strength and Conditioning Association (1990).

Also of concern to women are the muscle cuts, or definition and protruding veins, often observed in men; such changes are not as apparent in the typical woman who weight trains. It has been suggested that women's higher percentage of body fat serves to visually "smooth" accentuated muscle definition and, therefore, obscures the appearance of veins. The additional subcutaneous fat, the portions of storage fat deposited beneath the surface of the skin, might account for this. It has been reported to be 3 percent greater in females.

Women Can Tolerate Intense Weight Training Programs

There is also a misconception that females cannot tolerate the rigors of intensive weight training programs. It is obvious to the authors and to those who have weight trained women for many years that such a belief is without substance. Women approach training in the same way as men do, once they become familiar with the training area and develop appropriate expectations of training.

IMPLICATIONS FOR THE TRAINING PROGRAMS

Weight training programs are similar for women and men, except that women's programs typically use lighter loads or resistance. Women also need to include more upper body exercises, because they typically do not possess appropriate levels of upper body strength. The effects of hormonal fluctuations during the menstrual cycle on training intensity and outcomes are of growing interest, because they may provide insight into when training intensities should be increased or decreased to produce maximum results.

The parallel squat is a good lower body exercise for women, but only if performed correctly. It's a tremendous exercise for strengthening and toning the hips, buttocks, and thighs, and when it is performed and spotted as described in Appendix A, it is a very safe exercise. However, because women generally lack muscularity in the upper back and shoulder, they often experience discomfort from the bar resting on their shoulders. In addition to proper bar placement, tensing the upper back (especially the trapezius) and wearing a thick sweatshirt helps a great deal by elevating the bar off the scapula (shoulder blades). Another problem is that the bar will tend to slide down the back (from its initial position). Keeping the elbows high, instead of down by the sides next to the ribs, helps keep the bar stationary. These changes will make the parallel squat a comfortable and rewarding exercise for women.

Women, then, have a great potential for positive body compositional changes as a result of weight training. Improvements involve increases in strength and tone with minimal hypertrophy, decreases in subcutaneous fat, and a reshaping process that results in a more attractive appearance.

Preparing Your Body to Train

Warm-up activities such as brisk walking or jogging in place for about 5 minutes, followed by an appropriate stretching routine, help to physically and mentally prepare you to train hard. The stretching will also improve your flexibility, or your ability to move joints through a full range of motion, and in doing so may help prevent injury. Go through the series of static (held) and then dynamic stretching positions described and illustrated here. Be sure to do the dynamic stretches with slow movements and without bouncing. The stretches presented involve major joints and muscle groups, especially the antigravity muscles of the back of the legs, the upper and lower back, and the neck, which tend to become less flexible.

Include these stretching exercises *prior to* weight training and *immediately after* each training session. Brisk walking or jogging plus stretching increases blood and muscle temperatures, enabling muscles to contract and relax with greater ease. Stretching afterward helps speed your recovery from muscle soreness. Hold each of the stretching positions for 6 to 10 seconds, and repeat them two or three times if you wish to.

Chest and Shoulders

Grasp your hands together behind your back and slowly lift them upward, or simply reach back as far as possible if you are not able to grasp your hands. For an additional stretch, bend at the waist and raise your arms higher.

Upper Back, Shoulder, and Arm

With your right hand, grasp your left elbow and pull it slowly across your chest toward your right shoulder. You will feel tension along the outside of your left shoulder and arm. Repeat with the other arm. You can vary this stretch by pulling across and *down* over your chest and upper stomach.

Shoulder and Tricep (Back of Upper Arm)

Bring both arms overhead and hold your left elbow with your right hand. Allow your left arm to bend at the elbow, and let your left hand rest against the back of your right shoulder. Pull with your right hand to slowly move the left elbow behind your head until you feel a stretch. Repeat with the other arm.

Back and Hips

Sit with your right leg straight. Bend your left leg, crossing your left foot over and resting it to the outside of your right knee with the sole flat on the floor. Then push against the outside of your upper left thigh with your right elbow, just above the knee. Use your right elbow to keep this leg stationary as you perform the stretch. Next, place your left hand behind your buttocks, slowly turn your head to look over your left shoulder, and rotate your upper body toward your left hand and arm. You should feel tension in your lower back, hips, and buttocks. Repeat with the other leg.

Quadriceps

This stretch is performed in the standing position. Use a wall or stationary object for balance, and grasp your right foot with the left hand and pull so that your heel moves back toward your buttocks. You should feel tension along the front of your right thigh. Repeat with your left leg and right hand. You can add an additional stretch by leaning forward at the waist.

Hamstrings

While seated on the floor, straighten your right leg with the sole of your left foot slightly touching the inside of your right knee. Slowly bend forward from the hips toward your right foot until you feel tension in the back of your right thigh. Perform the same stretch with the left leg. Be sure to keep the toes of your right foot pointing up while your ankles and toes are relaxed.

Calves

Stand facing a wall or stationary object, about 2 feet away from it. With your feet together and your knees locked, lean forward. Apply a stretch on your calves by slowly moving your hips toward the wall. Be sure to keep your heels on the floor and your back straight. You can feel an additional stretch by slightly bending one knee at a time.

Step 1 Using Equipment Safely

When you walk into a well-equipped weight room you may be somewhat intimidated if you are new to weight training. You will see machines of various sizes and shapes, short and long bars, and weight plates (weights that fit onto the bars) of varying sizes and poundages with holes of different sizes. You will also notice that the room has benches, racks of various sizes, and areas where short and long bars are stored. Becoming familiar with this equipment is a logical first step as you begin to learn and develop the skills involved in weight training.

Although weight training involves many types of equipment, the steps (chapters) that follow discuss only the use of barbells, dumbbells, and weight machines. Step 1 introduces you to the various characteristics of these types of equipment and how to use them safely. If you are more experienced in weight training, use this as a quick equipment review, and give special attention to the safety guidelines provided and complete the drills at the end.

WHY IS BEING ABLE TO USE WEIGHT TRAINING EQUIPMENT IMPORTANT?

Learning what the various pieces of equipment are designed to do and how to use them properly has several implications. First, before you decide on the exercises to include in your training program, you need to be able to match up the types of equipment with the exercises that can be performed on them. To do this requires recognizing the types of equipment present in the training area(s) available to you. Another implication is that by learning the ''tools'' of weight training, you are able to train more efficiently (timewise), and you will become more proficient at creating desired effects on your muscles and joints. Even more important is the issue of safety. Knowing the ''whys and hows'' of equipment use will help you avoid injury.

WEIGHT TRAINING MACHINES

Machines typically found in the weight room provide a dynamic form of exercise. Dynamic exercises involve movement. In contrast, isometric exercises involve no observable movement. Dynamic exercises performed on weight machines involve both concentric and eccentric, or only concentric, muscle contractions (see the ''Physiological Considerations'' section).

Figure 1.1 shows (a) single-unit and (b) multi-unit machines. Single-unit machines are designed to work one muscle area. As you can see, the multi-unit machines have various stations attached to their large frame; these enable you to work many muscle areas simply by moving from station to station.

A closer look at the structure of these machines (Figure 1.2a) reveals how they are designed. The weight stack is lifted by pulling or pushing weight arms attached to fixed pivot points. In place of a weight arm may be a handle or bar that attaches to a cable, chain, or flat belt that rolls over a circular pulley. You will notice when using this type of equipment that some movement phases require more effort than others, as though someone were changing the weight stack on you. Really what has happened is that as the weight arm moves in response to being pushed or pulled, it changes the location of the weight stack (WS) in relation to the weight arm's pivot point (PP). This is illustrated in Figure 1.2b. As the distance between the weight stack and the pivot point becomes shorter, the exercise requires less effort, and as the distance between these two points becomes greater, the exercise requires more effort. If you are familiar with leverage concepts, you understand the specific reasons for all of this. Machines that feature a fixed pivot or the circular-shaped pulley design are commonly referred to as *fixed resistance* machines. The limitation of this type of equipment is that the muscles are not con-

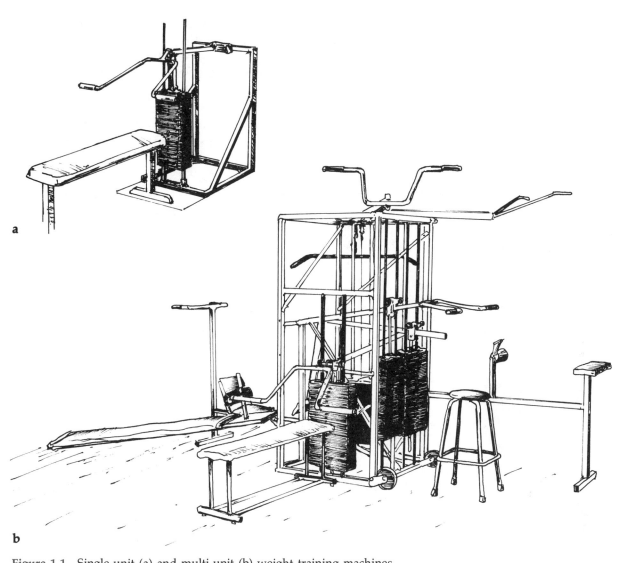

Figure 1.1   Single-unit (a) and multi-unit (b) weight training machines.

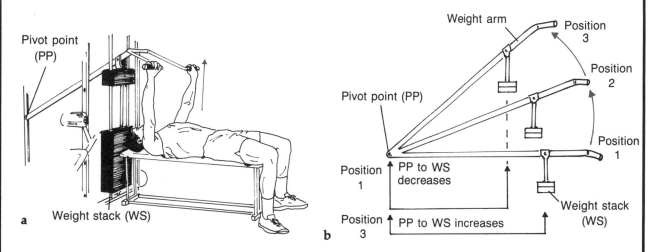

Figure 1.2   The structure of a fixed resistance machine (a). In b you can see that as the weight arm is moved from Position 1 to Position 3, the distance from the pivot point (PP) to the weight stack (WS) decreases, which makes the exercise easier to complete.

sistent throughout the exercise range. Free weights also fall into this category and present the same limitation.

In an effort to create a more consistent stress on muscles, some machines are designed with a weight stack that *varies* or moves, allowing the weight stack to roll or slide back and forth on the weight arm of the machine (Figure 1.3a). These machines are referred to as *variable resistance machines*. Note again the relationship between the weight stack and the pivot point as the stack moves. When the weight arm moves to a position that would require less effort with a fixed pivot, the weight stack moves away from the pivot point. When it is

pushed or pulled to a position requiring more effort, the weight stack moves closer to the pivot point. The result of these changes are seen in Figure 1.3b. There is more to understanding why a more consistent stress is imposed throughout the entire range of an exercise with the moving pivot, but the explanation here is sufficient to help you recognize the capabilities of these variable resistance machines.

Another type of variable resistance machine (Figure 1.4) features a somewhat kidney-shaped wheel or cam. The variation in the shape of the cam makes the cam function similarly to a moving pivot. This can be observed in Figure 1.4, a and b. As the chain (or a cable or belt) tracks over the peaks and valleys of the cam, the distance between the pivot point (the axle on which the cam rotates) and the weight stack varies to produce a more consistent stress on the muscles.

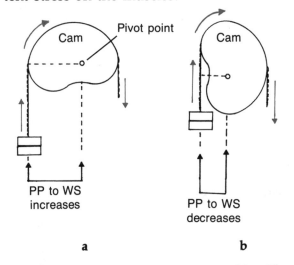

Figure 1.4 A variable resistance—cam machine. The cam functions similarly to the moving weight stack by varying the distance between the PP and the WS (a and b), thus stressing the muscles more consistently.

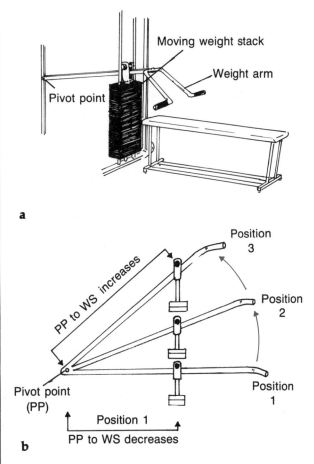

Figure 1.3 The structure of a variable resistance—moving weight stack machine (a). In b you can see that as the weight arm moves from Position 1 to Position 3, the distance from the PP to the WS increases, thus increasing the load. This change offsets the advantage gained by the moving machine arm and brings about a more uniform loading throughout the range of the exercise.

This design feature, like the moving pivot, is based on the leverage and strength capabilities of a typical person at specific points in an exercise. Actually, because the location of the moving pivot and the shape of the cam are designed to conform to the specific force characteristics of one body type (specific body height, arm, leg, trunk lengths, angle of muscle-tendon insertion onto bone, etc.), the likelihood of these machines actually accommodating or matching the force characteristics of many body types is remote. If you care to gain a better understanding of the principles involved in the equipment described here, consider reading Garhammer (1986), Stone and O'Bryant (1987), or Fleck and Kraemer (1987).

The fixed resistance and the variable resistance machines are the types of weight training equipment most commonly used in the schools, colleges, health clubs, and corporate settings, so these, along with the also-popular free weight equipment, are explained and illustrated in this text.

Isokinetic machines also involve dynamic exercise. Isokinetic movements are performed at constant speeds. Unlike the fixed- and variable-resistance machines that involve concentric and eccentric muscle contractions, isokinetic equipment involves only concentric contractions. And instead of using weight stacks, these machines create resistance by using hydraulic, pneumatic, or frictional features (Figure 1.5). Controls allow you to select movement speeds that relate to the level of resistance you will encounter, going from slower speeds that require great effort to faster speeds that require less effort per rep.

Figure 1.5 An isokinetic machine, which generates resistance through hydraulic, pneumatic, or frictional features, not weight stacks.

Isokinetic machines come closer to accommodating muscular force capabilities by producing a resistance to movement that is equivalent to the force you exert. The harder you push or pull, the greater will be the resistance you experience. The weaker the effort, the less the resistance. The difference between the cam and moving pivot and the isokinetic machines (disregarding weight stack and speed settings, respectively) is that with the former, the shape of the cam or the position of the roller dictates the effort you must exert. With isokinetic machines, how hard you push or pull determines the effort throughout the exercise movement. There is some dispute as to whether constant speed is really achieved with isokinetic machines, but there is little argument over their ability to control momentum, which is an important safety feature.

SAFETY CHARACTERISTICS OF MACHINES

Weight training machines are safer to train with than free weights, especially for those who have limited experience in the weight room. An important feature of these machines is that the weight stacks are located away from the person lifting; because the bars and weight plates cannot fall or be dropped, they won't cause the kinds of injuries we sometimes see with free weights. Consequently, there is no need for a spotter. The use of fixed- and variable-resistance machines, however, can result in injury to muscles, tendons, and joint structures if momentum is not controlled by performing exercises in a *slow, controlled* manner. The isokinetic machines that do not create momentum are safer. The stationary nature of all of the machines discussed here also permits safer travel to and from exercise stations. However, even though these machines are safer to use than free weights, there are still precautions that should be followed.

BEFORE USING MACHINES

Before using machines, *check* for frayed cables and belts, worn pulleys and chains, broken welds, loose pads, and uneven or rough movement. If any of these exist, do not use the machine until they have been repaired. Adjust levers and seats to accommodate your body size. When you are training on machines, assume a stable position on the seats, pads, and rollers. Fasten seat belts securely. Choose an appropriate load. Insert selector keys all the way. Perform exercises through the full range of motion in a *slow* and *controlled* manner. Do not allow the weight stacks to bounce during the lower phases of exercises or to hit the pulleys during the upward phases. *Never* place your hands between weight stacks to dislodge a selector key or to adjust loads, and keep them away from the chains, belts, pulleys, and cams.

FREE WEIGHT EQUIPMENT CHARACTERISTICS

The barbells and dumbbells have certain characteristics you should be familiar with (see Figure 1.6). On the typical barbell (Figure 1.6a), the middle section has both smooth and knurled, or roughened, areas, and *collars* on each side. The weight plates slide up to the collars, which stop the plates from sliding inward toward the hands. The *locks* slide up to the plates and keep them from sliding off the ends. A typical bar with collars and locks weighs approximately 5 pounds per foot, thus a 5-foot bar weighs approximately 25 pounds, a 6-foot bar, 30 pounds, and so on. Dumbbells (Figure 1.6, b and c) have a similar design

except they are shorter and the entire middle section of the bar, between the weight plates, is usually knurled. The dumbbell bar with collars and locks weighs approximately 3 pounds but is not usually considered when the weight of the dumbbell is recorded. For example, a dumbbell with a 10-pound plate on each side is described as weighing 20 pounds, not 23 pounds.

The longest barbell in a weight room, an *Olympic bar* (Figure 1.6d), is 7 feet long and weighs 45 pounds without locks. The locks vary in shape (Figure 1.6, e and f), and their weight (each) may range from less than a pound to 5 pounds. Therefore, an Olympic bar with locks can weigh as much as 55 pounds. An Olympic bar has the same diameter as most bars in the weight room except for the section between the collar and the end of the bar, where the diameter is greater. This is an important distinction to recognize when loading the bar. Only the *Olympic weight plates* (Figure 1.6g) (with larger diameter holes) will fit properly onto the Olympic bar. The plates with the smaller holes (Figure 1.6h) will not fit onto the Olympic bar.

Another type of bar is the *cambered*, or curl, bar (Figure 1.6i). It has the same characteristics as the barbell, except that it has curves that enable you to isolate certain muscle groups better than with a straight bar.

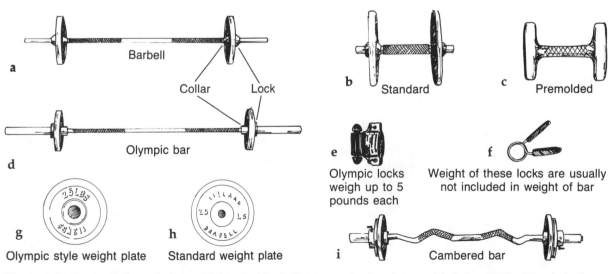

Figure 1.6 Free weight equipment: The typical barbell (a), standard and premolded dumbbells (b and c), the Olympic bar (d) and locks (e and f), the Olympic weight plate (g), the standard weight plate (h), and the cambered bar (i).

SAFETY CONSIDERATIONS FOR FREE WEIGHTS

The use of free weight barbells and dumbbells requires higher levels of motor coordination than do machines. The term *free* refers to their nonrestrictive effect on joint movement. This freedom of movement, however, easily translates into potential injury when correct lifting, loading, and spotting techniques are not used. This is not to say that free weight training is dangerous. When reasonable precautions are taken, it can be very safe, and it can even be more effective than machines in strengthening joint structures.

As you become more familiar with the free weight equipment, you will quickly realize that barbells and dumbbells offer tremendous versatility—your choice of exercises to perform is virtually unlimited. And if you plan to train at home, this versatility and the lower cost of free weight equipment will make it the preferred type of equipment.

However, you should take certain precautions to make free weight training safe and productive.

PRECAUTIONS IN THE WEIGHT ROOM

The following list of actions in the weight room will avoid potentially dangerous situations and make training safer.

Load Bars Properly

Take great care to load bars *evenly* and with the proper amount of load. If the ends of a suspended bar (on the "flat" or incline bench, and on the squat rack supports) are not loaded evenly, serious injury can result. Learning the weight of different bars and of the weight plates will help you in loading the bar evenly and in placing the proper amount of load on the bar.

Lock Barbells and Dumbbells

Lifting with unlocked barbells and dumbbells is truly dangerous. Plates not secured with locks easily slide off the bar and can land on feet or other body parts. *Locks* should be *checked for tightness* before each set of exercises. Do not assume that the last person using the barbell or dumbbell tightened the locks. Also check to see that the collars are secure.

Avoid Backing Into Others

Because of sudden losses in balance or simply being unaware that anyone is near you, you may back into someone. Take care to avoid this, as an untimely bump may cause a barbell or dumbbell held overhead to be dropped on the head (from a standing press) or a dumbbell to be dropped into the face (as in the supine dumbbell fly exercise) or any of a variety of other injuries.

Be Aware of Extended Bars

Extended bars are the bars that overhang or extend outward from machines, or barbells supported on racks (e.g., on the squat rack) or uprights (as for the bench press), or bars held in the hands. Of special concern are bars positioned at or above shoulder height. You can cause serious facial injuries if you are not careful as you move about the weight room. The lat pulldown bar and the free barbell held at or above shoulder height are the most likely sources of such injuries. Be especially cautious around people who are performing overhead exercises.

Store Equipment Properly

Each piece of equipment in the weight room should have a special storage location. Barbells, dumbbells, and weight plates left unattended, and those not replaced in their proper locations, are often tripped over or slipped on. See that the equipment you use is always placed in appropriate racks and locations. This applies to your equipment at home as well as to the equipment in a weight training facility. At home there may be an added danger if children are able to climb on equipment or attempt to lift plates and bars that are too heavy for them. Locate and secure weight training equipment so that children do not have access to it without your supervision.

Equipment-Related Drills

1. Equipment Recognition

This drill involves describing characteristics of different weight training equipment and determining whether the equipment exists in your weight room. Describe the characteristics of each type of equipment, then place a check mark (✔) to the left of each type of equipment that you are able to find in your weight room. You probably will not be able to check off all eight types listed.

Free Weight Equipment   *Characteristics*

____ Standard bar   _____

____ Olympic bar   _____

____ Cambered bar   _____

____ Dumbbells   _____

Machine Equipment

____ Fixed resistance   _____

Variable resistance:

____ Rolling pivot   _____

____ Cam   _____

____ Isokinetic—constant speed   _____

Success Goals =

   a. 8 out 8 types of equipment are described

   b. equipment that exists in the weight room is checked off

Your Scores =

   a. (#) ____ types of equipment described

   b. ____ check marks are recorded in the spaces for all types that exist in your weight room (yes or no)

2. Safety Checklists Drill

Below is a summary of the safety procedures and practices described earlier in this step. Without performing an exercise, demonstrate as many of the safety activities as possible. Mark a check (✔) to the left of the ones you complete. Then mark an X next to the left of those for which you understand what to do but that you cannot actually complete until you have an exercise to perform. Those that you cannot complete at this time have an asterisk (*) to their immediate left. At the conclusion of this drill, identify the activities that you have not completed. Then locate and read again the information that will enable you to understand and perform these when you are learning exercises and spotting techniques in Steps 4 through 10.

a. Machine Equipment Checklist Drill

If weight machines are available, perform this checklist of activites. Use check marks (ν) and Xs as described previously.

Before Using Machines

____ Check for frayed cables, belts, pulleys, worn chains, loose pads.
____ Check for smoothness of movement on guide rods.
____ Adjust levers and seats.
____ Insert selector keys all the way in.
____ Keep your hands away from the chains, belts, pulleys, and cams.
____ *Never* place your fingers or hands between weight stacks.

During Exercise Session

____ Assume a stable position on seats and pads.
____ Fasten belts securely (if applicable).
____ *Perform exercises through the full range of movement.
____ *Perform exercises in a *slow, controlled* manner.

Success Goals =

a. 6 out of 6 check marks are made in the ''Before Using Machines'' section

b. 2 out of 2 check marks are recorded in the ''During Exercise Session'' section

c. 2 out of 2 Xs are recorded in the ''During Exercise Session'' section

Your Scores =

a. (#) ____ check marks in the ''Before Using Machines'' section

b. (#) ____ check marks in the ''During Exercise Session'' section

c. (#) ____ Xs in the ''During Exercise Session'' section

b. Free Weight Equipment Safety Checklist

If free weights are available, perform this checklist of activities. Use a check mark (ν) or an X as described previously.

Before Using Free Weights

____ Check for tightness of collars.
____ If collars are welded, check for integrity of the welds.
____ Use locks, and tighten securely.
____ Be sure to load both ends of the bar evenly.

During Exercise Session

____ *Avoid walking into bars that extend outward.
____ *Avoid walking near persons performing overhead lifts.
____ *Do not perform overhead lifts or squats (back or front) in an area where others are performing supine exercises.
____ *Avoid backing into others.
____ *Perform exercises through the full range of movement.
____ *Perform exercises in a *slow, controlled* manner.

After Exercising

____ Place equipment back in its proper location.

Success Goals =

a. 4 out of 4 check marks are made in the "Before Using Free Weights" section

b. 6 out of 6 Xs are recorded in the "During Exercise Session" section

c. 1 check mark is made in the "After Exercising" section

Your Scores =

a. (#) ____ check marks in the "Before Using Free Weights" section

b. (#) ____ Xs in the "During Exercise Session" section

c. (#) ____ check mark in the "After Exercising" section

Summary

Becoming familiar with the various types of weight training equipment and how they are used safely is a logical starting point if you have not trained before. This involves being able to identify what the equipment is designed to do and how to use it, and determining whether it is in good working order. It is unwise to train on any piece of equipment until these things are understood. Be sure that you have completed all of the drills in this step and have a good understanding of the concepts covered before moving on to Step 2.

Safety and Technique Fundamentals

Step 2 Lifting and Spotting Fundamentals

Now that you have gained a knowledge of how to use weight training equipment safely, concentrate on the basic skill of lifting and handling a barbell, dumbbell, weight plate, or any heavy object off the floor. It is also important at this time to learn the fundamentals of spotting free weight exercises.

WHY ARE LIFTING AND SPOTTING FUNDAMENTALS IMPORTANT?

Lifting is a fundamental skill that is used every day in the weight room, at home or in the dormitory, and at work. Learning to do these basic fundamentals of weight training *correctly* decreases your likelihood of injuring yourself and increases your chances of getting the most out of training sessions. The cornerstone of safe and effective weight training programs is proper exercise technique. Exercises performed correctly avoid placing extraordinary stress on muscles, tendons, ligaments, bones, and the joints formed by these structures. Proper technique also produces quicker results, because it positions body parts in the angles at which muscles can best be taxed and stimulated to improve. Using proper breathing techniques helps prevent blackouts, which can lead to potentially life-threatening circumstances. The fundamentals learned in Step 2 can be applied to all exercises and spotting procedures described in this text. While you are learning these basic lifting and spotting skills, *always* use a very light bar, a dowel stick, or a light load selection on machines.

CORRECT LIFTING TECHNIQUES

The techniques of lifting involve focusing on four things: (a) having a good grip, (b) having a stable position from which to lift, (c) keeping the object being lifted close to the body, and (d) learning to use your legs, not your back, to do the lifting.

Gripping the Bar

There are two things to consider when establishing a grip: the *type* of grip used and *where* and *how far apart* the hands grip the bar. The grips that may be used to lift a bar off the floor are the *overhand*, or pronated, grip; the *underhand*, or supinated, grip; and the *alternate* grip. Note that the knuckles are up in the overhand grip (Figure 2.1a) and that the thumbs are toward each other. In the underhand grip (Figure 2.1b), the palms are up and the thumbs face away from each other. The alternate grip (Figure 2.1c) involves having one hand in an underhand grip and the other in an overhand grip. It does not matter which hand is used to grip the bar in the overhand or underhand fashion. In the alternate grip, sometimes called the mixed grip (Figure 2.1c), the thumbs point in the same direction.

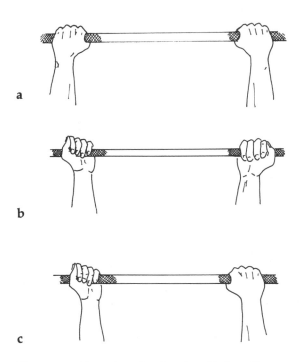

Figure 2.1 Bar grips: Overhand, with knuckles up (a), underhand, with palms up (b), and alternate (c).

All of these are termed *closed* grips, meaning that the fingers and thumbs are wrapped (closed) around the bar. When the thumbs do not wrap around the bar, the grip is referred to as an *open*, or false, grip. The open grip is very dangerous, because it is easy for the bar to roll out of the palms of the hand and onto the face or foot, causing severe injury. Always use a closed grip!

Width of Grip

Figure 2.2 shows several grip widths used in weight training. In some exercises the width of the grip places the hands at about shoulder width and equidistant from the weight plates. This is referred to as the "common" grip. Some exercises require a narrower grip, others a wider grip. You will need to learn the proper width for each exercise, as well as where to place your hands on the bar so that the bar is in a balanced position. An imbalanced grip can result in serious injury. Become familiar with the smooth and knurled (roughened) areas of the bar discussed in Step 1, and where the hands should be placed on these areas. Doing so will help you establish a balanced grip and get the most out of the exercise. Note that the grip used later in explaining proper lifting techniques is the common grip.

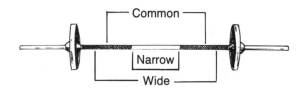

Figure 2.2 Common, narrow, and wide grip widths.

Preparatory Lifting Position

The preparatory lifting position shown in Figure 2.3, a and b, places the body in a stable position that calls upon the legs, not the back, to do the lifting, whereas the lifting position shown in Figure 2.3c places a lot of stress on the lower back. When lifting, think, "The bar

Figure 2.3 The correct preparatory lifting position (a and b) places stress on the legs, not on the lower back (c).

stays close, the hips stay low, and the back stays flat." The lifting mechanics presented here apply when lifting any heavy object, not just a barbell.

Take hold of the bar, using the common grip, and move into the correct preparatory position shown in Figure 2.3, a and b. Move up to the bar so that your shins are almost touching. Positioning the bar close to your shins keeps the weight being lifted closer to the lifting/pulling action, enabling you to exert a more effective force with your legs. Because lifting from this position places the load more on your legs than on your lower back, it is less apt to injure your lower back. Keep the applied force in line with the resistance (load), or as close as possible to it; this is a key concept to remember.

To establish a stable position, your feet must be flat on the floor, with the toes pointing slightly outward. Your feet should be positioned shoulder-width apart or slightly wider. Within reason, the wider your stance or "base of support," the greater your stability or balance. This is another important concept to adhere to when you are performing overhead exercises with dumbbells or barbells—or machine exercises that involve positioning your feet on the floor, or positioning your head, torso, hips, and legs on or against the equipment.

Now straighten your elbows and lower your hips. Your shoulders should be over or slightly ahead of the bar. Your head is up, and your eyes are looking straight ahead. Your back is in a "flat" or slightly arched position. Keep your chest out and your shoulders back by pulling the scapulae (shoulder blades) toward each other. Imagine the position typically assumed by a gorilla. Believe it or not, this is the position that is being described here, and getting into it is not as easy as it may appear. Oftentimes one or both heels will lift up when you move into the low position, causing you to step forward to catch your balance. If balance is a problem for you, work on Drill 2 at the end of this step. Also realize that proper head position (eyes straight ahead) is critical to maintaining proper body positioning. If there is a mirror available, watch yourself as you move into the low preparatory position. Does your back stay in a flat position, and do your heels stay in contact with the floor?

Lifting the Bar

Once you begin lifting (Figure 2.4a), say these things to yourself: "The bar stays close," "The hips stay low as the legs straighten," and "The back remains flat throughout the lifting." Keeping your head upright and your eyes looking straight ahead will help you accomplish these things. Get a mental picture of the head, shoulder, back, and hip positions shown. The most important things to remember are to keep the barbell, dumbbell, or weight plate as close as possible and to *use your leg muscles, not your back*! In preparation for pulling, breathe in to stabilize your upper torso. As you bring the bar to a point above your knees, exhale.

In the floor-to-thigh execution phase (Figure 2.4, a-c), you are pulling the barbell to your midthigh in a slow, controlled manner. At this height the barbell or object may be placed in a rack or handed to a partner, or be the first phase of an exercise (e.g., an initial pull of the bar to the shoulders in the overhead press, as described in Step 6). If you need to pull the barbell to your shoulders (Figure 2.4, d-f; thigh-to-shoulder execution phase), continue pulling; do not allow the bar to rest on your thighs. Instead, "brush" the bar against them as you continue to pull upward. During the pulling action, keep the bar close and your elbows straight until your legs straighten completely.

As you straighten your legs, your hips move forward quickly, followed by a rapid shoulder shrug of the trapezius muscles (between the neck and shoulder). Typically you will raise up on the balls of your feet at this point, as shown in Figure 2.4e. Visualize yourself jumping with the barbell while keeping your elbows straight. At the very peak of the shrug (and the bar's acceleration), your elbows flex and the bar is racked (caught) on the shoulders. Finish the racking movement by moving your elbows upward and forward (Figure 2.4f). Keep your elbows pointed outward and your wrists below the elbows (Figure 2.4g) for as long as possible during the pull (i.e., before flexing them in the racking movement). Time your racking of the bar on your shoulders so that your knees and hips are flexed as the bar makes contact. This will help to absorb the force of the bar's impact on your shoulders.

RETURNING THE BAR TO THE FLOOR

When lowering the bar or any heavy object to the floor, remember what you have learned about having a stable position, keeping the bar or weight close, keeping your back flat, using your legs, and moving the bar in a slow, controlled manner. If the bar is at shoulder height, allow its weight to slowly pull your arms to a straightened position, which should place the bar in a resting position (very briefly) on your thighs. Your hips and knees should be flexed so that, as the bar touches your thigh, its weight is absorbed. The bar is paused very briefly at midthigh before being lowered to the floor. Remember to keep your head up and back flat throughout the bar's return to the floor.

Breathing

Correct breathing involves *breathing out* during the *working or exertion phase* of exercise, and *inhaling during the relaxation phase*. Thus, when lifting a bar (or other object), exhale as the bar passes through the most difficult part of the lift (the ''sticking point''). If you are lifting the bar only to thigh level, the sticking point would be located just above your knees. If you are pulling the bar to your shoulders, the sticking point occurs at the peak of your shoulder shrug. Inhale as you lower the bar back to the floor. Be aware that you will have a tendency to hold your breath throughout the entire exertion phase. This should be avoided, because *it is dangerous*! By not exhaling, you reduce the return of blood to your heart, which in turn reduces the blood flow to your brain. If your brain is deprived of oxygen-rich blood, you will become dizzy and may faint. This is an inappropriate method of breathing for all exercises, and it is especially dangerous when you are performing overhead exercises. If you have high blood pressure, it is imperative that you use proper breathing during the execution of each exercise.

Also *avoid breathing rapidly* between efforts, as this may cause dizziness and nausea. If you are breathing rapidly, you are performing exercises too quickly, inhaling and exhaling at the wrong times, or both.

Figure 2.4 Keys to Success: Lifting Fundamentals

Preparation Phase

1. Use appropriate grip (Figure 2.4g shows overhand grip) ____
2. Grip slightly wider than shoulder width ____
3. Arms outside the knees ____
4. Bar close to shins (almost touching) ____
5. Feet shoulder-width apart ____
6. Feet flat on floor, toes pointed slightly outward ____
7. Hips low—''gorilla'' position ____
8. Arms straight ____
9. Shoulders over or slightly forward of bar ____
10. Head up, eyes focused straight ahead (throughout exercise) ____
11. Back slightly arched or flat, and tensed ____
12. Scapulae (shoulder blades) pulled toward each other ____
13. Chest held high ____

Execution
Phase, Upward

Floor to Thigh

1. Inhale before pulling ____
2. Slow, controlled pull ____
3. Back remains straight or slightly arched ____
4. Knees begin to straighten while hips stay low ____
5. Arms remain straight ____
6. Bar stays close to shins, knees, and thighs ____
7. Shoulders stay in position as knees straighten ____
8. Exhale when reaching midthigh ____

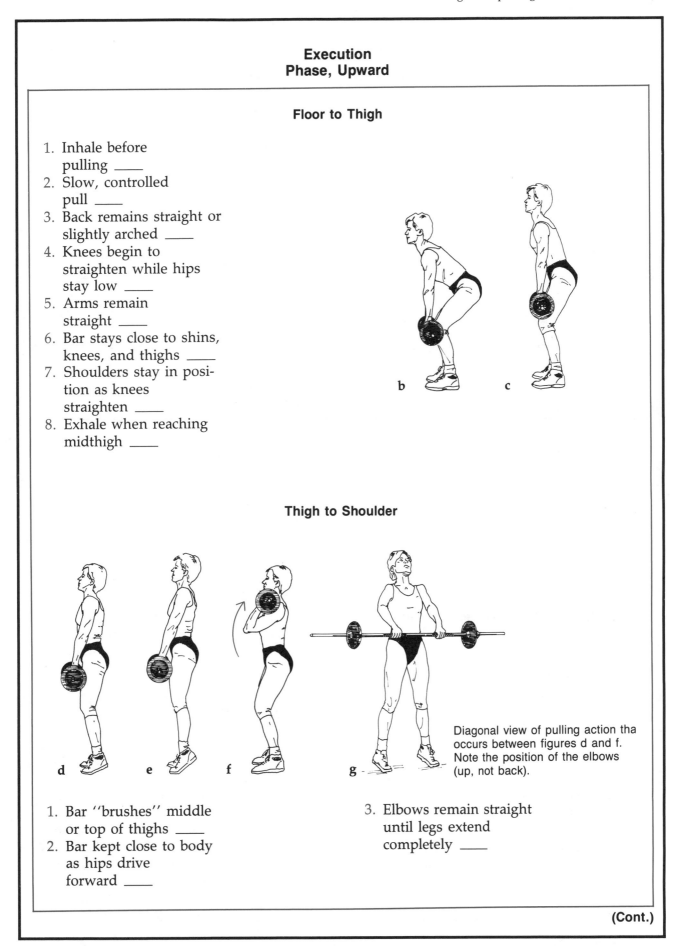

b   c

Thigh to Shoulder

d   e   f   g

Diagonal view of pulling action that occurs between figures d and f. Note the position of the elbows (up, not back).

1. Bar "brushes" middle or top of thighs ____
2. Bar kept close to body as hips drive forward ____

3. Elbows remain straight until legs extend completely ____

(Cont.)

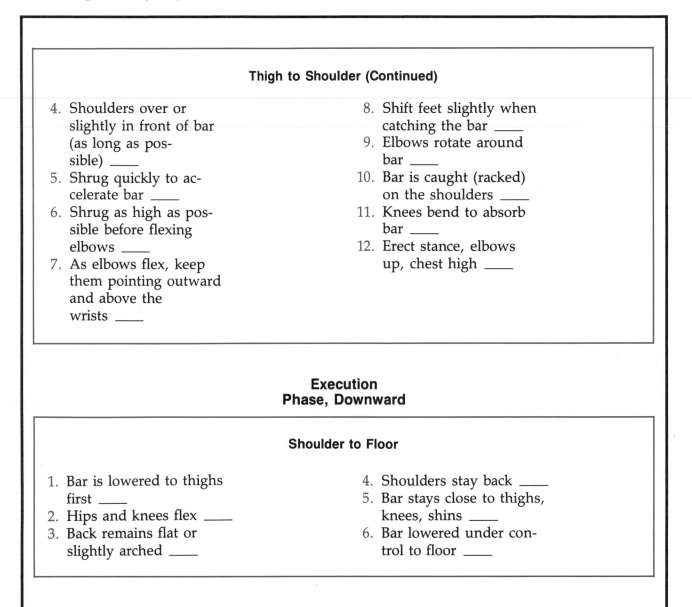

Thigh to Shoulder (Continued)

4. Shoulders over or slightly in front of bar (as long as possible) ____
5. Shrug quickly to accelerate bar ____
6. Shrug as high as possible before flexing elbows ____
7. As elbows flex, keep them pointing outward and above the wrists ____

8. Shift feet slightly when catching the bar ____
9. Elbows rotate around bar ____
10. Bar is caught (racked) on the shoulders ____
11. Knees bend to absorb bar ____
12. Erect stance, elbows up, chest high ____

**Execution
Phase, Downward**

Shoulder to Floor

1. Bar is lowered to thighs first ____
2. Hips and knees flex ____
3. Back remains flat or slightly arched ____

4. Shoulders stay back ____
5. Bar stays close to thighs, knees, shins ____
6. Bar lowered under control to floor ____

SPOTTER'S RESPONSIBILITIES

A spotter is someone who assists, as needed, in the execution of an exercise. Spotters in the weight room play a crucial role in making weight training a safe activity. As a spotter you must realize that being inattentive in the weight room can cause very serious injuries (muscle/tendon tears, facial and other bone fractures, broken teeth, etc.). Not all exercises require spotters, but exercises such as the free weight bench press and overhead press, which are included in your basic program, can result in serious injuries if not spotted correctly. The individuals you spot are depending on you. Do not underestimate the significance of your responsibilities as a spotter. Read and heed the following guidelines for spotting free weight exercises and for being responsible to the spotter when you are lifting. Specific instructions for spotting are provided later in this text for exercises requiring spotters.

Guidelines for Spotting Free Weight Exercises

1. Move all loose plates, barbells, and dumbbells away from the area to avoid slipping or tripping on them.
2. Know the Keys to Success Spotting Techniques/Procedures for the exercise.
3. Place your body in the proper position, with your hands as close to the bar as possible without obstructing the movement of the bar.
4. Place your body in a good lifting position in case you have to "catch" the bar

(keep your knees flexed and your back flat).

5. Effectively communicate with the person you are spotting (e.g., know how many reps he or she intends to complete).
6. Use the appropriate grip (a closed grip is a must!) with the proper hand location on the bar (if you need to grip the bar).
7. See that the bar is properly and evenly loaded.
8. Be knowledgeable about dangerous and potentially dangerous situations associated with the exercise being performed. (These will be identified throughout the text.)
9. Be alert and quick to respond to dangerous situations.
10. Know when and how, if needed, to guide the bar in the desired path.
11. Know when, and how much, lifting assistance is needed to complete the exercise.

12. As a last resort, assume all of the weight of the bar, but only if the person you are spotting might be injured if you didn't.
13. Suggest appropriate form changes as necessary.

Remember: *Spotters with poor technique can be injured, too!*

Your Responsibilities to the Spotter

1. Before the exercise begins, communicate how many reps you intend to complete.
2. During the exercise, indicate when you need assistance.
3. Always stay with the bar. That is, once the spotter needs to assist, remember to *not* release the bar or stop trying to complete the exercise. If you do, the entire weight of the bar is taken by the spotter, which may injure the spotter.
4. Learn your limits, and select appropriate loads and reps. (This is commonly a problem for individuals new to training.)

Detecting Errors in Lifting the Bar

Approach the detection of errors with the thought that recognizing errors will enable you to quickly develop excellent lifting skills. The errors that follow are typical. Of special concern are (a) the knees straightening immediately during the floor-to-thigh phase, (b) the elbows flexing too soon during the thigh-to-shoulder phase, and (c) not lowering the hips in the shoulder-to-floor phase.

ERROR   **CORRECTION**

Floor-to-Thigh Phase

1. Your heels raise up.

1. Too much weight is on the balls of your feet. You may be leaning too far forward. "Sit back" into the low position, and concentrate on putting more of your weight on your heels.

ERROR Ø	CORRECTION
2. Your upward pull is not smooth.	2. Straighten your elbows before pulling, and pull slowly.
3. Your hips raise up first when pulling.	3. This puts stress on your back rather than your legs. Your knees are straightening too soon! Think, ''Lead the upward movement with my shoulders''—not the hips. This will enable you to use your legs instead of your back to do the lifting.

Thigh-to-Shoulder Phase

1. Bar stops on your thighs.	1. The pull from the floor to your thighs should be continuous. Do not allow yourself to pause or stop the bar at your thighs.
2. Bar swings away from your thighs and hips.	2. Concentrate on pulling the bar up straight and keeping it in close to your thighs and hips.
3. Your elbows bend too soon.	3. Wait until your shrug is at its highest point before bending your elbows.
4. Your knees are straight when racking.	4. Having your knees flexed provides ''give'' to your shoulders as you rack the bar on them, and this dissipates much of the impact.

Shoulder-to-Floor Phase

1. Bar does not pause at your thighs.	1. Visualize the downward phase as a 2-count movement, ''1'' to the thigh, ''2'' to the floor.
2. Your hips remain high while lowering the bar from thigh-height to the floor.	2. This is stressful on the back! Once the bar reaches the thigh, squat down to lower the bar while keeping an upright and flat-back position.

Lifting Fundamental Drills

1. Grip Selection and Location

This series of drills involves lifting an empty bar or a dowel stick from the floor using the three types of grips in the three grip-width positions listed below. Your hands should be positioned on the bar so that the bar is balanced as you pull it to your thighs. Begin with a wide grip (see Figure 2.2) on the bar, using an underhand grip (see Figure 2.1). Using correct lifting technique, lift the bar to your thighs and then lower it back to the floor. Lift the bar twice more to your thighs, using first the overhand grip and then the alternated grip. Now move your hands to the common grip width and use the three different types of grips. Next move your hands to the narrow grip and do the same. Perform all grips with your thumbs around the bar.

Wide Grip Width—Underhand, Overhand, Alternated

   a. Three different grips are performed   Yes ____   No ____

   b. Spacing of the hands produces a balanced bar   Yes ____   No ____

   c. Grips performed with thumbs around bar   Yes ____   No ____

Common Grip Width—Underhand, Overhand, Alternated

   a. Three different grips are performed   Yes ____   No ____

   b. Spacing of the hands produces a balanced bar   Yes ____   No ____

   c. Grips performed with thumbs around bar   Yes ____   No ____

Narrow Grip Width—Underhand, Overhand, Alternated

   a. Three different grips are performed   Yes ____   No ____

   b. Spacing of the hands produces a balanced bar   Yes ____   No ____

   c. Grips performed with thumbs around bar   Yes ____   No ____

Success Goal = 9 "yes" responses to grip width and grip location questions

Your Score = (#) ____ "yes" responses

2. Preparation Position Drill

This drill will help you develop a better sense of balance and a greater awareness of proper body positioning. Squat down to the "gorilla" position with your hands clasped behind your head. Keep your balance without either heel rising up and without needing to step forward. Be sure to keep your head upright and your eyes looking straight ahead. Repeat this drill 10 times. Count the number of repetitions you are able to do without losing your balance.

Success Goal = 9 out 10 reps performed without losing balance

Your Score = (#) _____ reps performed with good balance

3. Floor-to-Thigh Drill

This drill is designed to assist you in learning to keep the bar in close to your shins, knees, and thighs, avoiding stress on your lower back.

From a standing position, move into the preparatory lifting position, and using the overhand grip, pull the bar to the middle of your thighs. Remember good lifting techniques: head up, back flat, and let the legs do the lifting. Lower the bar to the floor in the same manner. Repeat this drill 10 times. Doing this drill in front of a mirror is a great way to critique your technique. If a mirror is not available, have a qualified person observe and make appropriate comments about your technique. Count the number of times you are able to lift the bar and return it to the floor using good lifting technique.

Success Goal = 9 out of 10 reps performed with good lifting technique

Your Score = (#) _____ correctly performed reps

4. Thigh-to-Shoulder Drill

Most beginners have a great tendency to flex the elbows too soon during what is commonly referred to as the second pull—that is, the pull at the thigh that brings the bar to the shoulders. This drill will help you avoid this common technique flaw. Pick up the bar to your mid-thigh, using an overhand grip. With your knees and hips slightly flexed, perform a quick shoulder shrug, followed immediately by hip and knee extension while keeping your *elbows straight*. You may want to think of the movement as *jumping* with a bar while keeping your elbows straight. After each jump, return the bar to your thighs (not to the floor). Repeat this drill 10 times.

Success Goal = 9 out of 10 jumps (reps) performed with straight elbows

Your Score = (#) _____ correctly performed reps

5. Racking the Bar Drill

This drill will help you to develop the timing you need to flex your hips and knees when racking the bar on your shoulders. Follow the same procedures used in the previous drill, but instead of lowering the bar after the jump, pull the bar to your shoulders. Work on timing the "catch" of the bar at your shoulders with the flexing of your hips and knees and with your feet moving to a stance that is somewhat wider than in the initial position.

Success Goal = 8 out of 10 reps are racked with the hips, knees, and feet properly positioned

Your Score = (#) _____ correctly performed reps

6. Shoulder-to-Floor Drill

This drill will help you learn to smoothly, and without injury, return the bar to the floor. Lift the bar to the shoulders and return it to the floor 5 times.

Success Goals =

a. 4 out of 5 of the reps performed with a pause at the thighs before the bar is lowered to the floor

b. 5 out of 5 of the reps performed in an upright, flat-back position while the hips and knees flex to lower the bar from the thighs to the floor

Your Scores =

a. (#) _____ reps paused at the thigh

b. (#) _____ reps in which the hips and thighs flex to lower the bar to the floor

Summary

Good lifting technique requires a proper grip, a stable position from which to lift, keeping the object being lifted close to your body, and using your legs rather than your back. Remember, "Hips stay low as the legs straighten." This is true regardless of whether you are lifting a barbell (review Figure 2.4, a-g), lifting a box off the floor, or spotting in an exercise. By developing good fundamental techniques, you avoid injury and work your muscles in ways that will most effectively develop your strength.

Step 3 Identifying Practice Procedures

Steps 4 through 10 present explanations and illustrations of various weight training exercises. Step 3 explains how Steps 4 through 10 are organized and what is expected of you in them.

WHY IS THIS STEP ON IDENTIFYING PRACTICE PROCEDURES IMPORTANT?

Insight gained from this step will enable you to learn exercises quickly and safely, increasing your confidence, enjoyment, and success in the weight room.

Steps 4 through 10 begin with explanations and illustrations of exercises, which are followed by practice procedures and some drills. The following practice procedures (sometimes referred to simply as procedures) describe tasks that will help you learn how to perform exercises and determine loads to use when performing them.

1. Choose one exercise.
2. Practice grip, body positioning, and movement pattern.
3. Determine warm-up and trial loads.
4. Add proper range of motion, velocity, and breathing.
5. Visualize correct techniques.
6. Determine the training load.
7. Make needed load changes.

Each of these practice procedures will be described in detail.

1. CHOOSE ONE EXERCISE

In Steps 4 through 10 you will need to choose exercises to include in your weight training program. You will choose one exercise for each of the muscle groups shown in Figure 3.1, a and b. There are usually one free weight and two machine exercises from which to choose. Read the exercise technique explanations for each and view the Keys to Success. Consider the equipment and spotting requirements of each exercise.

2. PRACTICE GRIP, BODY POSITIONING, AND MOVEMENT PATTERN

This procedure has you practice the grip, body positioning, and movement pattern involved in the exercise selected. These must be correct, otherwise the outcomes designed for the exercise will be compromised.

Grips

As you know from Step 2, there are a variety of grips (and grip widths) that can be used. Use this practice procedure to learn which one

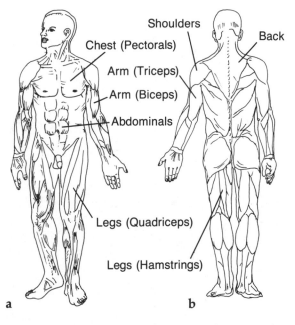

Figure 3.1 Anterior (a) and posterior (b) views of the muscle groups included in the basic program.

is correct for each exercise and to gain experience using it.

Body Positioning

Proper positioning in lying or standing exercises, or on equipment, provides a balanced and stable position. Positioning refers to the initial posture of the body, not arm or leg movements. Be sure you acquire the correct body position and use it in all future workouts.

Movement Pattern

The movement pattern refers to how the arms, legs, and trunk move during the execution of an exercise. Use this practice procedure to learn the correct movements for the involved body parts, and then practice them.

3. DETERMINE WARM-UP, TRIAL, AND TRAINING LOADS

It is important to use light loads in the early stages of learning weight training exercises so that you are able to concentrate on the techniques and do not have to worry about how hard to push or pull. Out of enthusiasm or curiosity, you may be tempted to use loads that are too heavy. When you select a load that is too heavy, even if your technique is perfect, you increase the chances that you will be injured.

In this practice procedure you will use the formulas shown in Figure 3.2 to determine the warm-up and trial loads for most exercises. After making your exercise selection, you will need to identify the chosen exercise in the formula. The letters FW (for free weight), C (for cam), and M (for multi-unit—can be single-unit too) are used to assist you in doing this. Realize that the coefficients are estimates. The unique differences of individuals combined with the variance in equipment design make it difficult, if not impossible, to derive coefficients that are without error. Those presented in this text are starting points for determining appropriate loads.

After you've identified the correct exercise, fill in your body weight in the appropriate space and multiply it by the number to the right of it (the coefficient). The use of body weight in determining appropriate loads is based upon the relationship that body weight has to strength. This is the reason for weight divisions in such sports as wrestling, boxing, and weight lifting. The coefficient is a number that has been derived from studies of males and females experienced and inexperienced in weight training. When multiplied by your body weight, the coefficient can be used in estimating warm-up and trial or training loads. Note, if you are a male who weighs more than 175 pounds simply record your body weight as 175. If you are a female and weigh over 140 pounds record your body weight as 140. The trial load will always be heavier than the warm-up load, because the coefficient used to determine it is about double that of the warm-up load. Sometimes the calculated warm-up loads for women are lighter than the lightest weight-stack plate on a machine. If this occurs, position a spotter so that he or she is able to safely assist (by pushing or pulling) in accomplishing the movement patterns involved in the exercise. The bars available for free weight exercises may pose the same problems. If so, very light dumbbells, a stripped-down dumbbell bar, or a single weight plate may be used in acquiring the warm-up and movement pattern of exercises.

To complete this practice procedure, round off numbers to the nearest 5-pound increment or to the closest weight-stack plate. The example in Figure 3.2 is of a female who weighs 120 pounds and has selected the free weight bench press from the three chest exercises available. In this example, the rounded-off warm-up (Figure 3.2a) and trial loads (Figure 3.2b) are 25 pounds and 40 pounds, respectively. The warm-up load is used in learning the techniques included in practice procedure 4, while the trial load is used in procedure 6 to determine the training load. Note that the term *trial load* is used because you will be "trying it out" in procedure 6 to see if it is an appropriate load to use later for training. Trial loads that are too heavy or light can be adjusted using Figure 3.3, provided in procedure 7.

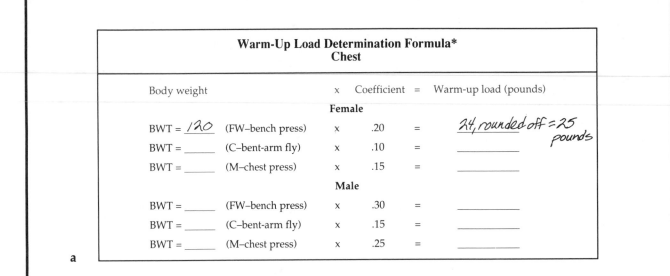

Warm-Up Load Determination Formula*
Chest

Body weight		x	Coefficient	=	Warm-up load (pounds)
			Female		
BWT = _120_	(FW–bench press)	x	.20	=	_24, rounded off = 25 pounds_
BWT = _____	(C–bent-arm fly)	x	.10	=	_____
BWT = _____	(M–chest press)	x	.15	=	_____
			Male		
BWT = _____	(FW–bench press)	x	.30	=	_____
BWT = _____	(C–bent-arm fly)	x	.15	=	_____
BWT = _____	(M–chest press)	x	.25	=	_____

a

Trial Load Determination Formula*
Chest

Body weight		x	Coefficient	=	Trial load (pounds)
			Female		
BWT = _120_	(FW–bench press)	x	.35	=	_42, rounded off = 40 pounds_
BWT = _____	(C–bent-arm fly)	x	.14	=	_____
BWT = _____	(M–chest press)	x	.27	=	_____
			Male		
BWT = _____	(FW–bench press)	x	.60	=	_____
BWT = _____	(C–bent-arm fly)	x	.30	=	_____
BWT = _____	(M–chest press)	x	.55	=	_____

b

*BWT = body weight, FW = free weight, C = cam, and M = multi- or single-unit machine exercise.

Figure 3.2 Determining warm-up loads (a) and trial loads (b).

4. ADD PROPER RANGE OF MOTION, VELOCITY, AND BREATHING

The term *range of motion* refers to moving the involved body part(s) through the entire movement pattern of the exercise. Performing an exercise in this manner enables the muscle(s) of those body parts to become more active and, therefore, better trained. During this practice procedure, notice the beginning and end points of the movement pattern, and be sure to reach them in each exercise.

Velocity is the speed of movement throughout the range of motion of an exercise. It is especially important during this practice procedure that you establish slow movement patterns. In doing so, you are better able to acquire the proper movement pattern and range of motion of the exercise, and to do so without injuring yourself.

Trying to remember when to exhale and inhale can be confusing, especially when there are other skills to remember. During this practice procedure, learn to identify the "sticking point" in an exercise—the point at which continuing the rep is most difficult—and tell yourself to *exhale* during it. After the sticking point has passed, and during the recovery movement phase, you should *inhale*.

5. VISUALIZE CORRECT TECHNIQUES

Visualization of the correct techniques is an excellent method to help establish in your mind correct exercise and spotting techniques. This practice procedure is designed to encourage you to use all of your senses while visualizing the correct execution of an exercise. Try to find a quiet location in the weight room, or develop the ability, even under noisy conditions, to clearly visualize the proper grip, body positioning, range of motion, velocity, and breathing for each exercise. Attempt to do this for 1 to 2 minutes during this practice procedure.

6. DETERMINE THE TRAINING LOAD

This practice procedure is designed to help you determine an appropriate training load, one that will result in muscular failure on the 12th to 15th rep (when giving a maximum effort). Simply use the trial load determined in practice procedure 3, and perform as many reps as possible. If the number of reps completed is 12 to 15, you have found an appropriate training load to use. You will need to

record this amount; later (in Step 11) you will transfer it to your workout chart. If you performed less than 12 or more than 15 reps, you have one more practice procedure to complete before moving on to Step 4.

7. MAKE NEEDED LOAD CHANGES

Because individuals differ in physical characteristics and experience, and because weight training equipment differs in design, trial loads may not produce the desired range of 12 to 15 reps. If you performed less than 12 reps with the trial load, it is *too heavy*. On the other hand, if you easily performed more than 15 reps, it is *too light*. In this practice procedure you will use your trial loads and a load adjustment chart to make necessary adjustments. Once training begins you may need to use the adjustment chart several times before an accurate training load is determined. Figure 3.3, a and b, shows how the Determining the Training Load Formula is used to make needed adjustments to the trial load. The example given in Figure 3.3 is of someone who performed 9 reps with 100 pounds. Because only 9 reps, instead of 12 reps (or more), were performed, there is a need to reduce the load.

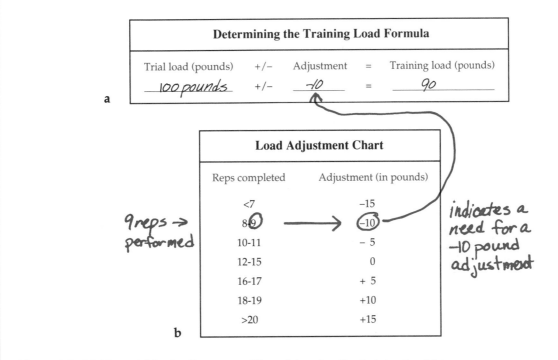

Figure 3.3 Making trial load adjustments (b) to determine the training load (a).

As you can see, 9 reps is associated with a 10-pound reduction. Thus, adjustments are added to, or subtracted from, the trial load to determine the training load. In this example, the 10-pound adjustment results in a training load of 90 pounds. In Step 11 you will transfer to your workout chart the training loads determined in this procedure.

Practice Procedure Quiz

Answer the following questions by checking off (✔) the correct answer:

1. The number of exercises you should choose in Steps 4 through 10 is [___ one, ___ two, ___ three].

2. In which practice procedure is the trial load used to determine your training load? [___ 2, ___ 3, ___ 6].

3. If you performed 12 to 15 reps with the trial load, you should continue on to [___ practice procedure 7, ___ the next step].

4. If you performed 17 reps with 100 pounds in practice procedure 6, what should your training load be? [___ 105 pounds, ___ 115 pounds, ___ 120 pounds].

5. If you performed 8 reps with 100 pounds in procedure 6, what should your training load be? [___ 80 pounds, ___ 90 pounds, ___ 100 pounds].

6. By making needed adjustments to the trial load, you arrive at the [___ adjusted load, ___ training load].

Answers to Practice Procedure Quiz

1. one
2. 6
3. practice procedure 7

4. 105 pounds
5. 90 pounds
6. training load

Summary

The practice procedures described here were organized so that you could concentrate on the specific techniques involved in each of the exercises presented in Steps 4 through 10, with loads light enough to allow you to do this safely. Follow the order of, and complete tasks included in, these practice procedures to discover how easy it is to learn weight training exercises, and how enjoyable training can be.

Step 4   Selecting a Chest Exercise

Some of the most popular exercises in weight training are those that work the chest muscles, or pectorals (pectoralis major, pectoralis minor), shown in Appendix B, anterior view. When developed properly, these muscles contribute a great deal to an attractive upper body and to added success in many recreational and athletic activities. The bench press, bent-arm fly, and chest press exercises described here provide an added benefit because they also work muscles of the shoulder (anterior deltoid). The bench press and chess press also work the back of the upper arm (tricep). Furthermore, the techniques involved are easily learned, and gains in muscular endurance and strength are made quickly. So don't be surprised if, after several workouts, you find that your chest exercise is your favorite exercise in your training program.

Free Weight Exercise

If you have access to free weights, you may select the bench press exercise to develop your chest. If you prefer working with machines, see the ''Machine Exercises'' section.

HOW TO PERFORM THE FREE WEIGHT BENCH PRESS

This exercise involves the use of a barbell and a special bench (called a bench-press bench). Begin by sitting down on the far end of the bench with your back to the upright supports. Now lie back and position yourself so that your buttocks, shoulders, and head are firmly and squarely on the bench, as shown in Figure 4.1a. Your legs should straddle the bench, and your feet should be flat on the floor, about shoulder-width apart. The three

contact points on the bench, plus your feet on the floor, equals four points of contact. This four-point position is important—especially the feet—because it provides a stable position when handling the bar over your chest and face.

From this position, slide toward the upright supports until your eyes are directly below the front edge of the shelf (of the uprights). This position helps prevent the bar from hitting the uprights during the upward execution phase, yet keeps the bar close enough to be easily placed back onto the shelf (''racked'') after the last repetition.

While the bar is supported on the uprights, grasp it with an evenly spaced, overhand grip, hands about shoulder-width apart or wider. An appropriate grip width on the bar positions the forearms perpendicular, or close to perpendicular, to the floor as the bar touches the chest. Keep in mind that a wide grip emphasizes a larger area of the chest than a narrow one and is usually the preferred grip width.

From this position, push the bar off the uprights to a straight-elbow position with your wrists directly over your elbows. Pause with the bar in the extended-arm position, and then lower the bar slowly to your chest as shown (in Figure 4.1b). The bar should contact your chest approximately an inch above or below the nipples. A woman may prefer to have the bar touch just below her breasts. Inhale as the bar is lowered to the chest. Once the bar touches the chest (do not bounce the bar off your chest), slowly push it straight upward to an extended-elbow position (see Figure 4.1c). Exhale through the sticking point, which occurs when the bar is about halfway up.

Throughout the exercise keep your head, shoulders, and buttocks in contact with the bench, and your feet flat on the floor. At the completion of the last repetition, signal by saying ''Okay.'' Then ''hook the bar back'' (guide the bar back) onto the shelf of the supports (this is termed "racking the bar"). *Be sure* to continue holding and supporting the bar until it is racked (see Figure 4.1d).

Spotting/Assistance Techniques

As the spotter, you should stand forward of your partner's head about 2 to 6 inches from the bench and centered between the uprights (see Figure 4.1a). To assist your partner in moving the bar off the supports (termed "handing off"), grip the bar using the alternate grip. Space your hands evenly between your partner's hands. At his or her command "Okay," carefully slide the bar off the supports and guide it to a straight-elbow position over the chest. Before releasing the bar, *be sure* that your partner's elbows are completely straight. Practice making your handoff as smooth as possible; it's a talent! If your handoff is too high or too low, or too far forward or too close (to the shelf), it will disturb your partner's stable position on the bench, which may contribute to a poor performance or injury.

Once the downward phase begins, your hands and eyes follow the bar's path to the chest (see Figure 4.1b) and should lead the bar's upward movement (see Figure 4.1c). As the elbows straighten during the last repetition and after your partner has given the "Okay" signal, assist by grasping the bar (with alternate grip) and racking the bar (see Figure 4.1d). *Be sure* that the bar is resting on the shelf of the upright supports before releasing the bar.

Special Caution

There are two times in this exercise when you, the spotter, need to be especially alert. The first is when the bar is about halfway in its upward movement; at this point there is a tendency for the wrists to extend (roll back), causing the bar to drop quickly toward your partner's neck or face. Should this occur, quickly catch the bar (with your knees bent) and help move it to the supports. Another time to be alert is when the bar is being racked. If instead of being placed on the shelf of the uprights, the bar is pushed into them or the shelf, the bar may drop toward your partner's face. As the spotter you need to *catch the bar immediately*, and then assist in guiding it onto the supports. You need to continue lifting and guiding the bar until it reaches the rack supports and you hear the "Okay" signal from your partner.

Figure 4.1   Keys to Success: *The Free Weight Bench Press Exercise*

Preparation Phase

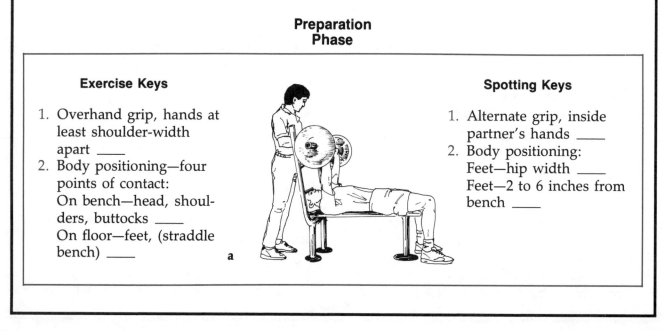

Exercise Keys

1. Overhand grip, hands at least shoulder-width apart ____
2. Body positioning—four points of contact:
   On bench—head, shoulders, buttocks ____
   On floor—feet, (straddle bench) ____

a

Spotting Keys

1. Alternate grip, inside partner's hands ____
2. Body positioning: Feet—hip width ____ Feet—2 to 6 inches from bench ____

Exercise Keys

3. Eyes below edge of shelf ____
4. Signal "Okay" to spotter ____
5. Move bar off supports ____
6. Push to straight-elbow position over chest ____

Spotting Keys

3. Knees flexed ____
4. Back flat ____
5. React to "Okay" command ____
6. Assist with bar off supports ____
7. Guide bar to straight-elbow position ____
8. Release bar smoothly ____

Execution
Phase, Downward

Exercise Keys

1. Inhale ____
2. Wrists straight ____
3. Wrists directly above elbows ____
4. Slow, controlled movement ____
5. Bar touches chest near nipples (or below breasts) ____

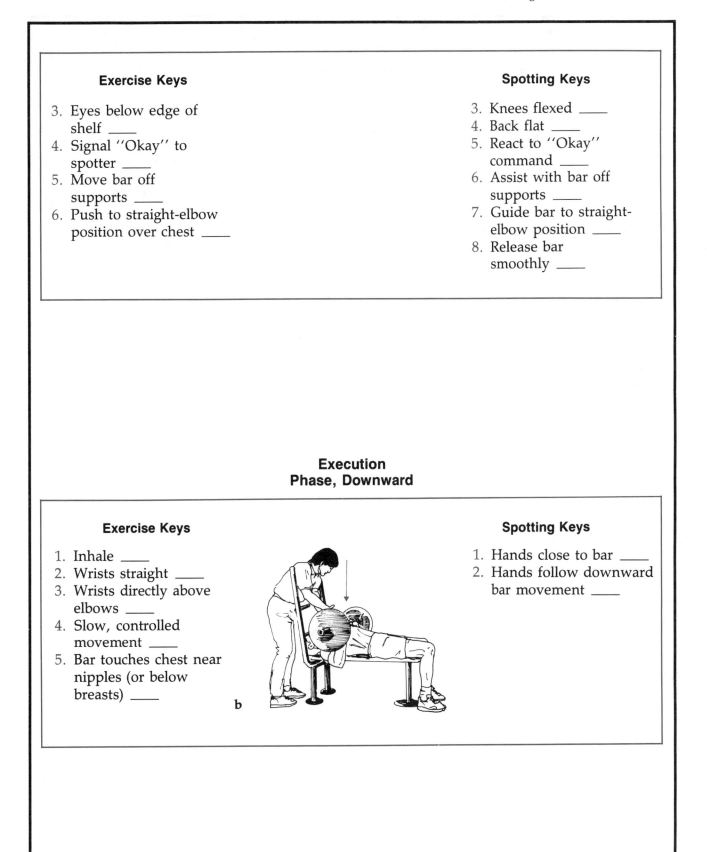

b

Spotting Keys

1. Hands close to bar ____
2. Hands follow downward bar movement ____

Execution
Phase, Upward

Exercise Keys

1. Push upward under control ____
2. Elbows extend evenly ____
3. Wrists directly above elbows ____
4. Exhale during upward movement ____
5. Controlled elbow extension near top ____
6. Pause at straight-elbow position ____
7. Inhale during downward movement ____
8. Continue upward and downward movements until completion of the set ____
9. Signal "Okay" on the last repetition ____

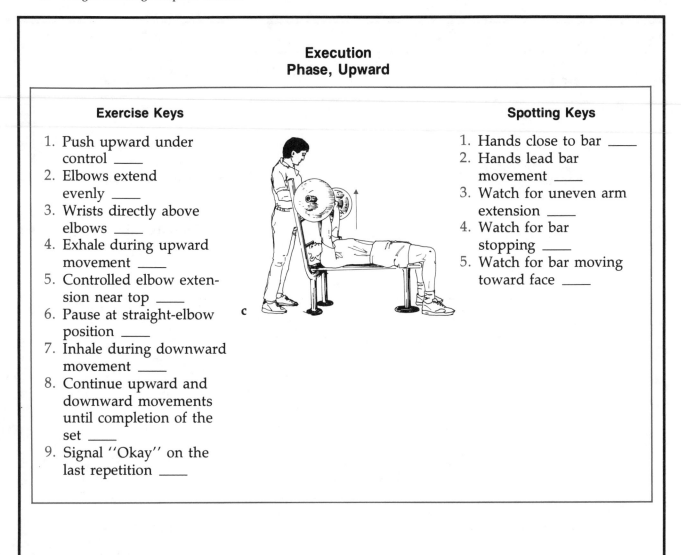

c

Spotting Keys

1. Hands close to bar ____
2. Hands lead bar movement ____
3. Watch for uneven arm extension ____
4. Watch for bar stopping ____
5. Watch for bar moving toward face ____

Racking the Bar
(After Last Repetition)

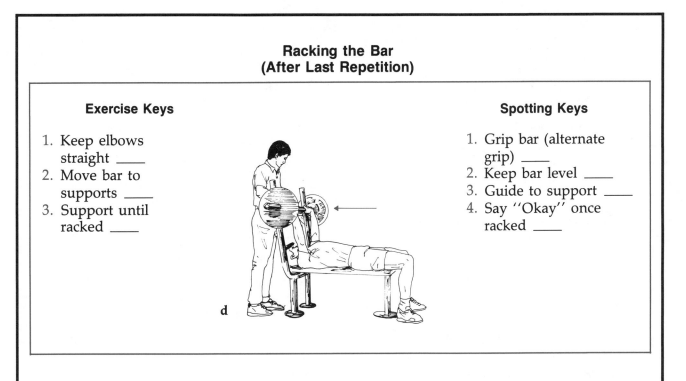

Exercise Keys

1. Keep elbows straight ____
2. Move bar to supports ____
3. Support until racked ____

Spotting Keys

1. Grip bar (alternate grip) ____
2. Keep bar level ____
3. Guide to support ____
4. Say "Okay" once racked ____

Detecting Free Weight Bench Press Errors

Most errors associated with this exercise are a result of bar speed—you tend to lower and raise the bar too quickly. All of the errors listed here are made worse as the speed of the movement increases. Thus, the first step in correcting errors is to make sure that the bar is moving slowly; then attempt to make the specific corrective changes described for the errors that affect you.

ERROR

CORRECTION

1. Your grip is not evenly spaced.

1. Evenly space your hands, using the markings on the bar and/or have your spotter help you locate a balanced position.

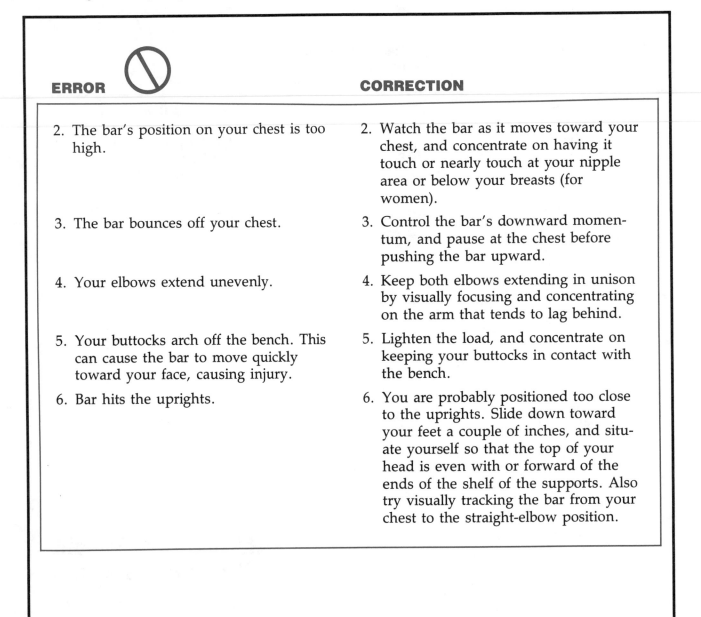

ERROR 🚫	CORRECTION
2. The bar's position on your chest is too high.	2. Watch the bar as it moves toward your chest, and concentrate on having it touch or nearly touch at your nipple area or below your breasts (for women).
3. The bar bounces off your chest.	3. Control the bar's downward momentum, and pause at the chest before pushing the bar upward.
4. Your elbows extend unevenly.	4. Keep both elbows extending in unison by visually focusing and concentrating on the arm that tends to lag behind.
5. Your buttocks arch off the bench. This can cause the bar to move quickly toward your face, causing injury.	5. Lighten the load, and concentrate on keeping your buttocks in contact with the bench.
6. Bar hits the uprights.	6. You are probably positioned too close to the uprights. Slide down toward your feet a couple of inches, and situate yourself so that the top of your head is even with or forward of the ends of the shelf of the supports. Also try visually tracking the bar from your chest to the straight-elbow position.

Machine Exercises

If you have access to either a cam or multi- or single-unit machine, you may select either the bent-arm fly or the chest press exercise to develop your chest.

HOW TO PERFORM THE BENT-ARM FLY EXERCISE

Assume a sitting position with your back firmly against the back pad. Adjust the seat until your shoulders are aligned with the overhead cam. Sit erect, looking straight ahead, and place your forearms on the arm pads, with the elbows parallel to the shoulders. Grip each handle between your thumb and index finger (see Figure 4.2a).

While in this position, push with your forearms until the pads touch in front of your chest (see Figure 4.2b). Exhale as your elbows come together. Pause in this position, and then slowly return to the starting position while inhaling (see Figure 4.2c).

Figure 4.2 *Keys to Success:*
Bent-Arm Fly Exercise (Pec Deck Chest Machine)

**Preparation
Phase**

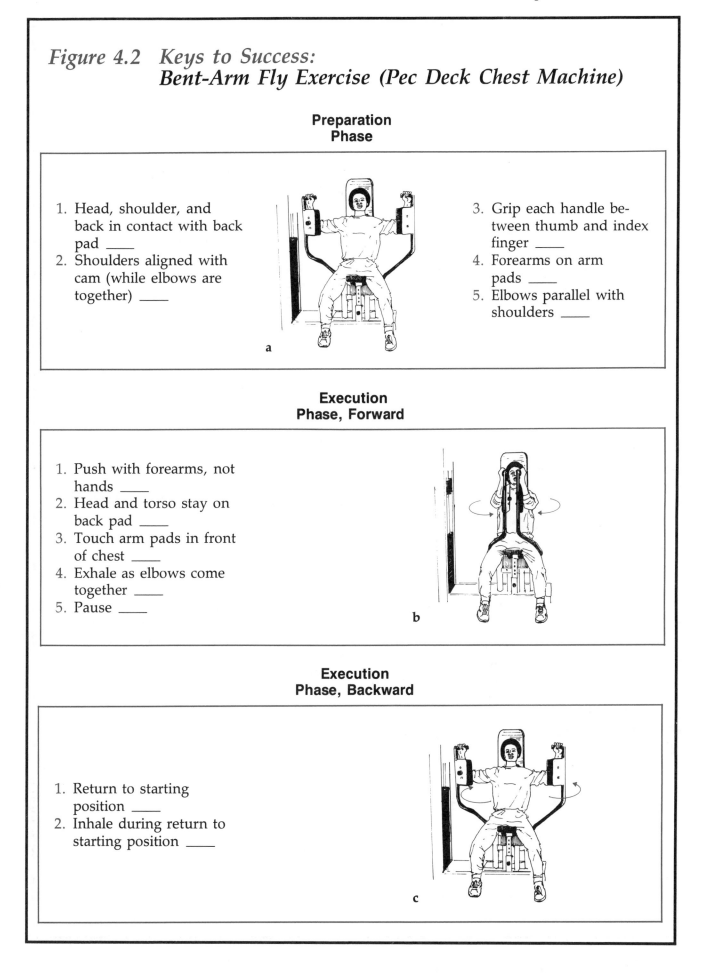

1. Head, shoulder, and back in contact with back pad ____
2. Shoulders aligned with cam (while elbows are together) ____

3. Grip each handle between thumb and index finger ____
4. Forearms on arm pads ____
5. Elbows parallel with shoulders ____

a

**Execution
Phase, Forward**

1. Push with forearms, not hands ____
2. Head and torso stay on back pad ____
3. Touch arm pads in front of chest ____
4. Exhale as elbows come together ____
5. Pause ____

b

**Execution
Phase, Backward**

1. Return to starting position ____
2. Inhale during return to starting position ____

c

Detecting Bent-Arm Fly Exercise Errors

Common errors in the bent-arm fly include body positioning on the equipment, an incorrect head and torso positioning during the exercise, and pressing with the hands instead of the forearms.

ERROR 🚫

CORRECTION

ERROR	CORRECTION
1. Your shoulders are not aligned with overhead cam.	1. Keep your torso in contact with back pads—if necessary, adjust seat so that your shoulders are aligned.
2. Your forearms are not on arm pads.	2. Press firmly with your forearms and elbows—not your hands.
3. Your head and torso lean forward.	3. Keep your head and shoulders against back pad—lighten load if necessary.
4. You are pressing with hands.	4. Think, ''Press elbows together.''

HOW TO PERFORM THE CHEST PRESS EXERCISE

Position yourself on the bench with head, shoulders, and buttocks in contact with it and feet flat on the floor about shoulder-width apart (four points of contact). Grip the bar handles with your hands shoulder-width apart, aligned with your nipples (see Figure 4.3a).

From this position, push to full elbow extension in a slow, controlled manner (see Figure 4.3b). Exhale through the sticking point of this exercise. Pause at full extension, then return to the starting position while inhaling (see Figure 4.3c).

Figure 4.3 Keys to Success: Chest Press (Multi- or Single-Unit Machine)

Preparation Phase

1. Head, shoulders, buttocks stay on bench, feet on floor (four points of contact) ____
2. Grip slightly wider than shoulders ____
3. Grip aligned with nipples on chest ____

CAUTION! Be sure your head is at least 2 inches from the weight stack.

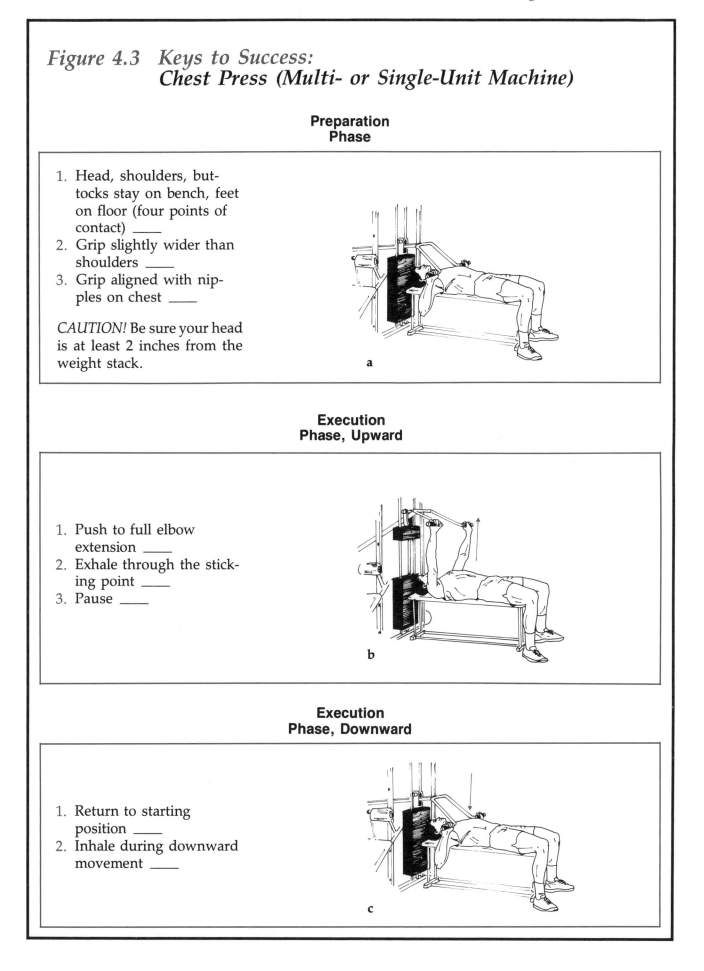

a

Execution Phase, Upward

1. Push to full elbow extension ____
2. Exhale through the sticking point ____
3. Pause ____

b

Execution Phase, Downward

1. Return to starting position ____
2. Inhale during downward movement ____

c

Detecting Chest Press Exercise Errors

Positioning the body too close to the weight stack, not executing each rep through the full range, and allowing the weight-stack plates to bang against each other are common errors.

ERROR 🚫

CORRECTION

ERROR	CORRECTION
1. Your body is positioned too close to the weight stack.	1. Dangerous—the selector key may strike your forehead. Slide toward your feet until there is approximately 2 inches of clearance.
2. The bar stack is stopped 2 or more inches above the weight stack.	2. Lower the bar stack to a point where the bar stack lightly touches the weight stack during each rep.

Practice Procedure Drills for Developing the Chest

1. Choose One Exercise

After reading about the characteristics and techniques involved in the three different exercises, and the type of equipment required of each, you are ready to put these details into action. Consider the availability of equipment and access to spotters in your situation, then select one of the following exercises to use in your program:

- Free weight bench press
- Bent-arm fly exercise (cam machine)
- Chest press (multi- or single-unit weight machine)

Later (in Step 11), you will copy your exercise choice and those from Steps 5 through 10, onto your workout chart.

Success Goal = List the 1 exercise you want to include in your program to develop the chest (remember to consider equipment and spotting requirements)

Your Choice = _____

2. *Practice Grip, Body Positioning, and Movement Pattern (and Spotting If You Have Selected the Free Weight Bench Press Exercise)*

When you first perform the exercise selected for developing the chest, use a dowel stick, a broomstick (with the broom section cut off), an empty bar, or the lightest machine weight stack. Regardless of what you select, focus on the following techniques:

- Proper grip
- Proper body positioning
- Proper movement pattern

If you selected a machine exercise, move on to the next paragraph and disregard the spotting keys that follow.

Spotting the Free Weight Bench Press Exercise

If you selected the free weight bench press exercise for developing your chest, you *need a spotter*, and you need to practice the skills of spotting. Identify a spotter and take turns with her or him when completing the Success Goals section. Instead of performing 15 reps in a continuous manner, rack the bar after each rep. There should be a handoff to begin each rep (until 15 reps are completed). Switch responsibilities so you and your partner both have a chance to develop proper grip, body positioning, and the movement patterns that are required in the bench press, and those used in spotting it.

Check your technique either by watching yourself in a mirror (if you're doing the bent-arm fly) or by asking a qualified person to observe and assess your performance in the basic techniques. Perform 15 reps in this chest exercise. Remember, if you have selected the free weight bench press exercise, the bar should be handed off and racked after each rep.

Success Goals =

a. **Machine/free weight**: 12 out of 15 reps are performed with the proper grip, body position, and movement pattern

b. **Free weight**: 12 out of 15 handoffs and rackings smoothly performed

Your Scores =

a. **Machine/free weight**: (#) _____ reps correctly performed with proper grip, body position, and bar/machine arm path

b. **Free weight**: (#) _____ smoothly performed handoffs and rackings

3. *Determine Warm-Up and Trial Loads*

This practice procedure answers the question, ''How much weight or load should I use?'' From Step 3 you will recall that the answer is based upon your body weight, which when multiplied by a coefficient approximates the appropriate load to use for warming up and training. (Remember, males over 175 pounds record 175 as your body weight, and females over 140 pounds use 140 as your body weight here and in Steps 5 through 10.)

Success Goals = Using the formulas below, determine both warm-up and trial loads for your chest exercise, then round your results to the nearest 5-pound increment, or to the closest weight-stack plate (be sure to use the coefficient assigned to the exercise you selected)

Warm-Up Load Determination Formula*
Chest

Body weight		x	Coefficient	=	Warm-up load (pounds)
		Female			
BWT = _____	(FW–bench press)	x	.20	=	_____
BWT = _____	(C–bent-arm fly)	x	.10	=	_____
BWT = _____	(M–chest press)	x	.15	=	_____
		Male			
BWT = _____	(FW–bench press)	x	.30	=	_____
BWT = _____	(C–bent-arm fly)	x	.15	=	_____
BWT = _____	(M–chest press)	x	.25	=	_____

Trial Load Determination Formula*
Chest

Body weight		x	Coefficient	=	Trial load (pounds)
		Female			
BWT = _____	(FW–bench press)	x	.35	=	_____
BWT = _____	(C–bent-arm fly)	x	.14	=	_____
BWT = _____	(M–chest press)	x	.27	=	_____
		Male			
BWT = _____	(FW–bench press)	x	.60	=	_____
BWT = _____	(C–bent-arm fly)	x	.30	=	_____
BWT = _____	(M–chest press)	x	.55	=	_____

*BWT = body weight, FW = free weight, C = cam, and M = multi- or single-unit machine exercise.

Your Scores =

a. (#) _____ pounds for warm-up load

b. (#) _____ pounds for trial load

(These loads will be used in the next two procedures.)

4. Add Proper Range of Motion, Velocity, and Breathing

Use your calculated *warm-up load*, and apply the previous basic techniques as well as focusing on these:

- Moving in a full range of motion
- Controlling velocity
- Timing your breathing

Check your technique either by watching yourself in a mirror (if you're doing the bent-arm fly) or by asking a qualified person to observe and assess your performance. Perform 15 reps with the warm-up load.

Success Goal = 12 out of 15 reps performed with full range, controlled velocity, and proper breathing

Your Score = (#) ＿＿＿ reps correctly performed with full range, controlled velocity, and proper breathing

5. Visualize Correct Techniques

Review the chest exercise keys and technique errors (presented in the previous section). Think about the techniques just practiced in procedures 2 and 4. Find a quiet spot in the weight room and mentally visualize yourself performing the selected chest exercise correctly. Use as many of your senses as possible to imagine the exact feel of the grip, body positioning, movement pattern, movement velocity, range of movement, and coordinated breathing. Remain undisturbed for 1 or 2 minutes. This helps you mentally ''set'' the proper technique in your mind, and also gives your body a rest before using the heavier trial load in your next drill.

Success Goal = 1 to 2 minutes of mental visualization of correct execution of selected chest exercise

Your Score = (#) ＿＿＿ minutes of visualization of correct execution

6. Determine the Training Load

This practice procedure is designed to help you determine an appropriate training load, one that is designed to produce 12 to 15 reps. Find your calculated trial load (practice procedure 3). *Do as many reps as possible* with this load, hopefully achieving 12 to 15 reps. Make sure that the reps are smoothly executed. If you are executing the free weight bench press, also check that your elbows extend evenly and that the bar touches on or near your nipples (or just below your breasts, for women). If you have selected a machine exercise, check that you are moving through the entire range of motion.

Success Goal = 12 to 15 reps smoothly executed of selected chest exercise with calculated trial load

Your Score = (#) ____ reps smoothly executed

If you smoothly executed 12 to 15 reps with the trial load, then your trial load equals what you need for training. Record this as your training load in practice procedure 7, and move on to the next chapter (Step 5). Note that this load is now referred to as your *training load.*

7. Make Needed Load Adjustments

If you performed less than 12 reps with your trial load, it is *too heavy,* and you should *lighten* the load. On the other hand, if you performed more than 15 reps, it is *too light,* and you should *increase* the load. Use the formula and Load Adjustment Chart (explained in Step 3) to make necessary adjustments.

Success Goal = Correctly determine your training load according to the following formula:

Determining the Training Load Formula

Trial load (pounds) +/– Adjustment = Training load (pounds)

_____ +/– _____ = _____

Load Adjustment Chart

Reps completed	Adjustment (in pounds)
<7	–15
8-9	–10
10-11	– 5
12-15	0
16-17	+ 5
18-19	+10
>20	+15

Your Score = (#) ____ pounds for training load (Note that this training load will later be recorded onto your workout chart in Step 11.)

Step 5 **Selecting a Back Exercise**

The bent over row using free weights, the rowing exercise using a cam machine, and the seated row using the low pulley on a multi- or single purpose machine are excellent exercises to develop the upper back (rhomboid, trapezius, latissimus dorsi, teres major—see Appendix B, posterior view). These muscles work in opposition to those of the chest. Also developed are the back of the shoulders (posterior deltoid, infraspinatus, teres minor), the front of the upper arm (biceps brachii), and the back of the forearm (brachioradialis). This exercise should be performed as often as the bench press to keep the anterior and posterior upper body musculature in balance.

Free Weight Exercise

If you have access to free weights, you may select the bent over row exercise to develop your back. If you prefer working with machines, see the "Machine Exercises" section.

HOW TO PERFORM THE BENT OVER ROW EXERCISE

The preparation position begins with your feet shoulder-width apart and your shoulders slightly higher than your hips (10 to 30 degrees). Your back should be flat, abdominals contracted, elbows straight, knees slightly flexed, and eyes looking forward. Grasp the bar in a palms-down overhand grip with thumbs around the bar. Your hands should be evenly spaced 4 to 6 inches wider than shoulder width. Exhale as the bar nears the chest during the upward movement, and inhale during the downward movement.

The execution phase begins as the bar is pulled in a straight line upward. Pull in a slow, controlled manner until the bar touches your chest near the nipples (or just below your breasts, for women). Your torso should remain straight and rigid throughout the exercise, with no bouncing or jerking. When the bar is touching your chest, pause momentarily in this position before beginning the downward movement. Slowly lower the bar in a straight line to the starting position without letting the weight touch the floor or bounce at the bottom. Be sure to keep the knees slightly flexed during the upward and downward movements to avoid putting undue stress on the lower back. Figure 5.1, a-c, shows the exercise Keys to Success for executing the bent over row.

Figure 5.1 Keys to Success:
Free Weight Bent Over Row Exercise

**Preparation
Phase**

1. Overhand grip, hands at least shoulder-width apart ____
2. Shoulders higher than hips ____
3. Lower back flat ____
4. Elbows straight ____
5. Knees slightly flexed ____
6. Head up, facing forward ____

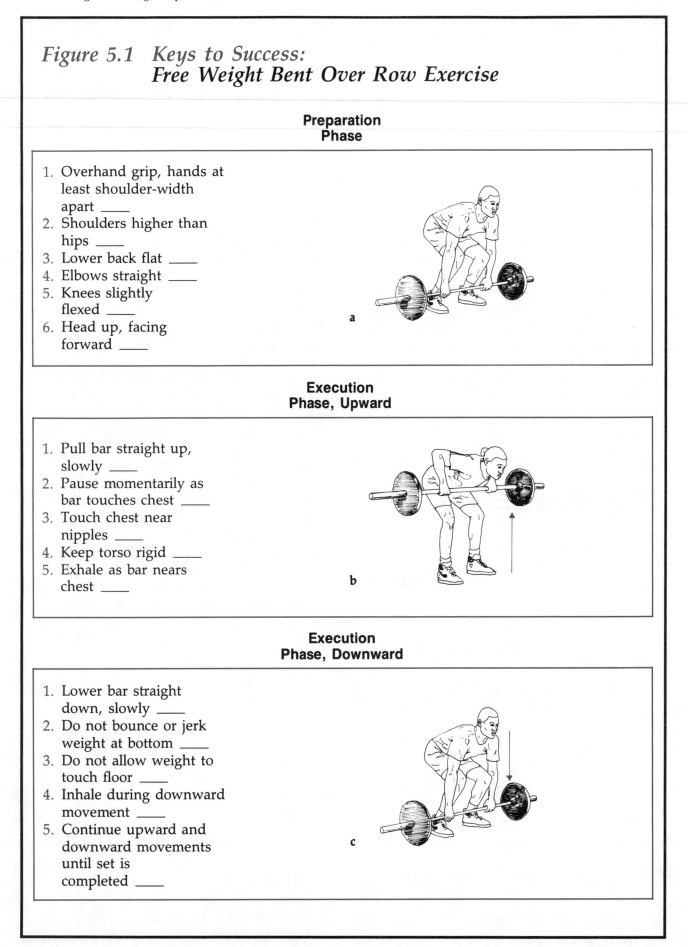

a

**Execution
Phase, Upward**

1. Pull bar straight up, slowly ____
2. Pause momentarily as bar touches chest ____
3. Touch chest near nipples ____
4. Keep torso rigid ____
5. Exhale as bar nears chest ____

b

**Execution
Phase, Downward**

1. Lower bar straight down, slowly ____
2. Do not bounce or jerk weight at bottom ____
3. Do not allow weight to touch floor ____
4. Inhale during downward movement ____
5. Continue upward and downward movements until set is completed ____

c

Detecting Free Weight Bent Over Row Errors

Most errors associated with the bent over row derive from using too much weight and from not maintaining the proper body position. When too much weight is used, the back muscles are not able to pull the bar all the way to the chest, which reduces the extent to which the back muscles can be worked and developed. You will tend to jerk the bar, using momentum to get the bar to the chest, then let it free-fall back to the starting position.

Avoiding the temptation of using heavy loads will enable you to more effectively work the back muscles because the bar is being pulled all the way to the chest. It is also important to establish and maintain the proper body position. A correct shoulder-to-back position places the back muscles in an ideal alignment for strengthening, and reduces the likelihood of injury to the lower back.

ERROR

CORRECTION

ERROR	CORRECTION
1. The bar does not touch your chest.	1. Reduce the weight on the bar and concentrate on touching your chest with the bar.
2. Your shoulders are lower than your hips.	2. Elevate your shoulders 10 to 30 degrees above your hips.
3. Your knees are locked out.	3. Flex your knees slightly, to reduce stress on your lower back.
4. Your upper back is rounded.	4. Lift your head up and look straight forward.
5. Your upper torso is not stable and moves up and down.	5. Use a mirror to watch and maintain the proper position, or have someone place their hand on your upper back.

Machine Exercises

If you have access to either a cam or multi- or single-unit machine, you may select either the rowing or the seated row exercise to develop your back.

HOW TO PERFORM THE ROWING EXERCISE

Assume a sitting position with your back toward the weight stack. Sit erect, looking straight ahead, and place your upper arms between the pads with your forearms crossed (see Figure 5.2, a-c). While maintaining this position, pull your arms in a rowing movement as far back as possible. Exhale at this time. Pause and then return slowly to the starting position while inhaling. Keep your forearms parallel to the floor at all times.

Figure 5.2 Keys to Success:
Rowing Exercise (Cam Rowing Machine)

**Preparation
Phase**

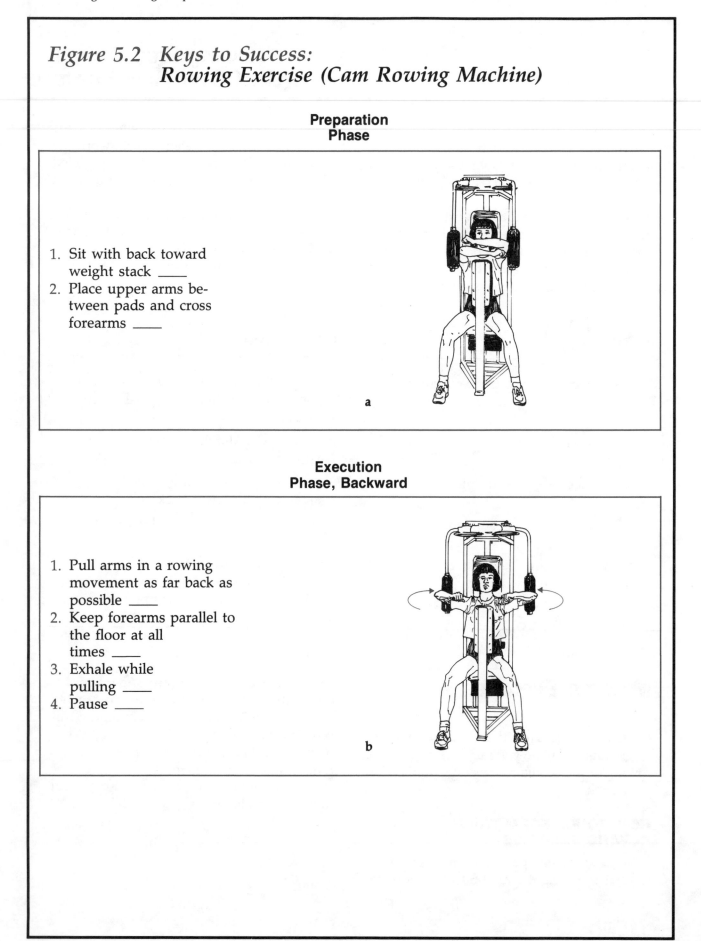

1. Sit with back toward weight stack ____
2. Place upper arms between pads and cross forearms ____

a

**Execution
Phase, Backward**

1. Pull arms in a rowing movement as far back as possible ____
2. Keep forearms parallel to the floor at all times ____
3. Exhale while pulling ____
4. Pause ____

b

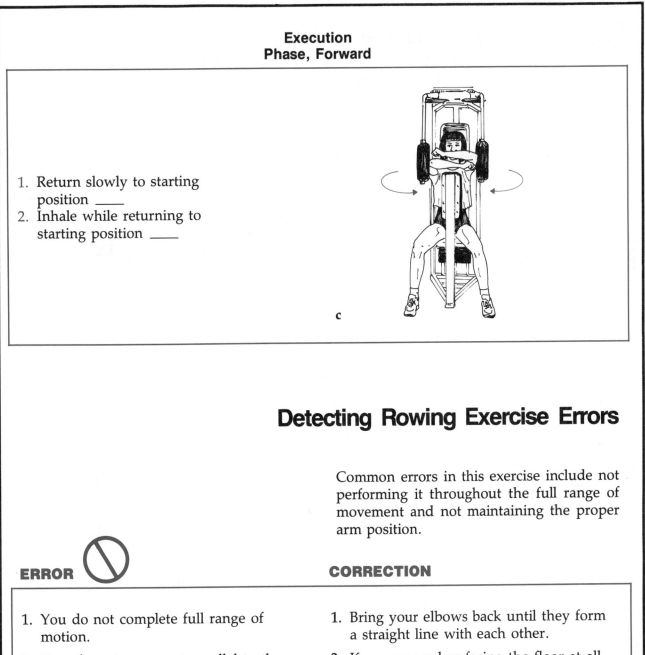

**Execution
Phase, Forward**

1. Return slowly to starting position ____
2. Inhale while returning to starting position ____

c

Detecting Rowing Exercise Errors

Common errors in this exercise include not performing it throughout the full range of movement and not maintaining the proper arm position.

ERROR 🚫

CORRECTION

1. You do not complete full range of motion.

2. Your forearms are not parallel to the floor.

1. Bring your elbows back until they form a straight line with each other.

2. Keep your palms facing the floor at all times.

HOW TO PERFORM THE SEATED ROW EXERCISE

At the Low Pulley Station, assume a seated position with your knees slightly flexed. Keep your torso erect, with your lower back and abdominal muscles contracted. Take an overhand grip, with palms facing inward. Maintain this position while pulling the bar slowly and smoothly to your chest. Exhale as the bar nears your chest. Pause, then return to the starting position while inhaling. Your upper torso should not be allowed to move back and forth (see Figure 5.3, a-c).

Figure 5.3 Keys to Success:
Seated Row Exercise (Rowing Station—Multi- or Single-Unit Machine)

**Preparation
Phase**

1. Assume a seated position, knees slightly flexed ____
2. Keep upper torso erect, lower back flat ____
3. Take an overhand grip ____

**Execution
Phase, Backward**

1. Pull bar slowly and smoothly to chest ____
2. Do not use torso movements to pull weight ____
3. Exhale as bar nears chest ____
4. Pause ____

**Execution
Phase, Forward**

1. Return to starting position ____
2. Inhale during the return ____

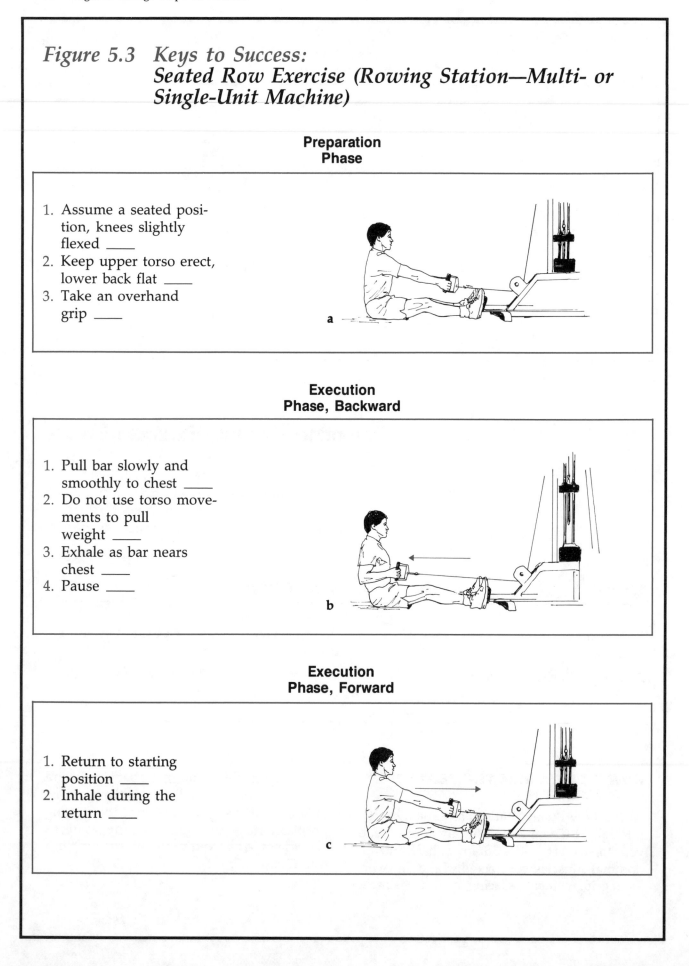

Detecting Seated Row Exercise Errors

The most common error observed in the seated row exercise is that of allowing the upper body to move forward and backward, instead of remaining erect throughout the exercise.

When this happens, the lower back muscles become involved in pulling. This compromises the benefit to the upper back muscles, for which this exercise was designed and selected.

ERROR 🚫

CORRECTION

1. Your knees are not flexed.	1. Make sure your knees are slightly flexed to decrease pressure on your lower back.
2. Your torso is not erect.	2. Keep your torso erect by contracting your abdominal and lower back muscles.
3. You allow the weight plate to fall quickly to the weight stack.	3. Pause at your chest—then slowly return the bar to the starting position.
4. You use torso movement to pull the bar to your chest.	4. Keep your upper torso rigid—lighten the weight if necessary.

Practice Procedural Drills for Developing the Back

1. Choose One Exercise

After reading about the characteristics and techniques involved in the three different exercises, and the type of equipment required of each, you are ready to put these details into action. Consider the availability of equipment in your situation, then select one of the following exercises to use in your program.

- Free weight bent over row
- Rowing exercise (cam rowing machine)
- Seated row (multi- or single-unit weight machine)

Later (in Step 11), you will copy your exercise choice onto your workout chart.

Success Goal = List the 1 exercise that you want to include in your program to develop the back

Your Choice = _____

2. Practice Grip, Body Positioning, and Movement Pattern

When you first perform the exercise selected for developing the back, use a dowel stick, an empty bar, or the lightest machine weight stack. Regardless of what you select, focus on the following techniques:

- Proper grip
- Proper body positioning
- Movement pattern

Check your technique either by watching yourself in a mirror or by asking a qualified person to observe and assess your performance in the basic techniques. Perform 15 reps of this back exercise.

Success Goals = **Machine/free weight**: 12 out of 15 reps are performed with the proper grip, body position, and movement pattern

Your Scores =   (#) _____ reps correctly performed with the proper grip, body position, and movement pattern

3. Determine Warm-up and Trial Loads

This practice procedure answers the question, "How much weight or load should I use?" Be sure to use the correct coefficient for the exercise you select.

Success Goals = Using the formulas below, determine both warm-up and trial loads, then round off your results to the nearest 5-pound increment, or to the closest weight-stack plate. Be sure to use the coefficient assigned to the exercise you selected.

<table>
<tr><td colspan="5" align="center">Warm-Up Load Determination Formula*
Back</td></tr>
<tr><td>Body weight</td><td></td><td>x   Coefficient =</td><td></td><td>Warm-up load (pounds)</td></tr>
<tr><td colspan="5" align="center">Female</td></tr>
<tr><td>BWT = _____</td><td>(FW–bent over row)</td><td>x</td><td>.20</td><td>=</td><td>_____</td></tr>
<tr><td>BWT = _____</td><td>(C–rowing exercise)</td><td>x</td><td>.10</td><td>=</td><td>_____</td></tr>
<tr><td>BWT = _____</td><td>(M–seated row)</td><td>x</td><td>.15</td><td>=</td><td>_____</td></tr>
<tr><td colspan="5" align="center">Male</td></tr>
<tr><td>BWT = _____</td><td>(FW–bent over row)</td><td>x</td><td>.25</td><td>=</td><td>_____</td></tr>
<tr><td>BWT = _____</td><td>(C–rowing exercise)</td><td>x</td><td>.20</td><td>=</td><td>_____</td></tr>
<tr><td>BWT = _____</td><td>(M–seated row)</td><td>x</td><td>.25</td><td>=</td><td>_____</td></tr>
</table>

Trial Load Determination Formula*
Back

Body weight		x	Coefficient	=	Trial load (pounds)
			Female		
BWT = _____	(FW–bent over row)	x	.35	=	_____
BWT = _____	(C–rowing exercise)	x	.20	=	_____
BWT = _____	(M–seated row)	x	.25	=	_____
			Male		
BWT = _____	(FW–bent over row)	x	.45	=	_____
BWT = _____	(C–rowing exercise)	x	.40	=	_____
BWT = _____	(M–seated row)	x	.45	=	_____

*BWT = body weight, FW = free weight, C = cam, and M = multi- or single-unit machine exercise.

Your Scores =

a. (#) _____ pounds for warm-up load

b. (#) _____ pounds for trial load

(These loads will be used in the next two procedures.)

4. Add Proper Range of Motion, Velocity, and Breathing

Use your calculated warm-up load, and apply the previous basic techniques as well as focusing on these:

- Moving in the full range of motion
- Controlling velocity
- Timing your breathing

Check your technique either by watching yourself in a mirror or by asking a qualified person to observe and assess your performance. Perform 15 reps with the warm-up load.

Success Goal = 12 out of 15 reps performed with full range of motion, controlled velocity, and proper breathing

Your Score = (#) _____ reps correctly performed with full range of motion, controlled velocity, and proper breathing

5. Visualize Correct Techniques

Review the back exercise technique errors (presented in the previous section). Think back to the previous activity. Locate a quiet spot in the weight room and mentally visualize yourself performing the selected back exercise correctly. Use as many of your senses as possible to imagine the exact feel of the grip, body positioning, and coordinated breathing. Remain undisturbed for 1 or 2 minutes. This helps you mentally set the proper technique in your mind, and also gives your body a rest before using the heavier trial load in your next drill.

Success goal = 1 to 2 minutes of mental visualization of correct execution of selected back exercise

Your Score = (#) _____ minutes of visualization of correct execution

6. *Determine the Training Load*

This practice procedure is designed to help you determine an appropriate training load, one that is designed to produce 12 to 15 reps. Find your calculated trial load (practice procedure 3). *Do as many reps as possible* with this load, hopefully achieving 12 to 15 reps. Make sure that all reps are smoothly executed. If you are executing the free weight bent over row, also check that your hips are lower than your back, and that the bar touches on or near the nipples. If you have selected a machine exercise, check that you are moving through the full range of motion.

Success Goal = 12 to 15 reps smoothly executed of selected back exercise with calculated trial load

Your Score = (#) _____ reps smoothly executed

If you smoothly executed 12 to 15 reps with your trial load, then your trial load is the weight you need for training. Record this trial load as your training load in practice procedure 7, and move on to the next chapter (Step 6). Note that this load is now referred to as your training load.

7. *Make Needed Load Adjustments*

If you did not perform 12 reps with your trial load, it is *too heavy* and you should *lighten the load*. On the other hand, if you performed more than 15 reps, it is *too light*, and you should *increase the load*. Use the formula and Load Adjustment Chart to make necessary adjustments.

Success Goal = Correctly determine your training load according to the following formula:

Determining the Training Load Formula

Trial load (pounds)	+/−	Adjustment	=	Training load (pounds)
_____	+/−	_____	=	_____

Load Adjustment Chart

Reps completed	Adjustment (in pounds)
<7	−15
8-9	−10
10-11	− 5
12-15	0
16-17	+ 5
18-19	+10
>20	+15

Your Score = (#) ____ pounds for training load

(Note that this training load will later be recorded onto your workout chart in Step 11.)

Step 6 Selecting a Shoulder Exercise

Overhead pressing exercises using free weights, a pulley/pivot machine, or a cam machine are excellent for developing the front and middle of the shoulder (anterior and middle heads of the deltoid shown in Appendix B, posterior view). Also developed is the back of the upper arm (triceps). These exercises contribute to shoulder-joint stabilization and muscle padding for protection, as well as to balanced muscular development of the chest and upper back. The free weight standing press, also called the military press, is generally considered to be the best combined shoulder and arm exercise.

Free Weight Exercise

If you have access to free weights, you may select the overhead press exercise to develop your shoulders. If you prefer working with machines, see the ''Machine Exercises'' section.

HOW TO PERFORM THE FREE WEIGHT STANDING PRESS

Preparation for performing this exercise involves placing the bar on a squat rack or a set of supports at shoulder height. If racks or supports are not available, you must lift the bar from the floor, utilizing the techniques presented in Step 2. Grasp the bar in an overhand grip, with your hands equidistant from the center of the bar and slightly more than shoulder-width apart. Hold your wrists firmly in a slightly extended position with elbows under the bar. The bar should be resting on your shoulders, clavicles (collarbone), and hands (see Figure 6.1a).

Push the bar upward in a straight line above the shoulders at a slow to moderate speed, until your elbows are extended (see Figure 6.1b). You will need to move your head slightly backward as the bar starts moving off of and returning to the shoulders. Otherwise the head should be maintained in an upright position throughout this exercise. Avoid leaning back or hyperextending the spine (exaggerating the lower back curvature) during the press. Pause momentarily at the top of this exercise, then lower the bar slowly to the ready position (see Figure 6.1c). Do not bounce the bar on your upper chest. You should inhale as you lower the bar and exhale as the bar passes through the sticking point on ascent. *Caution!* Be very careful to not hold your breath through the sticking point because this may cause you to black out (while the bar is overhead). If you must lower the bar to the floor after completing the exercise, use the shoulder-to-floor lowering techniques presented in Step 2.

Spotting/Assistance Techniques

Spotters must be approximately the same height as their partners. While spotting, stand directly behind your partner, as close as possible without touching or interfering with the exercise. If assistance is necessary, use both hands in an overhand grip placed just inside your partner's hands. Your main function is to assist through the sticking point, being especially alert for unexpected backward movements of the bar.

Special Caution

There is one time during this exercise when the spotter needs to be especially alert. This occurs during the upward phase when the bar is at the sticking point (at about eye level).

There is a tendency to close the eyes and lean back. Both are dangerous; closing the eyes can cause the lifter to become disoriented, and leaning back can injure her or his lower back. Should either of these occur, quickly assist, and caution your partner to open her or his eyes and stand erect.

The most difficult thing to learn when spotting the free weight overhead press is to spot without interfering. During the upward movement—especially at the sticking point—you will have a tendency to push the bar forward as you assist by lifting upward. This will cause your partner to become unbalanced. To help you develop the ability to apply only upward lift on the bar, ask a training partner to give you verbal feedback when you are spotting. At the completion of a set, ask your partner if your spotting assistance disturbed his or her balance. Figure 6.1, a-c, shows both the exercise and the spotting Keys to Success for executing the free weight standing press.

Figure 6.1 Keys to Success: Free Weight Standing Press Exercise

Preparation Phase

Exercise Keys

1. Overhand grip, evenly spaced, shoulder-width or slightly wider ____
2. Head upright, facing forward ____
3. Elbows under bar, wrists extended ____
4. Bar resting in hands on shoulders, clavicles ____

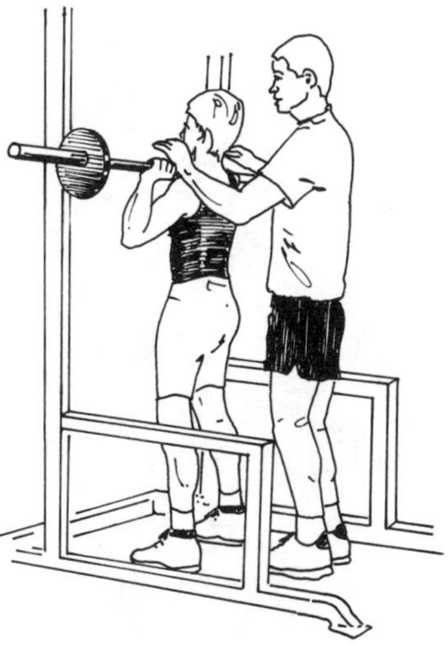

Spotting Keys

1. Stand directly behind partner ____
2. Stand as close as possible without touching ____
3. Eyes watching bar ____
4. Feet shoulder-width apart ____

a

Execution
Phase, Upward

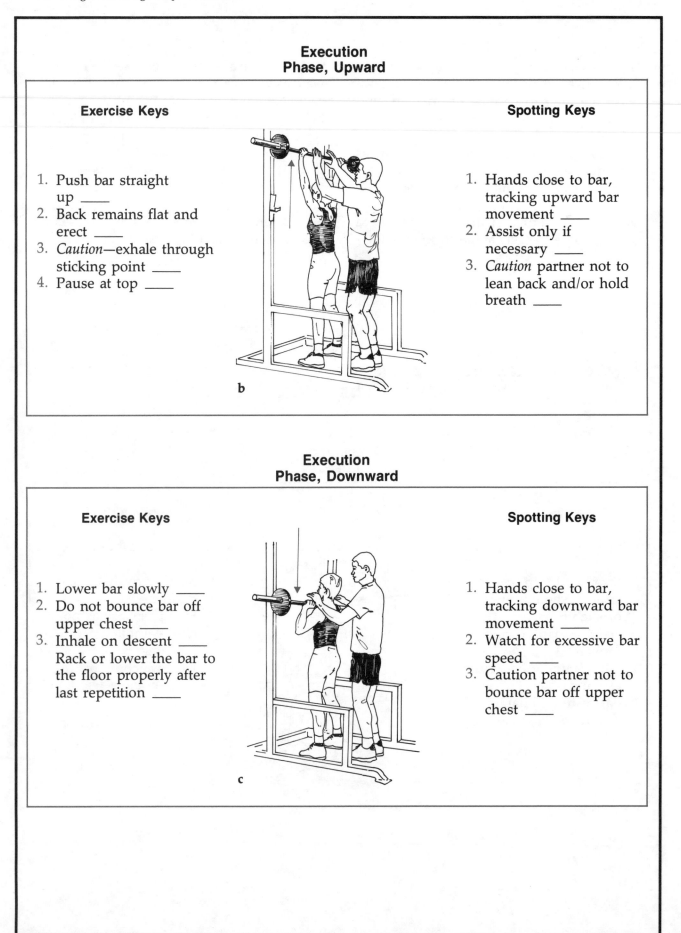

Exercise Keys

1. Push bar straight up ____
2. Back remains flat and erect ____
3. *Caution*—exhale through sticking point ____
4. Pause at top ____

Spotting Keys

1. Hands close to bar, tracking upward bar movement ____
2. Assist only if necessary ____
3. *Caution* partner not to lean back and/or hold breath ____

b

Execution
Phase, Downward

Exercise Keys

1. Lower bar slowly ____
2. Do not bounce bar off upper chest ____
3. Inhale on descent ____ Rack or lower the bar to the floor properly after last repetition ____

Spotting Keys

1. Hands close to bar, tracking downward bar movement ____
2. Watch for excessive bar speed ____
3. Caution partner not to bounce bar off upper chest ____

c

Racking the Bar

Exercise Keys	Spotting Keys
1. Walk forward until bar contacts rack ＿＿	1. Walk with partner until bar is racked ＿＿
2. Bend the knees until bar is in the rack ＿＿	2. Tell your partner when the bar is safely racked ＿＿
3. Never lean forward to rack bar ＿＿	

Detecting Free Weight Standing Press Errors

Of the errors commonly seen when observing the standing press, leaning back too far is the most common. This should be avoided because it places a lot of stress on the lower back. This and other common errors, and suggestions for correcting them, are presented next.

ERROR 🚫   **CORRECTION**

ERROR	CORRECTION
1. Your grip is too wide.	1. Evenly space your hands using the markings on the bar for reference.
2. Your torso leans back too far.	2. This typically occurs at the bar's sticking point. Think, "Torso, head, and bar form a straight line."
3. Your eyes are closed.	3. Concentrate on focusing on some object straight ahead, especially when reaching the sticking point.
4. You hold your breath.	4. Remember to begin exhaling as the bar reaches the sticking point.
5. Your arms are extended unevenly.	5. Keep both of your arms extending in unison by visually focusing and concentrating on the arm that lags behind.
6. You start the bar upward with a knee kick (flexion, then quick extension).	6. Start with your knees in a fully extended position, and keep them that way throughout the upward and downward movements.

Machine Exercises

If you have access to either a cam or multi- or single-unit machine, you may select either of the seated press exercises to develop your shoulders.

HOW TO PERFORM THE SEATED PRESS EXERCISES (WEIGHT MACHINE)

Assume an erect sitting position on the stool so that the front of your shoulders are directly below the handles. Take a palms-forward grip approximately shoulder-width apart. Push the handles upward until your elbows extend completely. Keep your shoulders directly under the handles throughout the exercise, and keep your lower back flat by statically contracting the muscles of your lower back and abdominal area. Exhale as your elbows near the fully extended (sticking point) position. Pause when the elbows are fully extended, then slowly return to the starting position (see Figure 6.2, a-c).

Figure 6.2 Keys to Success: Seated Press Exercise (Multi- or Single-Unit Weight Machine)

Preparation Phase

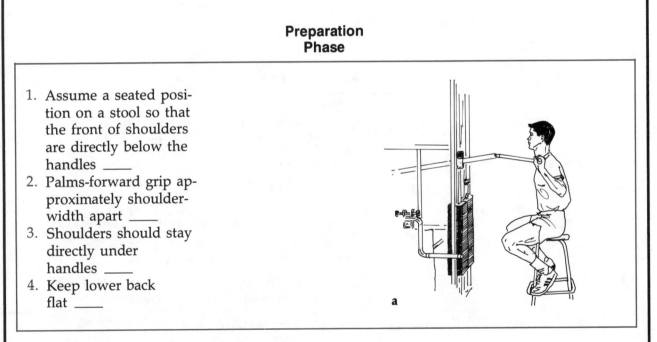

1. Assume a seated position on a stool so that the front of shoulders are directly below the handles ____
2. Palms-forward grip approximately shoulder-width apart ____
3. Shoulders should stay directly under handles ____
4. Keep lower back flat ____

Execution
Phase, Upward

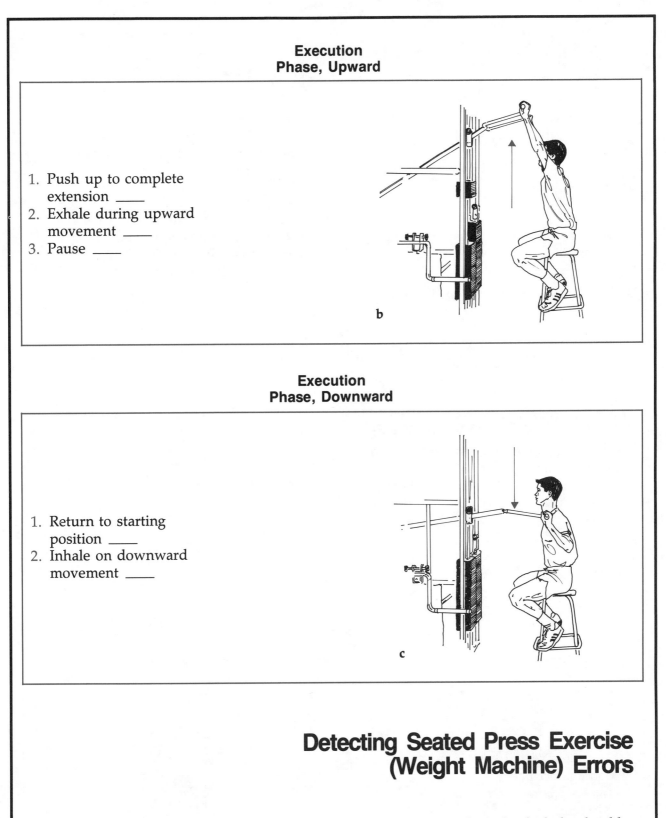

1. Push up to complete extension ____
2. Exhale during upward movement ____
3. Pause ____

b

Execution
Phase, Downward

1. Return to starting position ____
2. Inhale on downward movement ____

c

Detecting Seated Press Exercise (Weight Machine) Errors

The most common errors observed when this exercise is performed is hyperextending (excessively arching) the lower back and not lowering the handles to shoulder level. Hyperextending the lower back subjects it to a lot of stress, and not lowering the handles reduces the range through which the shoulder muscles work, thus minimizing their development. These and other commonly observed errors, and suggestions for correcting them, are discussed next.

ERROR 🚫	CORRECTION
1. You arch your back excessively when reaching the sticking point.	1. Keep your back flat by contracting your abdominal and lower back muscles. Think, ''Head to buttocks forms a straight line.''
2. You hold your breath.	2. Begin exhaling as the handles reach the sticking point.
3. You don't lower the handles to shoulder level.	3. Try to lower the handles enough to have the weight plate lightly touch (not bang) the weight stack.
4. The weight plates bang against each other.	4. Control the handles' downward momentum, and pause at shoulder level before pushing upward.

HOW TO PERFORM THE OVERHEAD PRESS EXERCISE (CAM MACHINE)

Position yourself on the seat with your back against the pad and your shoulders aligned under the handles. Grasp the handles with a palms-inward grip. From this position push to full elbow extension in a slow, controlled manner (see Figure 6.3, a-c). Exhale when passing through the sticking point. Pause at full extension, then return to the starting position while inhaling.

Figure 6.3 Keys to Success: Shoulder Press (Cam Machine)

Preparation Phase

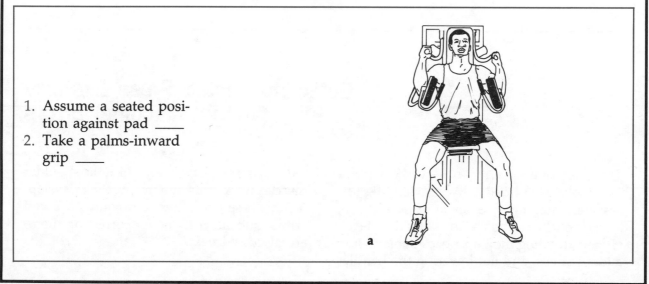

1. Assume a seated position against pad ____
2. Take a palms-inward grip ____

a

Execution
Phase, Upward

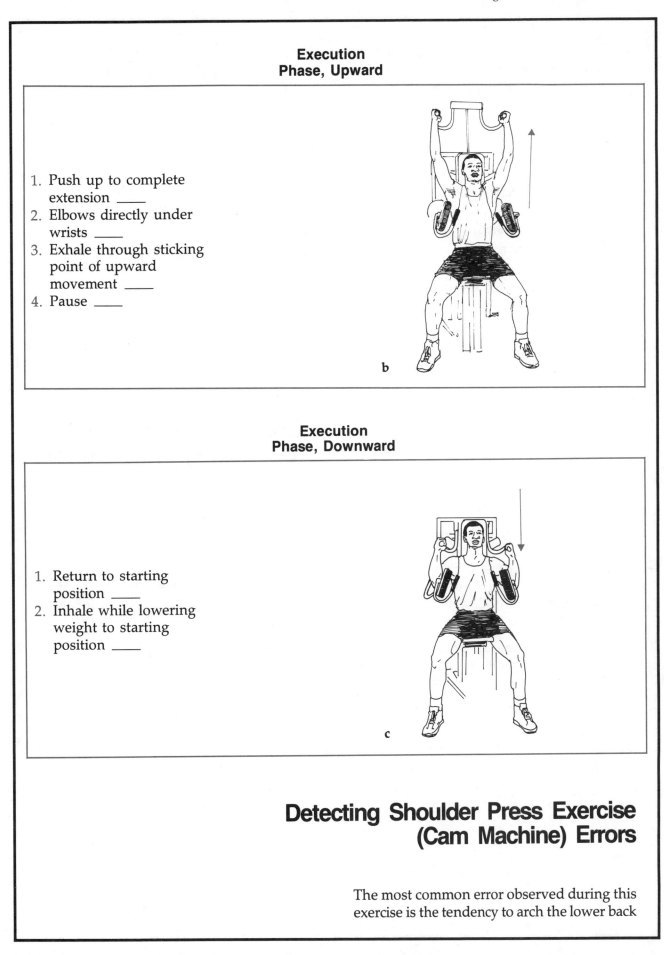

1. Push up to complete extension ____
2. Elbows directly under wrists ____
3. Exhale through sticking point of upward movement ____
4. Pause ____

b

Execution
Phase, Downward

1. Return to starting position ____
2. Inhale while lowering weight to starting position ____

c

Detecting Shoulder Press Exercise (Cam Machine) Errors

The most common error observed during this exercise is the tendency to arch the lower back when the sticking point is reached. The back should be kept flat against the pad because the arched back position inappropriately stresses the lower back. This error and others common to the overhead press exercise, along with suggestions for correction, are presented next.

ERROR   **CORRECTION**

1. Your lower back is not against the pad.

2. Your lower back arches when the sticking point is reached.

3. You hold your breath during the sticking point.

1. Slide back on the seat until your lower back is against the pad.

2. Concentrate on keeping your buttocks and lower back pressed against the pad.

3. Begin exhaling as the bar nears the extended elbow position.

Practice Procedure Drills for Developing the Shoulders

1. Choose One Exercise

After reading about the characteristics and techniques involved in the three different exercises and the type of equipment required for each, you are ready to put this information into action. Consider the availability of equipment and your situation, then select one of the following exercises to use in your program.

- Free weight standing press
- Seated press (multi- or single-unit weight machine)
- Shoulder press (cam machine)

Later (in Step 11), you will copy your exercise choice onto your workout chart.

Success Goal = List the 1 exercise you want to include in your program to develop the shoulder

Your Choice = _____

2. *Practice Grip, Body Positioning, and Movement Pattern (and Spotting, if You Have Selected the Free Weight Standing Press Exercise)*

When you first perform the exercise selected for developing the shoulders, use a dowel stick, an empty bar, or the lightest machine or cam weight stack. Whatever you select, focus on the following techniques:

- Proper grip
- Proper body positioning
- Proper movement pattern

If you selected a machine exercise, move on to the Success Goals section and disregard spotting keys.

Spotting the Free Weight Standing Press Exercise

If you selected the free weight standing press exercise for developing your shoulders, *you need a spotter* and you need to practice the skills of spotting. Identify a spotter and take turns with him or her when completing the Success Goals section. Switch responsibilities so you and your partner have a chance to develop proper grip, body positioning, and movement patterns involved in spotting the standing press.

Check your spotting technique either by watching yourself in a mirror or by asking a qualified person to observe and assess your performance in the techniques. Also request feedback from those you spot.

Success Goals =

a. **Machine/free weight**: 12 out of 15 reps are performed using the proper grip, body position, and movement pattern

b. **Free weight**: 12 out of 15 spotting assists are performed without interfering with the movement pattern and the balance of the person you are spotting

Your Scores =

a. **Machine/free weight**: (#) ____ reps correctly performed with proper grip, body position, and movement pattern

b. **Free weight**: (#) ____ smoothly performed spotting assists

3. *Determine Warm-Up and Trial Loads*

The next practice procedure answers the question, "How much weight or load should I use?" Be sure to use the correct coefficient for the exercise you select.

Success Goals = Using the formulas that follow, determine both warm-up and trial loads, then round off your results to the nearest 5-pound increment, or the closest weight-stack plate.

Warm-Up Load Determination Formula*
Shoulder

Body weight		x	Coefficient	=	Warm-up load (pounds)
	Female				
BWT = _____	(FW–standing press)	x	.10	=	_____
BWT = _____	(M–seated press)	x	.10	=	_____
BWT = _____	(C–shoulder press)	x	.10	=	_____
	Male				
BWT = _____	(FW–standing press)	x	.15	=	_____
BWT = _____	(M–seated press)	x	.15	=	_____
BWT = _____	(C–shoulder press)	x	.20	=	_____

Trial Load Determination Formula*
Shoulder

Body weight		x	Coefficient	=	Trial load (pounds)
	Female				
BWT = _____	(FW–standing press)	x	.22	=	_____
BWT = _____	(M–seated press)	x	.15	=	_____
BWT = _____	(C–shoulder press)	x	.25	=	_____
	Male				
BWT = _____	(FW–standing press)	x	.38	=	_____
BWT = _____	(M–seated press)	x	.35	=	_____
BWT = _____	(C–shoulder press)	x	.40	=	_____

*BWT = body weight, FW = free weight, M = multi- or single-unit machine exercise, and C = cam, .

Your Scores =

a. (#) _____ pounds for warm-up load

b. (#) _____ pounds for trial load

(These loads will be used in the next two drills.)

4. Add Proper Range of Motion, Velocity, and Breathing

Using your calculated warm-up load, apply the previous basic techniques while focusing on the following ones:

- Moving in a full range of motion
- Controlling velocity
- Timing your breathing

Check your technique either by watching yourself in a mirror (machine exercises only) or by asking a qualified person to observe and assess your performance. Perform 15 reps with the warm-up load.

Success Goal = 12 out of 15 reps performed with full range, controlled velocity, and proper breathing

Your Score = (#) _____ reps correctly performed with full range, controlled velocity, and proper breathing

5. *Visualize Correct Techniques*

Review the shoulder exercise keys and technique errors (presented in the previous section). Think back to the previous drill. Find a quiet spot in the weight room, and mentally visualize yourself performing the selected shoulder exercise correctly. Use as many of your senses as possible to imagine the exact feel of the grip, body positioning, movement pattern, movement velocity, full range of movement, and coordinated breathing. Remain undisturbed for 1 or 2 minutes. This helps you mentally set the proper technique in your mind and also gives your body a rest before using the heavier trial load in your next drill.

Success Goal = 1 to 2 minutes of mental visualization of correct execution of selected shoulder exercise

Your Score = (#) _____ minutes of visualization of correct execution

6. *Determine the Training Load*

This practice procedure is designed to help you determine an appropriate training load, one that is designed to produce from 12 to 15 reps. To do so, find your calculated trial load (practice procedure 3). *Do as many reps as possible* with this load, hopefully achieving 12 to 15 reps. Make sure that all reps are smoothly executed. If you are performing the free weight standing press, also check that your elbows extend evenly and that you avoid leaning backward. If you have selected a machine exercise, check that you are moving through the full range of movement.

Success Goal = 12 to 15 reps smoothly executed in selected shoulder exercise with calculated trial load

Your Score = (#) _____ reps smoothly executed

If you smoothly executed 12 to 15 reps with your trial load, then your trial load is the weight you need for training. Record this as your training load in practice procedure 7, and move on to the next chapter (Step 7). Note that this is now referred to as your training load.

7. Make Needed Load Adjustments

If you did not complete 12 reps with your trial load, it is *too heavy*, and you should *lighten* the load. On the other hand, if you performed more than 15 reps, it is *too light* and you should *increase* the load. Use the formula and Load Adjustment Chart to make the necessary adjustments.

Success Goal = Correctly determine your training load according to the following formula:

Determining the Training Load Formula

Trial load (pounds)	+/−	Adjustment	=	Training load (pounds)
_____	+/−	_____	=	_____

Load Adjustment Chart

Reps completed	Adjustment (in pounds)
<7	−15
8-9	−10
10-11	− 5
12-15	0
16-17	+ 5
18-19	+10
>20	+15

Your Score (#) _____ pounds for training load

(Note that this training load will later be recorded onto your workout chart in Step 11.)

Step 7   Selecting a Bicep (Arm) Exercise

Exercises that develop the upper arm are very popular, especially with beginning weight trainers and body builders. These muscles respond quickly when properly trained, and changes in this area are noticed more and sooner than changes in other body parts. The anterior and posterior portions of the upper arm are commonly known as the bicep (covered in this step) and the tricep (covered in Step 8).

The free weight bicep curl, the preacher curl using the cam-type of machine, and the low pulley bicep curl using a single- or multipurpose weight machine are ideal exercises to develop the front of the upper arm (bicep muscles shown in Appendix B, anterior view). Also developed are muscles in the front of the forearm (anterior forearm muscles). The bicep is the traditional ''show me your muscle'' muscle admired by many. Development of this muscle contributes to elbow stabilization and, to some extent, shoulder stabilization.

Free Weight Exercise

If you have access to free weights, you may select the bicep curl exercise to develop your bicep muscles. If you prefer working with machines, see the ''Machine Exercises'' section.

HOW TO PERFORM THE FREE WEIGHT BICEP CURL EXERCISE

The preparation position involves gripping the bar in an underhand grip about shoulder width. Your hands should be evenly spaced. Hold your upper arms against your ribs and perpendicular to the floor. Your elbows should be fully extended.

The bar should be touching the front of your thighs in this position. Your back should be straight, and your head looking straight forward. Your knees should be slightly flexed to reduce the stress on the lower back.

The execution phase begins by pulling the bar upward toward your shoulders, keeping your elbows and upper arms perpendicular to the floor and close to your sides. Avoid allowing your elbows and upper arms to move back or out to the sides. Your body must remain straight and erect throughout the exercise; no rocking, swinging, or jerking should occur. Begin to exhale as the bar nears your shoulders (sticking point). After flexing the elbows as far as possible, inhale as you slowly lower the bar back to your thighs (see Figure 7.1, a-c). Your elbows should be fully extended and there should be a momentary pause at the thighs between each rep.

Figure 7.1   Keys to Success:
Free Weight Bicep Curl Exercise

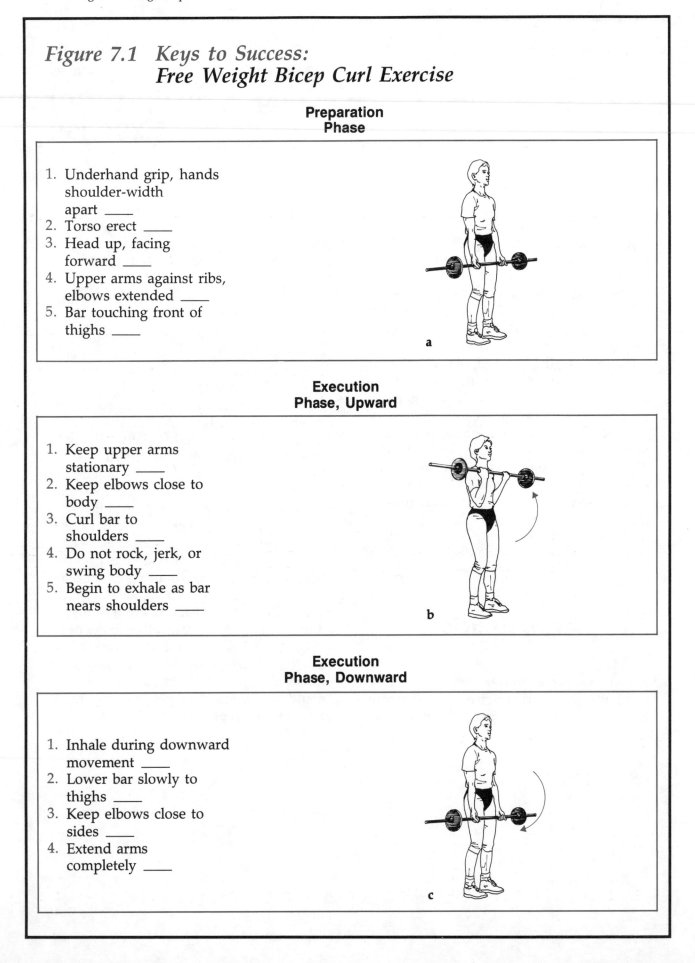

Preparation Phase

1. Underhand grip, hands shoulder-width apart ____
2. Torso erect ____
3. Head up, facing forward ____
4. Upper arms against ribs, elbows extended ____
5. Bar touching front of thighs ____

a

Execution Phase, Upward

1. Keep upper arms stationary ____
2. Keep elbows close to body ____
3. Curl bar to shoulders ____
4. Do not rock, jerk, or swing body ____
5. Begin to exhale as bar nears shoulders ____

b

Execution Phase, Downward

1. Inhale during downward movement ____
2. Lower bar slowly to thighs ____
3. Keep elbows close to sides ____
4. Extend arms completely ____

c

Detecting Free Weight Bicep Curl Errors

The free weight bicep curl is probably one of the easiest exercises to perform, but unfortunately it is probably the one that is most often performed incorrectly. The most common errors are not extending the elbows completely between reps, leaning backward, and using momentum to complete the reps.

ERROR 🚫

CORRECTION

ERROR	CORRECTION
1. Your elbows are slightly flexed in the preparatory position.	1. Stand erect, with your shoulders back and your elbows extended.
2. Your upper arms move backward.	2. Squeeze the inside of your upper arms against your ribs.
3. You use momentum to complete the rep.	3. Keep your upper body erect. If this problem persists, stand with your back against the wall.
4. Your elbows do not extend completely between reps.	4. Pause long enough to watch your elbows extend before curling the bar upward.

Machine Exercises

If you have access to either a cam or multi- or single-unit machine, you may select either the preacher curl or the low pulley bicep curl exercise to develop your bicep muscles.

HOW TO PERFORM THE PREACHER CURL

Assume a sitting position with chest against the pad. Place your elbows on the pad in line with axes of the cams. Adjust the seat so that your elbows are slightly lower than your shoulders. Grasp the bar in an underhand grip. Begin the exercise at full elbow extension. Curl the bar upward as far as possible, pausing briefly at the top position. Exhale as the bar passes through the sticking point. Inhale as you slowly lower the bar to the starting position, being careful not to allow the elbows to hyperextend (see Figure 7.2, a-c).

Figure 7.2 Keys to Success:
          Preacher Curl (Cam Machine)

**Preparation
Phase**

1. Sit with chest against the pad ___
2. Place elbows on pad in line with axes of cams ___
3. Adjust seat so elbows are slightly lower than shoulders ___
4. Use underhand grip ___

**Execution
Phase, Upward**

1. Curl upward as far as possible ___
2. Exhale through the sticking point ___

**Execution
Phase, Downward**

1. Inhale while slowly lowering the bar to starting position ___

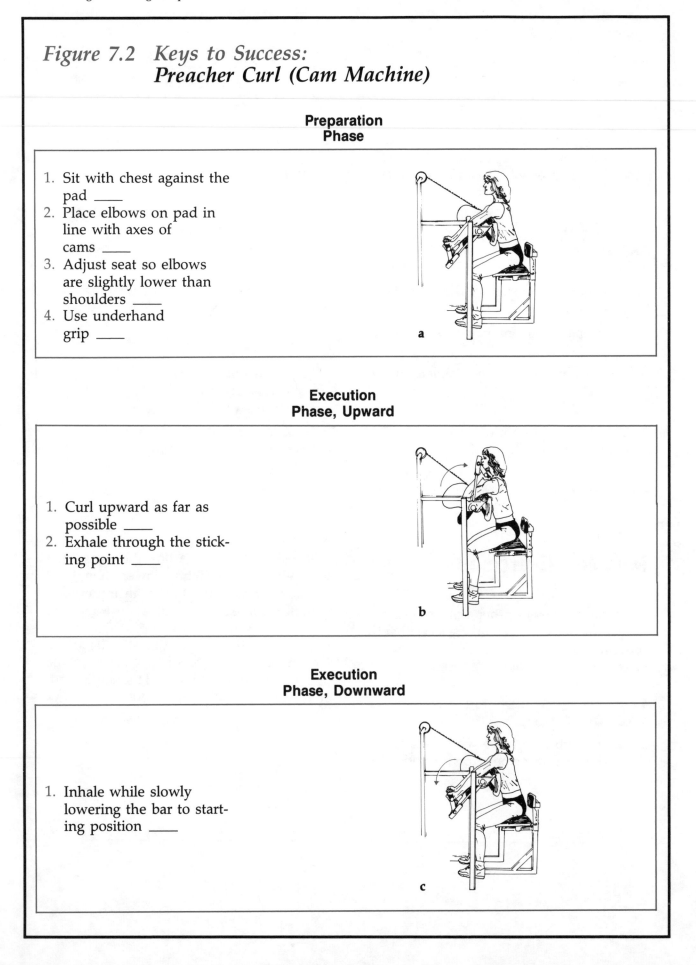

Detecting Preacher Curl Exercise Errors

Common errors in this exercise include not keeping the entire upper arm on the pad, and not pausing at the extended elbow position.

These and other commonly observed errors, and corrections for them, are presented next.

ERROR

CORRECTION

ERROR	CORRECTION
1. Your elbows are not in line with the axes of the cams.	1. Position arms so that your elbows are in line with the axes of the cams.
2. Your elbows are flexed at the start of the exercise.	2. Start the exercise with your elbows fully extended.
3. You do not go through the full range of motion.	3. Curl upward until your hands almost touch your shoulders and lower until the elbows are fully extended.
4. You allow weights to drop quickly.	4. Slowly lower the bar, being careful not to hyperextend your elbows.
5. You do not breathe properly.	5. Exhale when passing through the sticking point; inhale when lowering the bar.

HOW TO PERFORM THE LOW PULLEY BICEP CURL

Assume a position facing the weight machine with your feet approximately 18 inches from the machine. Keep your torso erect, with your head up and looking forward. Your knees should be slightly flexed and your shoulders leaning back. Grasp the bar in an under-hand grip and begin the exercise with the bar touching the front of the thighs and your elbows fully extended. Curl the bar until it almost touches your chin. Avoid allowing your upper arms to move backward or out to the sides. Exhale as you pass through the sticking point and inhale while lowering the bar (see Figure 7.3, a-c).

Figure 7.3 Keys to Success:
Low Pulley Bicep Curl (Multi- or Single-Unit Weight Machine)

**Preparation
Phase**

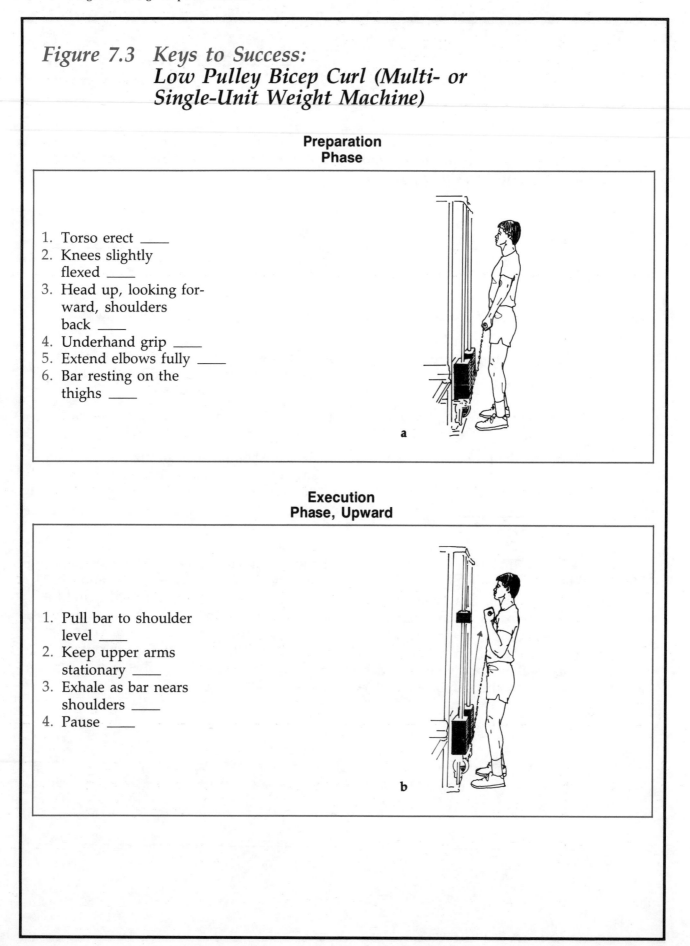

1. Torso erect ____
2. Knees slightly flexed ____
3. Head up, looking forward, shoulders back ____
4. Underhand grip ____
5. Extend elbows fully ____
6. Bar resting on the thighs ____

a

**Execution
Phase, Upward**

1. Pull bar to shoulder level ____
2. Keep upper arms stationary ____
3. Exhale as bar nears shoulders ____
4. Pause ____

b

**Execution
Phase, Downward**

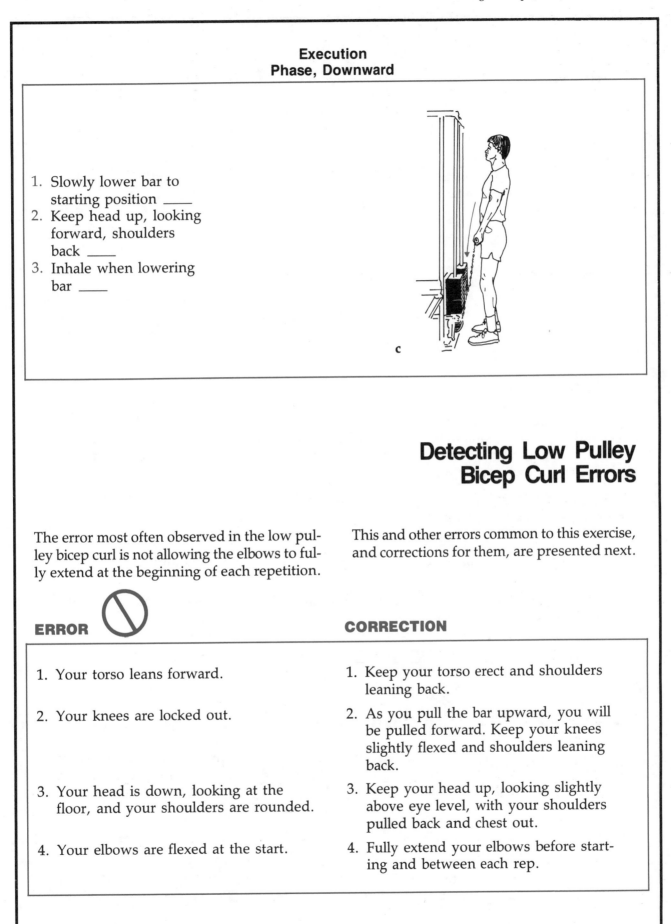

1. Slowly lower bar to starting position ____
2. Keep head up, looking forward, shoulders back ____
3. Inhale when lowering bar ____

c

Detecting Low Pulley Bicep Curl Errors

The error most often observed in the low pulley bicep curl is not allowing the elbows to fully extend at the beginning of each repetition.

This and other errors common to this exercise, and corrections for them, are presented next.

ERROR 🚫

CORRECTION

ERROR	CORRECTION
1. Your torso leans forward.	1. Keep your torso erect and shoulders leaning back.
2. Your knees are locked out.	2. As you pull the bar upward, you will be pulled forward. Keep your knees slightly flexed and shoulders leaning back.
3. Your head is down, looking at the floor, and your shoulders are rounded.	3. Keep your head up, looking slightly above eye level, with your shoulders pulled back and chest out.
4. Your elbows are flexed at the start.	4. Fully extend your elbows before starting and between each rep.

ERROR 🚫	CORRECTION
5. You do not go through full range of motion.	5. Raise the bar until it almost touches your shoulder, and fully extend your elbows.
6. You allow the weight plates to drop quickly to the weight stack.	6. Slowly lower the weight, allowing the weight plate to touch, not bang, against the weight stack.

Practice Procedure Drills for Developing the Bicep

1. Choose One Exercise

After reading about the characteristics and techniques involved in the three different exercises, and the type of equipment required for each, you are ready to put these details into action. Consider the availability of equipment and your situation, then select one of the following exercises to use in your program.

- Free weight bicep curl
- Preacher curl (cam machine)
- Low pulley bicep curl (multi- or single-unit weight machine)

Later (in Step 11), you will copy your exercise choice onto your workout chart.

Success Goal = List the 1 exercise you want to include in your program to develop the bicep muscles

Your Choice = _____

2. Practice Grip, Body Positioning, and Movement Pattern

When you first perform the exercise selected for developing the biceps, use a dowel stick, an empty bar, or the lightest machine weight stack. Regardless of what you select, focus on the following techniques:

- Proper grip
- Proper body positioning
- Proper movement pattern

Check your technique either by watching yourself in a mirror or by asking a qualified person to observe and assess your performance in the basic techniques. Perform 15 reps in the bicep exercise.

Success Goal = **Machine/free weight**: 12 out of 15 reps are performed with the proper grip, body position, and movement pattern

Your Score = (#) _____ reps correctly performed with the proper grip, body position, and movement pattern

3. Determine Warm-Up and Trial Loads

This practice procedure answers the question, "How much weight or load should I use?" Be sure to use the correct coefficient for the exercise you selected.

Success Goals = Complete the following formulas to determine both warm-up and trial loads, then round off your results to the nearest 5-pound increment, or to the closest weight-stack plate

Warm-Up Load Determination Formula*			
Arm–Bicep			

Body weight		x	Coefficient	=	Warm-up load (pounds)
	Female				
BWT = _____	(FW–bicep curl)	x	.10	=	_____
BWT = _____	(C–preacher curl)	x	.10	=	_____
BWT = _____	(M–low pulley bicep curl)	x	.10	=	_____
	Male				
BWT = _____	(FW–bicep curl)	x	.15	=	_____
BWT = _____	(C–preacher curl)	x	.10	=	_____
BWT = _____	(M–low pulley bicep curl)	x	.10	=	_____

Trial Load Determination Formula*			
Arm–Bicep			

Body weight		x	Coefficient	=	Trial load (pounds)
	Female				
BWT = _____	(FW–bicep curl)	x	.23	=	_____
BWT = _____	(C–preacher curl)	x	.12	=	_____
BWT = _____	(M–low pulley bicep curl)	x	.15	=	_____
	Male				
BWT = _____	(FW–bicep curl)	x	.30	=	_____
BWT = _____	(C–preacher curl)	x	.20	=	_____
BWT = _____	(M–low pulley bicep curl)	x	.25	=	_____

*BWT = body weight, FW = free weight, C = cam, and M = multi- or single-unit machine exercise.

Your Scores =
a. (#) _____ pounds for warm-up load
b. (#) _____ pounds for trial load

(These loads will be used in the next two drills.)

4. *Add Proper Range of Motion, Velocity, and Breathing*

Use your calculated warm-up load, and apply the previous basic techniques while focusing on the following ones:

- Moving in a full range of motion
- Controlling velocity
- Timing your breathing

Check your technique either by watching yourself in a mirror or by asking a qualified person to observe and assess your performance. Perform 15 reps with the warm-up load.

Success Goal = 12 out of 15 reps performed with full range, controlled velocity, and proper breathing

Your Score = (#) _____ reps correctly performed with full range, controlled velocity, and proper breathing

5. *Visualize Correct Techniques*

Review the bicep exercise technique errors (presented in the previous section). Think back to the previous activity. Try to locate a quiet spot in the weight room and mentally visualize yourself performing the selected bicep exercise correctly. Use as many of your senses as possible to imagine the exact feel of the grip, body positioning, and coordinated breathing. Remain undisturbed for 1 or 2 minutes. This helps you mentally set the proper technique in your mind and also gives your body a rest before using the heavier trial load in your next drill.

Success Goal = 1 to 2 minutes of mental visualization of correct execution of selected bicep exercise

Your Score = (#) _____ minutes of visualization of correct execution

6. *Determine the Training Load*

This practice procedure is designed to help you determine an appropriate training load, one that is designed to produce from 12 to 15 reps. To do so, find your calculated trial load (practice procedure 3). *Do as many reps as possible* with this load, hopefully achieving 12 to 15 reps. Make sure that all reps are smoothly executed. If you are performing the free weight bicep curl, also check that you do not use body momentum to complete the exercise. If you selected a machine exercise, check that you are moving through the full range of motion.

Success Goal = 12 to 15 reps smoothly executed of selected bicep exercise with calculated trial load

Your Score =   (#) ____ reps smoothly executed

If you smoothly executed 12 to 15 reps with your trial load, then your trial load is the weight you need for training. Record this trial load as your training load in practice procedure 7, and move on to the next chapter (Step 8). Note that this load is now referred to as your training load.

7. *Make Needed Load Adjustments*

If you did not complete 12 reps with your trial load, it is *too heavy*, and you should *lighten the load*. On the other hand, if you performed more than 15 reps, it is *too light*, and you should *increase the load*. Use the formula and Load Adjustment Chart to make necessary adjustments.

Success Goal = Correctly determine your training load according to the following formula:

Determining the Training Load Formula			
Trial load (pounds)	+/− Adjustment	=	Training load (pounds)
_____	+/− _____	=	_____

Load Adjustment Chart	
Reps completed	Adjustment (in pounds)
<7	−15
8-9	−10
10-11	− 5
12-15	0
16-17	+ 5
18-19	+10
>20	+15

Your Score = (#) ____ pounds for training load

(Note that this training load will later be recorded onto your workout chart in Step 11.)

Step 8 Selecting a Tricep (Arm) Exercise

The free weight and cam machine tricep extension and the press-down exercise on a multi- or single-unit weight machine are excellent exercises for developing the back of the upper arm (tricep, shown in Appendix B, posterior view) When properly developed, the tricep muscles contribute to elbow joint stabilization and, to a lesser extent, shoulder stabilization (long head of tricep). Development of this muscle group contributes to activities that require any type of pushing or throwing motion.

Free Weight Exercise

If you have access to free weights, you may select the tricep extension exercise to develop your tricep muscles. If you prefer working with machines, see the ''Machine Exercises'' section.

HOW TO PERFORM THE FREE WEIGHT TRICEP EXTENSION EXERCISE

The preparation position involves holding the bar in a narrow overhand grip with hands ap-proximately 6 inches apart. Use the fundamental lifting techniques presented in Step 2 to take the bar from the floor to the shoulders, and those in Step 6 to position the bar in a fully extended elbow position overhead.

The execution phase begins by lowering the bar in a slow, controlled manner behind your head to shoulder level by flexing the elbows. The upper arms maintain a vertical position with elbows pointed straight up.

From a fully flexed position, push the bar back to the overhead starting position. During the upward movement, your elbows will have a tendency to move forward and bow out. Pull your upper arms close to your ears and keep the elbows pointing straight up. You should exhale through the sticking point, which occurs as the bar approaches the top position. Inhale while the bar is being lowered. Do not move the legs or body in any way to assist in moving the bar upward (see Figure 8.1, a-c).

Figure 8.1 Keys to Success:
      Free Weight Tricep Extension Exercise

**Preparation
Phase**

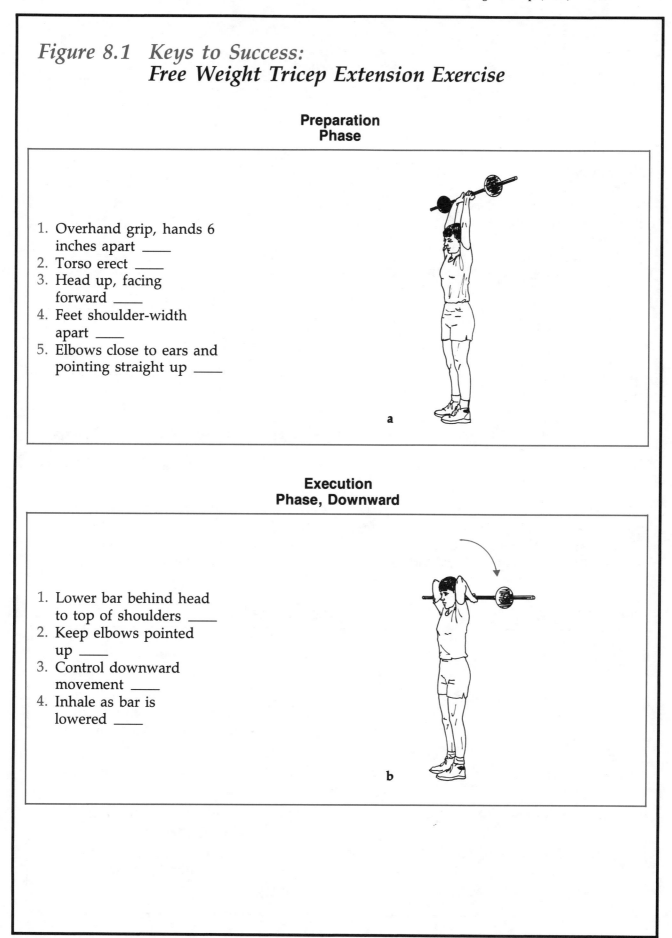

1. Overhand grip, hands 6 inches apart ____
2. Torso erect ____
3. Head up, facing forward ____
4. Feet shoulder-width apart ____
5. Elbows close to ears and pointing straight up ____

a

**Execution
Phase, Downward**

1. Lower bar behind head to top of shoulders ____
2. Keep elbows pointed up ____
3. Control downward movement ____
4. Inhale as bar is lowered ____

b

**Execution
Phase, Upward**

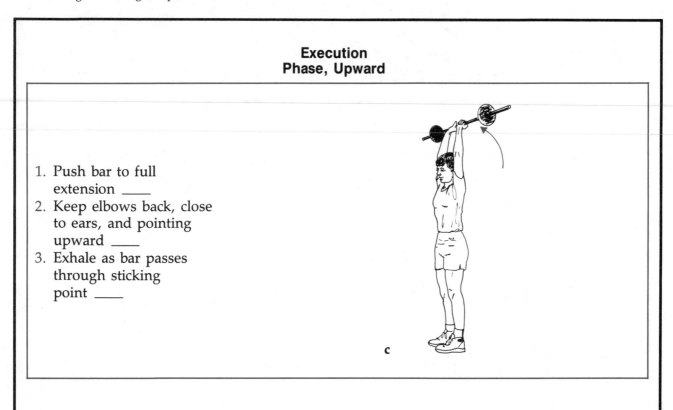

1. Push bar to full extension ____
2. Keep elbows back, close to ears, and pointing upward ____
3. Exhale as bar passes through sticking point ____

c

Detecting Free Weight Tricep Extension Errors

Most errors associated with the tricep extension exercises involve moving the upper arms out of position. When using free weights, your elbows will tend to move forward and bow out during the upward phase. You should concentrate on keeping your elbows close to the ears and pointing straight up. This and other common errors are described next.

ERROR 🚫

CORRECTION

1. Your hands are too far apart.

2. You drop the bar instead of lowering it.

3. Your elbows move forward during upward phase.

4. Your elbows bow out away from your head.

5. You do not lower the bar to the top of your shoulders.

1. Space your hands no more than 6 inches apart.

2. Think "Lower" not "Drop." Control the bar's downward momentum, and pause at shoulder level before pushing upward.

3. Concentrate on keeping your elbows pointing straight up.

4. Concentrate on keeping your upper arms close to your ears.

5. Perform exercise in front of mirror and lower the bar to shoulder level during each rep.

Machine Exercises

If you have access to either a cam or a multi- or single-unit machine, you may select either the tricep extension (cam) or the press-down exercise to develop your tricep muscles.

HOW TO PERFORM THE TRICEP EXTENSION EXERCISE

Assume a sitting position with your back firmly against the pad. Adjust the seat until your shoulders are close to the same height as your elbows. Your elbows should be in line with the axes of the cam. Place your hands, upper arms, and elbows on the pads. From this position push with your hands until your elbows are completely straight. Do not allow your upper arms to lift off the pads. Pause in the extended position, then slowly return to the starting position. You should exhale when pushing upward through the sticking point and inhale during the return (see Figure 8.2, a-c).

Figure 8.2 Keys to Success: Tricep Extension (Cam Machine)

Preparation Phase

1. Place back firmly against pad ____
2. Adjust seat so that shoulders are close to the same height as elbows ____
3. Place upper arms and hands on pads ____

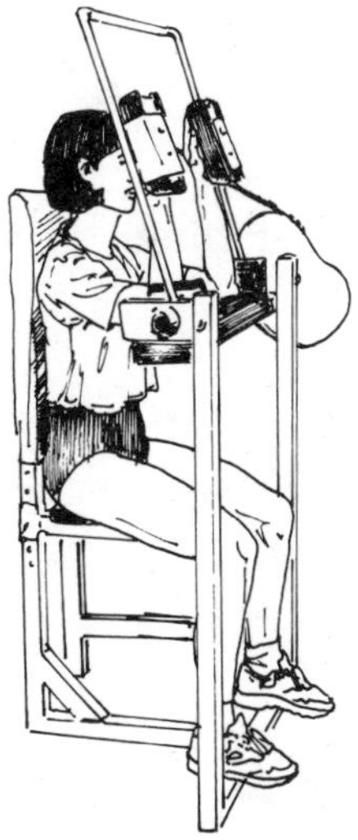

a

**Execution
Phase, Downward**

1. Extend elbows completely ____
2. Upper arms stay back and elbows point forward ____
3. Exhale while passing through sticking point ____

b

**Execution
Phase, Upward**

1. Slowly return to starting position ____
2. Inhale during return to starting position ____

c

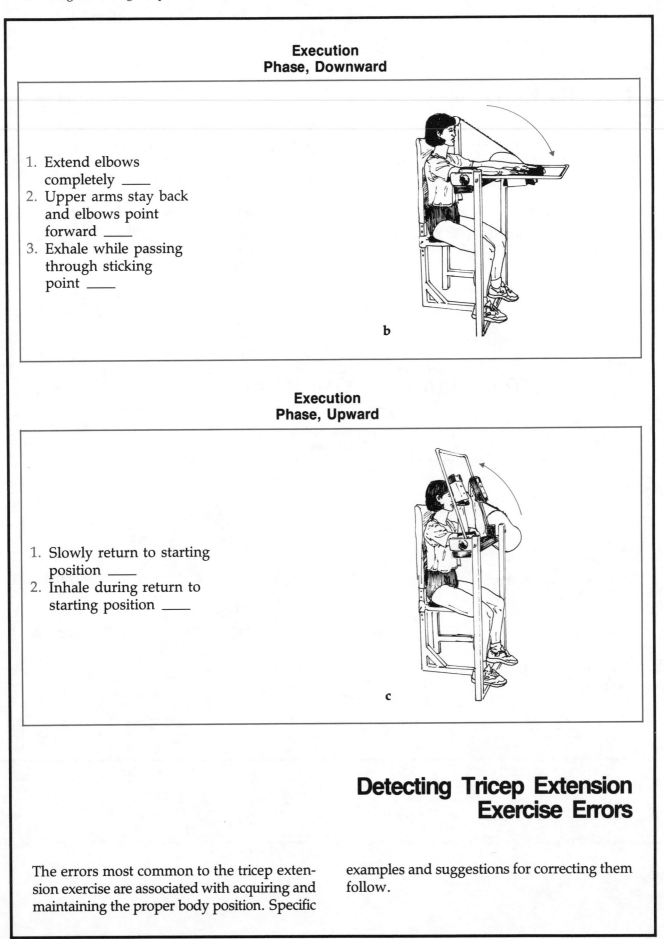

Detecting Tricep Extension Exercise Errors

The errors most common to the tricep extension exercise are associated with acquiring and maintaining the proper body position. Specific examples and suggestions for correcting them follow.

ERROR	CORRECTION
1. Your elbows are higher than your shoulders.	1. Adjust the seat to position your elbows to be more level with your shoulders.
2. Your upper arms and elbows lift off the pads.	2. Keep pressing your upper arms and elbows against the pads—lighten your load if necessary.
3. Your elbows are not in line with the axes of the cam.	3. Adjust the positioning of the upper arms so elbows are in line with the axes of the cam.
4. You do not breathe properly.	4. Exhale when passing through the sticking point, and inhale during the return.

HOW TO PERFORM THE TRICEP PRESS-DOWN EXERCISE

Assume an erect position facing the weight machine, with your feet approximately shoulder-width apart. Grasp the lat bar in an overhand grip, with your hands no more than 6 inches apart. Begin the exercise with the bar at chest height and upper arms pressed firmly against your ribs.

From this position extend your forearms until your elbows are straight and the bar touches your thighs. Pause, then slowly return the bar to chest height without moving your upper arms and torso. Exhale after passing the sticking point, and inhale during the return (see Figure 8.3, a-c).

Figure 8.3 Keys to Success:
Press-Down on Lat Bar
(Multi- or Single-Unit Weight Machine)

**Preparation
Phase**

1. Stand erect ____
2. Feet shoulder-width apart ____
3. Overhand grip ____
4. Hands no more than 6 inches apart ____
5. Bar chest-high to begin ____
6. Squeeze upper arms against ribs ____

a

**Execution
Phase, Downward**

1. Extend forearms until
   bar touches thighs ____
2. Do not move upper arms
   or torso ____
3. Exhale when passing
   through sticking
   point ____
4. Pause ____

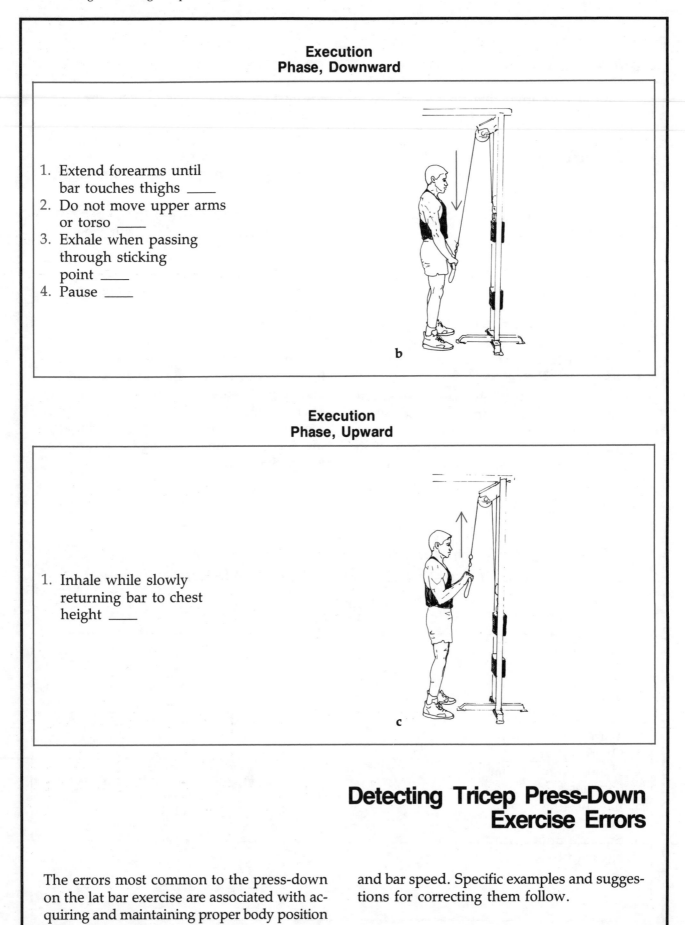

b

**Execution
Phase, Upward**

1. Inhale while slowly
   returning bar to chest
   height ____

c

Detecting Tricep Press-Down Exercise Errors

The errors most common to the press-down on the lat bar exercise are associated with acquiring and maintaining proper body position and bar speed. Specific examples and suggestions for correcting them follow.

ERROR ⊘	CORRECTION
1. Your hands are too far apart.	1. Space your hands no more than 6 inches apart.
2. You allow the bar to move above the shoulders.	2. The bar should begin at chest height and not be allowed to move higher than shoulder level—think, "knuckles below the shoulders.".
3. Your upper arms move away from the side of your ribs during press-down.	3. Squeeze your upper arms against your ribs, and pause at the fully extended and flexed elbow positions.
4. Your elbows are not extended completely.	4. Continue pressing down until your elbows completely straighten and bar touches thighs.
5. You move the bar rapidly up to chest height.	5. This causes many of the bar location and arm position errors presented here and imposes stress on the elbows and joints. Slowly return bar to chest height.
6. Your torso moves back and forth.	6. Maintain a stable, upright position, one in which your head, shoulders, hips, and feet form a straight line. Lighten the load if necessary.

Practice Procedure Drills for Developing the Tricep

1. Choose One Exercise

After reading about the characteristics and techniques involved in the three different exercises, and the type of equipment required for each, you are ready to put these details into action. Consider the availability of equipment and your situation, then select one of the following exercises to use in your program.

- Free weight tricep extension
- Tricep extension (cam machine)
- Press-down on lat bar (multi- or single-unit weight machine)

Later (in Step 11), you will copy your exercise choice onto your workout chart.

Success Goal = List the 1 exercise you want to include in your program to develop the tricep

Your Choice = _____

2. *Practice Grip, Body Positioning, and Movement Pattern*

When you first perform the exercise selected for developing the tricep, use a dowel stick, an empty bar, or the lightest machine weight stack. Whatever you select, focus on the following techniques:

- Proper grip
- Proper body positioning
- Proper movement pattern

Check your technique either by watching yourself in a mirror or by asking a qualified person to observe and assess your performance in the basic techniques. Perform 15 reps in this tricep exercise.

Success Goal = Machine/free weight: 12 out of 15 reps are performed with the proper grip, body position, and movement pattern

Your Score = (#) ____ reps correctly performed with the proper grip, body position, and movement pattern

3. *Determine Warm-Up and Trial Loads*

This practice procedure answers the question "How much weight or load should I use?" Be sure to use the correct coefficient for the exercise you selected.

Success Goals = Using the formulas below, determine both warm-up and trial loads, then round off your results to the nearest 5-pound increment, or to the closest weight-stack plate

<table>
<tr><td colspan="6" align="center">**Warm-Up Load Determination Formula***
Arm–Tricep</td></tr>
<tr><td>Body weight</td><td></td><td>x</td><td>Coefficient</td><td>=</td><td>Warm-up load (pounds)</td></tr>
<tr><td colspan="6" align="center">**Female**</td></tr>
<tr><td>BWT = _____</td><td>(FW–tricep extension)</td><td>x</td><td>.05</td><td>=</td><td>_____</td></tr>
<tr><td>BWT = _____</td><td>(C–tricep extension)</td><td>x</td><td>.05</td><td>=</td><td>_____</td></tr>
<tr><td>BWT = _____</td><td>(M–press-down on lat bar)</td><td>x</td><td>.10</td><td>=</td><td>_____</td></tr>
<tr><td colspan="6" align="center">**Male**</td></tr>
<tr><td>BWT = _____</td><td>(FW–tricep extension)</td><td>x</td><td>.10</td><td>=</td><td>_____</td></tr>
<tr><td>BWT = _____</td><td>(C–tricep extension)</td><td>x</td><td>.20</td><td>=</td><td>_____</td></tr>
<tr><td>BWT = _____</td><td>(M–press-down on lat bar)</td><td>x</td><td>.15</td><td>=</td><td>_____</td></tr>
</table>

Trial Load Determination Formula*
Arm–Tricep

Body weight		x	Coefficient	=	Trial load (pounds)
Female					
BWT = _____	(FW–tricep extension)	x	.12	=	_____
BWT = _____	(C–tricep extension)	x	.13	=	_____
BWT = _____	(M–press-down on lat bar)	x	.19	=	_____
Male					
BWT = _____	(FW–tricep extension)	x	.21	=	_____
BWT = _____	(C–tricep extension)	x	.35	=	_____
BWT = _____	(M–press-down on lat bar)	x	.32	=	_____

*BWT = body weight, FW = free weight, C = cam, and M = multi- or single-unit machine exercise.

Your Scores =

a. (#) ____ pounds for warm-up load

b. (#) ____ pounds for trial load

(These loads will be used in the next two drills.)

4. Add Proper Range of Motion, Velocity, and Breathing

Use your calculated warm-up load, and apply the previous basic techniques while focusing on the following ones:

- Moving in a full range of motion
- Controlled velocity
- Timing and breathing

Check your technique either by watching yourself in a mirror or by asking a qualified person to observe and assess your performance. Perform 15 reps with the warm-up load.

Success Goal = 12 out of 15 reps performed with full range, controlled velocity, and proper breathing

Your Score =   (#) ____ reps correctly performed with full range, controlled velocity, and proper breathing

5. *Visualize Correct Techniques*

Review the tricep exercise technique errors (presented in the previous section). Think back to the previous activity. Find a quiet spot in the weight room and mentally visualize yourself performing the selected tricep exercise correctly. Use as many of your senses as possible to imagine the exact feel of the grip, body positioning, and coordinated breathing. Remain undisturbed for 1 or 2 minutes. This helps you mentally ''set'' the proper technique in your mind and also gives your body a rest before using the heavier trial load in your next drill.

Success Goal = 1 to 2 minutes of visualization of correct execution

Your Score = (#) _____ minutes of visualization of correct execution

6. *Determine the Training Load*

This practice procedure is designed to help you determine an appropriate training load, one that is designed to produce from 12 to 15 reps. To do so, find your calculated trial load (practice procedure 3). *Do as many reps as possible* with this load, hopefully achieving 12 to 15 reps. Make sure that all reps are smoothly executed. If you are executing the free weight tricep extension, also check that your elbows point straight up and your upper arms stay close to your ears. If you have selected a machine exercise, check that you are moving through the full range of motion.

Success Goal = 12 to 15 reps smoothly executed of selected tricep exercise with
    calculated load

Your Score = (#) _____ reps smoothly executed

If you smoothly executed 12 to 15 reps with your trial load, then your trial load is the weight you need for training. Record this as your training load in practice procedure 7, and move on to the next chapter (Step 9). Note that this load is now referred to as your training load.

7. *Make Needed Load Adjustments*

If you did not perform 12 reps with your trial load, it is *too heavy*, and you should *lighten the load*. On the other hand, if you performed more than 15 reps, it is *too light*, and you should *increase the load*. Use the formula and Load Adjustment chart to make necessary adjustments.

Success Goal = Correctly determine your training load according to the following
    formula:

Determining the Training Load Formula				
Trial load (pounds)	+/−	Adjustment	=	Training load (pounds)
_____	+/−	_____	=	_____

Load Adjustment Chart	
Reps completed	Adjustment (in pounds)
<7	−15
8-9	−10
10-11	− 5
12-15	0
16-17	+ 5
18-19	+10
>20	+15

Your Score = (#) _____ pounds for training load

(Note that this training load will later be recorded onto your workout chart in Step 11.)

Step 9 Selecting a Leg Exercise

Exercises that develop the upper leg are considered to be very physically demanding, due to the large muscle area involved. The exercises selected are the lunge (free weights) and leg press (machine). These exercises are excellent for the front of the thigh (quadriceps), shown in Appendix B, anterior view, the back of the thigh (hamstrings), and the hip (gluteals), shown in Appendix B, posterior view. These exercises contribute to knee and hip joint stabilization, muscle padding for protection of the hip, and lower body "sculpturing." The leg and hip strength gained through these exercises is especially beneficial to those involved in athletic activities.

Free Weight Exercise

If you have access to free weights, you may select the lunge exercise to develop your legs. If you prefer working with machines, see the "Machine Exercise" section.

HOW TO PERFORM THE LUNGE EXERCISE

The lunge is a relatively difficult exercise to perform because of the balance required. You should try lunges first without weights to develop the needed balance. When you feel comfortable with the forward and backward movements and with your balance, begin using hand-held dumbbells. The preparation phase begins with your feet shoulder-width apart, eyes straight ahead, head up, shoulders back, chest out, and back straight. *This erect posture should be maintained throughout the exercise* (see Figure 9.1a).

The forward execution phase begins with a slow, controlled step forward (Figure 9.1b) on your preferred leg, being careful not to overstride. As shown in Figure 9.1c, your hips are lowered enough so that the top of your (forward) thigh is slightly below parallel and your knee is directly over your ankle. Your front foot should be straight ahead and your back knee relatively extended to stretch your hip flexor muscles. The knee that is back should not quite touch the floor.

The backward execution phase begins by pushing off your front foot and returning to the starting position smoothly without using upper-torso momentum (see Figure 9.1, d-f). Step forward with the other foot in the next rep and continue alternating until the set is completed. At first you might have to slide (stutter step) your foot on the floor in order to return to the starting position. As you gain strength and develop better balance, this may not happen. Inhale as you take the forward step. Exhale as you push off the forward foot on the way back to the starting position.

Figure 9.1 *Keys to Success:*
Lunge Exercise (Dumbbells)

**Preparation
Phase**

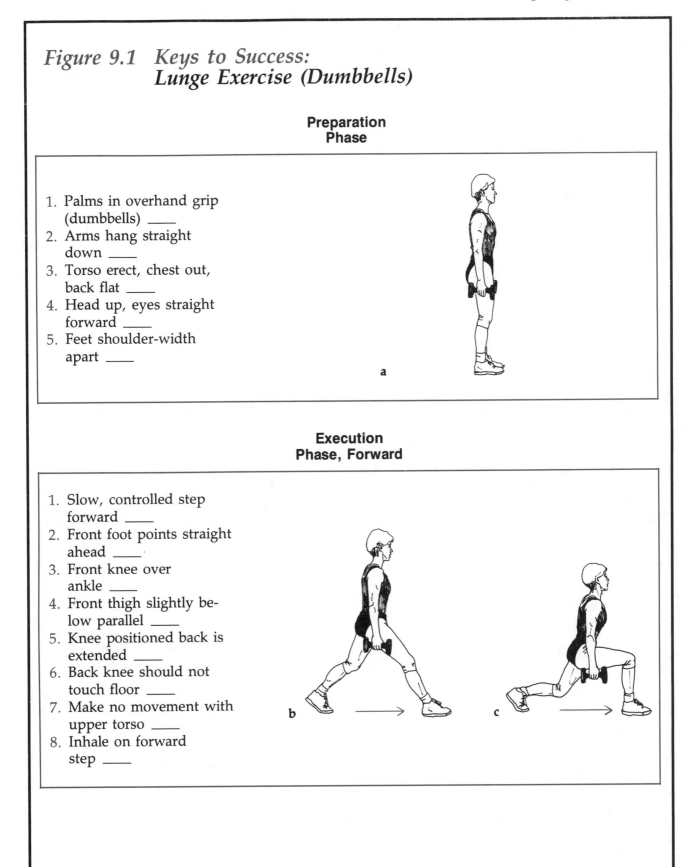

1. Palms in overhand grip
   (dumbbells) ____
2. Arms hang straight
   down ____
3. Torso erect, chest out,
   back flat ____
4. Head up, eyes straight
   forward ____
5. Feet shoulder-width
   apart ____

a

**Execution
Phase, Forward**

1. Slow, controlled step
   forward ____
2. Front foot points straight
   ahead ____ ·
3. Front knee over
   ankle ____
4. Front thigh slightly below parallel ____
5. Knee positioned back is
   extended ____
6. Back knee should not
   touch floor ____
7. Make no movement with
   upper torso ____
8. Inhale on forward
   step ____

b

c

Execution
Phase, Backward

1. Push off front foot to return to starting position ____
2. Maintain erect torso position ____
3. Keep eyes looking straight ahead ____
4. Exhale during push-off ____

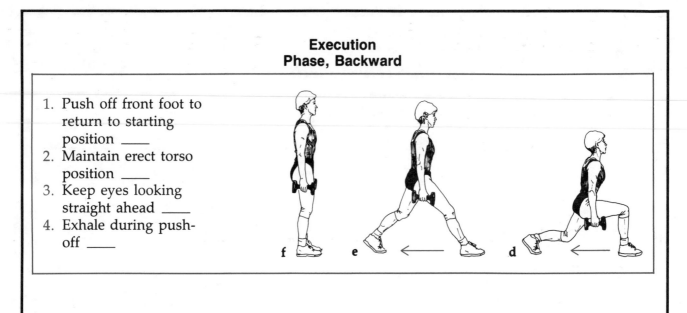

Detecting Lunge Errors

Most errors associated with the lunge are the result of stride length and torso movement. You will tend to overstride or understride. It is also common to use torso momentum to return to the starting position.

ERROR

CORRECTION

1. Your front foot is pointed out.

2. Your back knee is not extended.

3. Your upper torso leans forward.

1. Keep your front foot pointed forward. Think, ''The thigh, knee, and foot form a straight line.''

2. Use a mirror to determine needed changes in hip and knee position.

3. Concentrate on keeping your head and shoulders back and your chest out.

Machine Exercise

If you have access to either a multi- or single-unit machine, you may select the leg press exercise to develop your legs.

HOW TO PERFORM THE LEG PRESS

This exercise involves the use of a leg press machine, either the pulley/pivot or the cam type. The preparation phase begins by adjusting the seat so that there is a 90-degree angle or less at the knees. Sit erect, with your lower back against the back of the seat and with your feet parallel and flat against the pedal surface. Grasp the handrails to stabilize your body (see Figure 9.2a).

The forward execution phase (Figure 9.2b) is initiated by pushing your legs to the extended knee position while maintaining an upright position. Avoid twisting your body as you extend your legs. Do *not* "lock out" the knees *at any time*. Exhale during your press outward, and inhale on your return to the starting position.

The backward execution phase (Figure 9.2c) involves allowing your legs to move back to your body as far as possible without your buttocks lifting up and/or the weight touching the stack.

Figure 9.2 *Keys to Success:* *Leg Press (Multi- or Single-Unit Machine)*

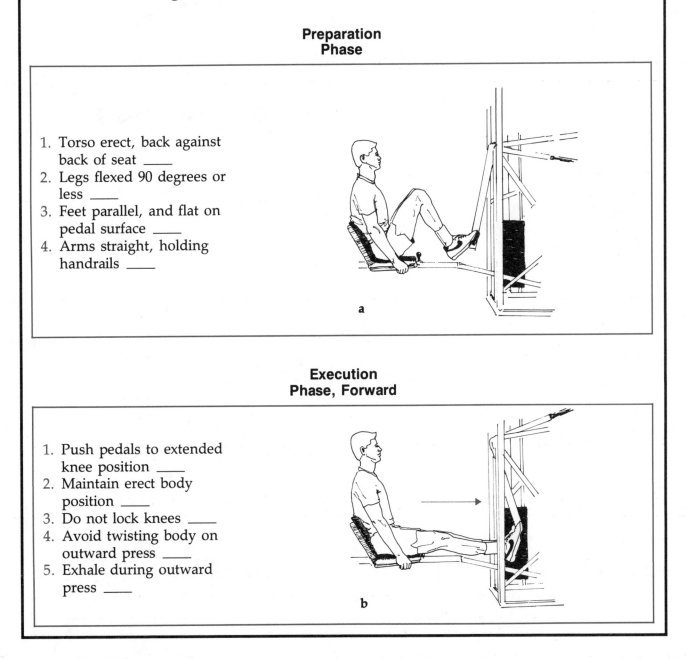

Preparation Phase

1. Torso erect, back against back of seat ____
2. Legs flexed 90 degrees or less ____
3. Feet parallel, and flat on pedal surface ____
4. Arms straight, holding handrails ____

a

Execution Phase, Forward

1. Push pedals to extended knee position ____
2. Maintain erect body position ____
3. Do not lock knees ____
4. Avoid twisting body on outward press ____
5. Exhale during outward press ____

b

**Execution
Phase, Backward**

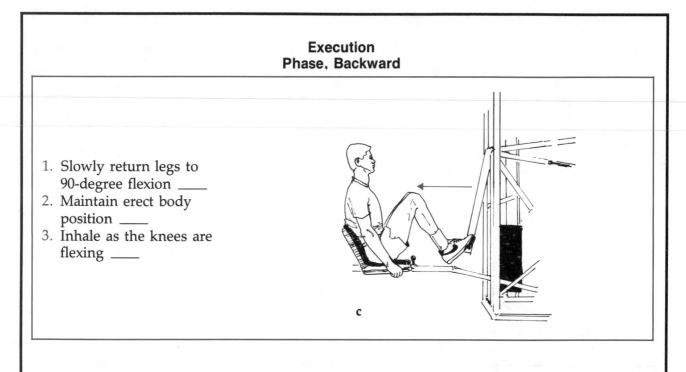

1. Slowly return legs to 90-degree flexion ____
2. Maintain erect body position ____
3. Inhale as the knees are flexing ____

c

Detecting Leg Press Errors

Most errors associated with the leg press involve the speed of extension and flexion, and locking the knees. There is a tendency to press out too quickly, causing the knees to lock out. The danger here is that you might hyperextend the knees and cause injury to them by doing this. Another common error is letting the weight free-fall back to the starting position. Thus, the first step in correcting errors is to slowly extend the knees, then make a slow, controlled movement back to touch, not bang, the weight stack.

ERROR 🚫

CORRECTION

1. Your feet are not flat on the pedal surface.

1. There is a tendency to push with the balls of the feet only. Keep your heels on the surface—elevated heels place stress on your knees and may result in your feet slipping off the pedals.

2. Your upper and lower legs do not form a 90 degree angle.

2. Use a mirror or ask someone for feedback to establish a 90 degree angle.

3. Your torso leans forward.

3. Sit erect with the back and hips pushed against the seat.

4. Your knees are fully locked out at the end of the forward execution phase.

4. This can cause serious injury to your knees. Control your forward speed, and be sure that you stop before your knees are locked out.

Practice Procedure Drills for Developing the Legs

1. Choose One Exercise

After reading about the characteristics and techniques involved in these two exercises, and the type of equipment required for each, you are ready to put these details into action. Consider the availability of equipment in your situation, then select one of the following exercises to use in your program.

- Lunge (free weights)
- Leg press (multi- or single-unit weight machine)

Later (in Step 11), you will copy your exercise choice onto your workout chart.

Success Goal = List the 1 exercise you want to include in your program to develop the legs

Your Choice = _____

2. Practice Foot Placement, Body Positioning, and Movement Pattern

When you perform the exercise selected for developing the legs, use only your body weight in the lunge exercise, or the lightest machine weight stack in the leg press exercise. Whatever you select, focus on the following techniques:

- Proper foot placement
- Proper body positioning
- Proper movement pattern

Check your technique either by watching yourself in a mirror or by asking a qualified person to observe and assess your performance in the basic techniques. Perform 15 reps in this leg exercise.

Success Goal = **Machine/free weight**: 12 out of 15 reps are performed with the proper foot placement, body position, and movement pattern

Your Score = (#) ____ reps correctly performed with the proper foot placement, body position, and movement pattern

3. Determine Warm-Up and Trial Loads

This practice procedure answers the question "How much weight or load should I use?" You should use the following formulas only if you selected the leg press exercise.

Success Goals = Determine both warm-up and trial loads, then round off your results to the closest weight-stack plate

Warm-Up Load Determination Formula* Legs				
Body weight		x	Coefficient =	Warm-up load (pounds)
	Female			
	(FW–lunge)	x	=	no load
BWT = _____	(M–leg press)	x	.50 =	_____
	Male			
	(FW–lunge)	x	=	no load
BWT = _____	(M–leg press)	x	.70 =	_____

Trial Load Determination Formula* Legs				
Body weight		x	Coefficient =	Trial load (pounds)
	Female			
	(FW–lunge)	x	=	5 lb (each hand)
BWT = _____	(M–leg press)	x	1.0 =	_____
	Male			
	(FW–lunge)	x	=	10 lb (each hand)
BWT = _____	(M–leg press)	x	1.3 =	_____

*BWT = body weight, FW = free weight, and M = multi- or single-unit machine exercise.

With the Lunge Exercise

Practice without weight until you develop the necessary balance, then begin to add weight by holding hand-held dumbbells.

Females should add in *10-pound* increments (5 pounds in each hand), and *males* should add in *20-pound* increments (10 pounds in each hand). Continue to add weight slowly until you establish a training load that produces 12 to 15 reps.

Your Scores =

  a. (#) ____ pounds for warm-up load

  b. (#) ____ pounds for trial load

(These loads will wil be used in the next two drills.)

4. Add Proper Range of Motion, Velocity, and Breathing

Use your warm-up load, and apply the previous basic techniques while focusing on the following ones:

- Moving in the full range of motion
- Controlling velocity
- Timing your breathing

Check your technique either by watching yourself in a mirror or by asking a qualified person to observe and assess your performance. Perform 15 reps with the warm-up load.

Success Goal = 12 out of 15 reps performed with full range, controlled velocity, and proper breathing

Your Score =   (#) ____ reps correctly performed with full range, controlled velocity, and proper breathing

5. Visualize Correct Techniques

Review the leg exercise technique errors (presented in the previous section). Think back to the previous activity. Find a quiet spot in the weight room and mentally visualize yourself performing the selected leg exercise correctly. Use as many of your senses as possible to imagine the exact feel of the foot placement, body positioning, and coordinated breathing. Remain undisturbed for 1 or 2 minutes. This helps you mentally set the proper technique in your mind and also gives your body a rest before using the heavier trial load in your next drill.

Success Goal = 1 to 2 minutes of mental visualization of correct execution of selected leg exercise

Your Score =   (#) ____ minutes of visualization of correct execution

6. Determine the Training Load

This practice procedure is designed to help you determine an appropriate training load, one that is designed to produce from 12 to 15 reps. If you selected the leg press exercise, find your calculated trial load (practice procedure 3). *Do as many reps as possible* with this load, hopefully achieving 12 to 15 reps. If you selected the lunge exercise, you should gradually increase the weight of the dumbbells until the 12-15 rep range is achieved. Men begin with 10-pound dumbbells and women with 5-pound dumbbells (one in each hand). Make sure that all reps are smoothly executed and that you are moving through the full range of motion.

Success Goal = 12 to 15 reps smoothly executed of selected leg exercise with calculated trial load

Your Score =   (#) _____ reps smoothly executed

If you smoothly executed 12 to 15 reps with your trial load, then your trial load equals the load you need for training. Record this trial load as your training load in practice procedure 7, and move on to the next chapter (Step 10). Note that this load is now referred to as your training load.

7. Make Needed Load Adjustments

If you performed less than 12 reps with your trial load, it is *too heavy*, and you should *lighten the load*. On the other hand, if you performed more than 15 reps, the load is *too light*, and you should *increase it*. Use the formula and Load Adjustment Chart (described in Step 3) to make necessary adjustments (for the leg press). If you selected the lunge exercise, gradually increase training loads until the 12-15 rep range is reached.

Success Goal = Correctly determine your training load according to the following formula (leg press) or by gradually increasing dumbbell loads for the lunge exercise:

Determining the Training Load Formula				
Trial load (pounds)	+/–	Adjustment	=	Training load (pounds)
_____	+/–	_____	=	_____

Load Adjustment Chart	
Reps completed	Adjustment (in pounds)
<7	–15
8-9	–10
10-11	– 5
12-15	0
16-17	+ 5
18-19	+10
>20	+15

Your Score = (#) _____ pounds for training load

(Note that this training load will later be recorded onto your workout chart in Step 11.)

Step 10 Selecting an Abdominal Exercise

The abdominal muscles are the major supporting muscles for the stomach area. They not only support and protect internal organs, but they aid the muscles of the lower back to properly align and support the spine for proper posture as well as in lifting activities. Properly developed abdominal muscles serve as a biological girdle to flatten your waistline. Although there is no such thing as spot reducing (fat reduction in only one area), strong abdominal muscles make the area smaller and look tighter even though the fat may still be there. The abdominal muscles (shown in Appendix B, anterior view) include the rectus abdominis, which causes the trunk to bend or flex, and the external obliques, which assist the rectus abdominis and cause trunk rotation and bending to the side.

The exercises described here will be the twisting trunk curl and the machine abdominal curl. These exercises should be performed on a regular basis, three to five times each week. The straight-leg (knees straight) sit-up is not included here because it relies heavily on hip flexors (rectus femoris and iliopsoas) and does not emphasize working the abdominal muscles, and because it may contribute to lower back problems.

No Weight Exercise

You may select the twisting trunk curl exercise to develop your abdominal muscles. Or, if you prefer working with machines, see the "Machine Exercise" section.

HOW TO PERFORM THE TWISTING TRUNK CURL EXERCISE

Prepare for this exercise by lying with your back on the floor and your feet on a bench or chair. Fold your arms across your chest, with your hands on opposite shoulders.

The upward execution phase begins as you pull your chin to your chest and contract the abdominal muscles to move your torso upward. Alternately curl your shoulders toward the opposite knees and exhale when nearing the point of greatest flexion (upward position). Pause at the point of greatest flexion.

The downward execution phase follows the pause at the top. Begin to inhale at this point. Be sure to keep your chin on your chest until your shoulders touch the floor (see Figure 10.1, a-c). Then allow your head to touch. Your lower back and hips should remain in contact with the floor throughout the exercise. A high number of reps is encouraged to promote tone, muscular endurance, strength and muscle definition.

Figure 10.1 Keys to Success: Twisting Trunk Curl Exercise

Preparation Phase

1. Back flat on floor ___
2. Feet on bench or chair ___
3. Arms folded across chest ___

a

Execution Phase, Upward

1. Chin to chest first ___
2. Alternately curl shoulders and upper back toward opposite knees ___
3. Exhale when nearing highest position ___
4. Pause momentarily ___

b

Execution Phase, Downward

1. Return slowly to starting position ___
2. Keep chin to chest until shoulders touch ___
3. Inhale during downward movement ___

c

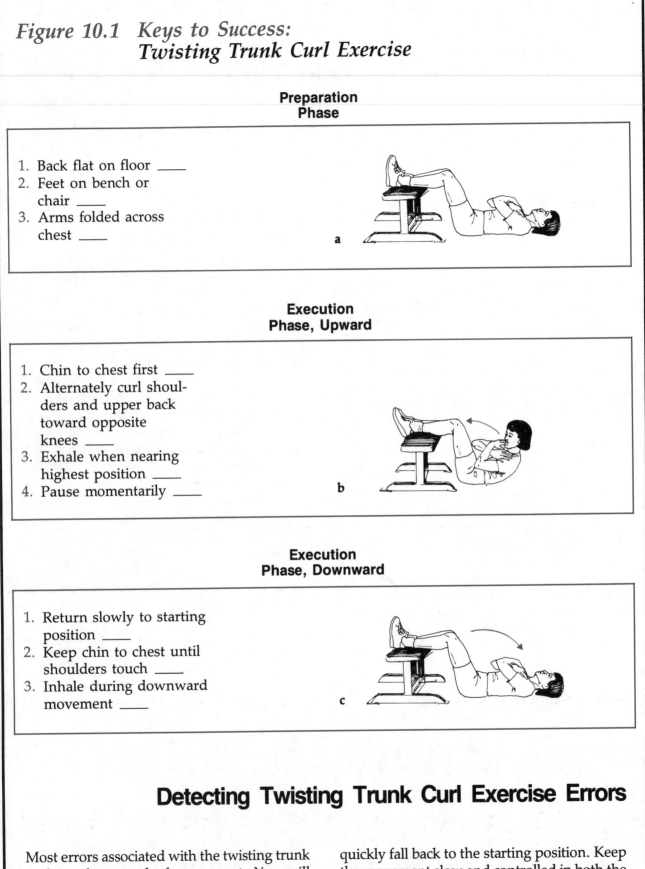

Detecting Twisting Trunk Curl Exercise Errors

Most errors associated with the twisting trunk curl involve speed of movement. You will have a tendency to lunge forward and then quickly fall back to the starting position. Keep the movement slow and controlled in both the upward and the downward position.

ERROR ⊘	CORRECTION
1. Your buttocks lift off the floor just prior to upward movement.	1. Start the exercise with your head, shoulders, upper back, and lower back in contact with the floor. Keep your lower back and buttocks in contact with the floor throughout each rep. Pause on the floor before beginning another rep.
2. Your chin is not on your chest.	2. Curl your chin to your chest to begin the upward movement.
3. Your shoulders lower rapidly, followed by bouncing action upward.	3. Slowly lower your upper back, shoulders, and head to the starting position. Pause on the floor before beginning another rep.

Machine Exercise

If you have access to a cam machine, you may select the trunk curl exercise to develop your abdominal muscles.

HOW TO PERFORM THE TRUNK CURL

Assume an erect sitting position, with your shoulders and upper arms firmly against the pads. Adjust the height of the seat so that the axis of rotation is level with the lower part of your sternum (midchest). Place your ankles behind the roller pad, with your knees spread and your hands grasping the roller in front of you (see Figure 10.2a). While maintaining this position, shorten the distance between your rib cage and navel by contracting your abdominals only (see Figure 10.2b). Pause in the fully contracted position, then return slowly to the starting position (see Figure 10.2c). Exhale during the contraction phase, and inhale during the relaxation phase.

Figure 10.2 Keys to Success:
Trunk Curl (Cam Machine)

Preparation Phase

1. Sit with shoulders and upper arms firmly against the pads ____
2. Adjust seat so axis of rotation is level with lower part of sternum ____
3. Place ankles behind roller pad ____
4. Spread knees and sit erect ____
5. Grasp roller ____

a

Execution Phase, Downward

1. Shorten distance between rib cage and navel by contracting abdominals only ____
2. Keep legs relaxed as chest is lowered ____
3. Exhale during contraction ____
4. Pause in contracted position ____

b

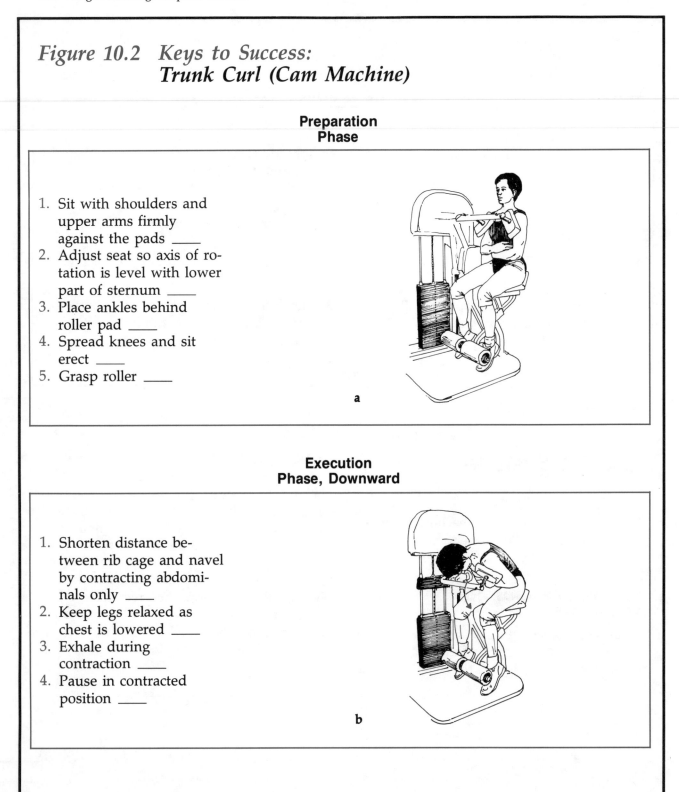

**Execution
Phase, Upward**

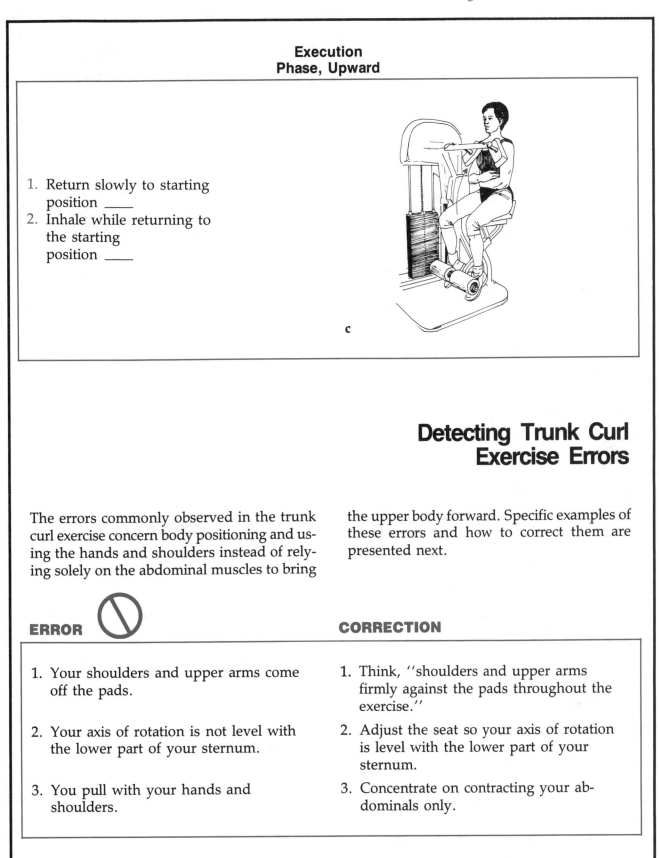

1. Return slowly to starting position ____
2. Inhale while returning to the starting position ____

c

Detecting Trunk Curl Exercise Errors

The errors commonly observed in the trunk curl exercise concern body positioning and using the hands and shoulders instead of relying solely on the abdominal muscles to bring the upper body forward. Specific examples of these errors and how to correct them are presented next.

ERROR 🚫   **CORRECTION**

ERROR	CORRECTION
1. Your shoulders and upper arms come off the pads.	1. Think, ''shoulders and upper arms firmly against the pads throughout the exercise.''
2. Your axis of rotation is not level with the lower part of your sternum.	2. Adjust the seat so your axis of rotation is level with the lower part of your sternum.
3. You pull with your hands and shoulders.	3. Concentrate on contracting your abdominals only.

Practice Procedure Drills for Developing the Abdominals

1. Choose One Exercise

After reading about the characteristics and techniques involved in the two different exercises, and the type of equipment required for each, you are ready to put these details into action. Consider what equipment is available to you, then select one of the following exercises to use in your program.

- Twisting trunk curl (no weight)
- Trunk curl (cam machine)

Later (in Step 11), you will copy your exercise choice onto your workout chart.

Success Goal = List the 1 exercise you want to include in your program to develop the abdominals

Your Choice = _____

2. Practice Body Positioning and Movement Pattern

When you perform the machine trunk curl, use the lightest weight stack. With both trunk curl exercises, focus on the following techniques:

- Proper body positioning
- Proper movement pattern

Check your technique either by watching yourself in a mirror or by asking a qualified person to observe and assess your performance in the basic techniques. Perform 15 reps of this abdominal exercise.

Success Goal = 12 out of 15 reps are performed with the proper body position and movement pattern

Your Score = (#) ____ reps correctly performed with the proper body position and movement pattern

3. Determine Warm-Up and Trial Loads

This practice procedure answers the question "How much weight or load should I use?" For the trunk curl (cam machine) exercise, use the formulas below.

If you chose the twisting trunk curl, you will not need to establish warm-up, trial, and training loads. Continue on with the following practice procedures and ignore comments concerning warm-up and training loads. If you chose the machine trunk curl, follow the procedures as they are described.

Success Goals = Determine both warm-up and trial loads, then round off your results to the closest weight-stack plate

Warm-Up Load Determination Formula* Abdominals				
Body weight		x	Coefficient =	Warm-up load (pounds)
	Female			
	(twisting trunk curl)	x	=	no load
BWT = _____	(C–trunk curl)	x	.20 =	_____
	Male			
	(twisting trunk curl)	x	=	no load
BWT = _____	(C–trunk curl)	x	.20 =	_____

Trial Load Determination Formula* Abdominals				
Body weight		x	Coefficient =	Trial load (pounds)
	Female			
	(twisting trunk curl)	x	=	no load
BWT = _____	(C–trunk curl)	x	.20 =	_____
	Male			
	(twisting trunk curl)	x	=	no load
BWT = _____	(C–trunk curl)	x	.20 =	_____

*BWT = body weight, and C = cam.

Your Scores =

 a. (#) ____ pounds for warm-up load

 b. (#) ____ pounds for trial load

(These loads will be used in the next two drills.)

4. Add Proper Range of Motion, Velocity, and Breathing

Use your calculated warm-up load, and apply the previous basic techniques while focusing on the following ones:

- Moving in a full range of motion
- Controlling velocity
- Timing your breathing

Check your technique either by watching yourself in a mirror or by asking a qualified person to observe and assess your performance. Perform 15 reps with the warm-up load.

Success Goal = 12 out of 15 reps performed with full range, controlled velocity, and proper breathing

Your Score = (#) ___ reps correctly performed with full range, controlled velocity, and proper breathing

5. Visualize Correct Technique

Review the appropriate trunk curl exercise Keys to Success and technique errors (presented in the previous section). Find a quiet spot in the weight room and mentally visualize yourself performing the selected abdominal exercise correctly. Use as many of your senses as possible to imagine the exact feel of the body positioning, movement pattern, movement velocity, full range of motion, and coordinated breathing. Remain undisturbed for 1 or 2 minutes. This helps you mentally set the proper technique in your mind and also gives your body a rest before using the heavier trial load in your next drill.

Success Goal = 1 to 2 minutes of mental visualization of correct execution of the trunk curl

Your Score = (#) ___ minutes of visualization of correct execution

6. Determine the Training Load

This practice procedure is designed to help you determine an appropriate training load, one that is designed to produce from 12 to 15 reps. To do so, find your calculated trial load (practice procedure 3). *Do as many reps as possible* with this load, hopefully achieving 12 to 15 reps. Make sure that all reps are smoothly executed. If you selected the twisting trunk, no calculation is needed. Simply perform as many twisting trunk curls as possible.

Success Goal = 12 to 15 reps smoothly executed of selected abdominal exercise with calculated trial load

Your Score =   (#) ＿＿ reps smoothly executed

If you smoothly executed 12 to 15 reps with your trial load, your trial load is the load you need for training. Record this trial load as your training load in practice procedure 7, and move on to the next chapter (Step 11). Note that this load is now referred to as your training load.

7. Make Needed Load Adjustments

If you performed less than 12 reps with your trial load, it is *too heavy*, and you should *lighten the load*. On the other hand, if you performed more than 15 reps, the load is *too light*, and you should *increase it*. Use the formula and Load Adjustment Chart to make necessary adjustments (for the trunk curl).

Success Goal = Correctly determine your training load according to the following formula:

Determining the Training Load Formula			
Trial load (pounds)	+/− Adjustment	=	Training load (pounds)
＿＿＿＿＿＿	+/− ＿＿＿＿	=	＿＿＿＿＿＿

Load Adjustment Chart	
Reps completed	Adjustment (in pounds)
<7	−15
8-9	−10
10-11	− 5
12-15	0
16-17	+ 5
18-19	+10
>20	+15

Your Score = (#) ＿＿ pounds for training load

(Note, this training load will later be recorded onto your workout chart in Step 11.)

Step 11 Completing Your First Workout Chart

Now the fun really begins, because this is when you start training! This step directs you through a series of tasks necessary to complete your workout.

When the 11 checkpoints presented here are consistently followed, your workouts will produce some exciting changes, both in the confidence you have in the weight room and in your physical development.

Checkpoints for Completing Your First Workout

In preparation for your first workout, you will need to copy the exercises you selected and the training load information from the practice procedures section in Steps 4 through 10 to the workout chart located in Appendix C. An example of how to do this is shown in Figure 11.1, using the bench press as the chosen exercise (from Step 4). **Locate and copy this information now onto the workout chart in Appendix C**. Be sure to record the exercise selected for the chest first (at the top), then (below it) the exercises selected for the back, shoulders, arms (front, biceps—back, triceps), legs, and abdomen, **in that order**.

1. Workout #1

For your first workout, follow the sequence of activities as they are described in the following checklist. After completing the workout, come back to the listing of tasks and check all that you completed.

Workout #1 Checklist

1.____ **Warm Up Properly**
Refer to the "Preparing Your Body to Train" section if you are not sure you remember the warm-up exercises.

2.____ **Perform Exercises in Order Listed on Your Workout Chart**
Start at the top of the workout chart with the chest exercise and work down.

3.____ **Use Proper Exercise and Spotting (With Free Weights) Techniques**
You may want to refer back to the Keys to Success as references.

4.____ **Complete One Set of Each Exercise**
The first workout includes only one set. Your succeeding workouts will include more.

1. Choose One Exercise

After reading about the characteristics and techniques involved in the three different exercises, and the type of equipment required of each, you are ready to put these details into action. Consider the availability of equipment and access to spotters in your situation, then select one of the following exercises to use in your program:

- Free weight bench press
- Bent-arm fly exercise (cam machine)
- Chest press (multi- or single-unit weight machine)

Later (in Step 11), you will copy your exercise choice and those from Steps 5 through 10, onto your workout chart.

Success Goal = List the 1 exercise you want to include in your program to develop the chest (remember to consider equipment and spotting requirements)

Your Choice = *Bench press*

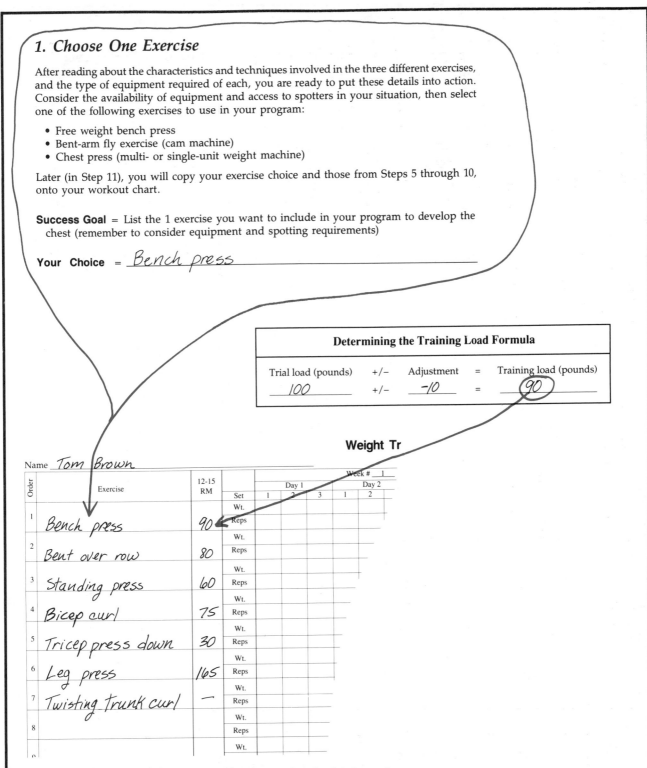

Determining the Training Load Formula

Trial load (pounds)	+/−	Adjustment	=	Training load (pounds)
100	+/−	*−10*	=	*90*

Weight Tr

Name *Tom Brown*   Week # ___1___

Order	Exercise	12-15 RM	Set	Day 1 1	Day 1 2	Day 1 3	Day 2 1	Day 2 2
1	*Bench press*	*90*	Wt. Reps					
2	*Bent over row*	*80*	Wt. Reps					
3	*Standing press*	*60*	Wt. Reps					
4	*Bicep curl*	*75*	Wt. Reps					
5	*Tricep press down*	*30*	Wt. Reps					
6	*Leg press*	*165*	Wt. Reps					
7	*Twisting trunk curl*	*—*	Wt. Reps					
8			Wt. Reps					
			Wt.					

Figure 11.1 Copying exercise selection and training load information.

5.___ Complete 12 to 15 Reps in Each Set

If the training loads are correct, you should be able to perform 12 to 15 reps; if not, you will need to make adjustments as described below.

6.____ **Use Correct Loads**
Check to see that your load selection is correct and that bars are loaded evenly. Learn to recognize the weight of the plates and bars by remembering their sizes and shapes.

7.____ **Be Sure That Locks (on Free Weights) Are Used and Tightened and/or That Selector Keys (Machine) Are Fully Inserted**
This is very important, especially when you are performing overhead exercises (e.g., standing press, tricep extension).

8.____ **Allow 1 Minute of Rest Between Each Set**
After completing a set of an exercise, rest approximately 1 minute before starting the next exercise.

9.____ **After Completing Each Set, Record Load and Reps Completed**
Record this information under "Day 1", first column 1 (refers to first set), on the workout chart. Figure 11.2 illustrates where to write in loads and reps performed.

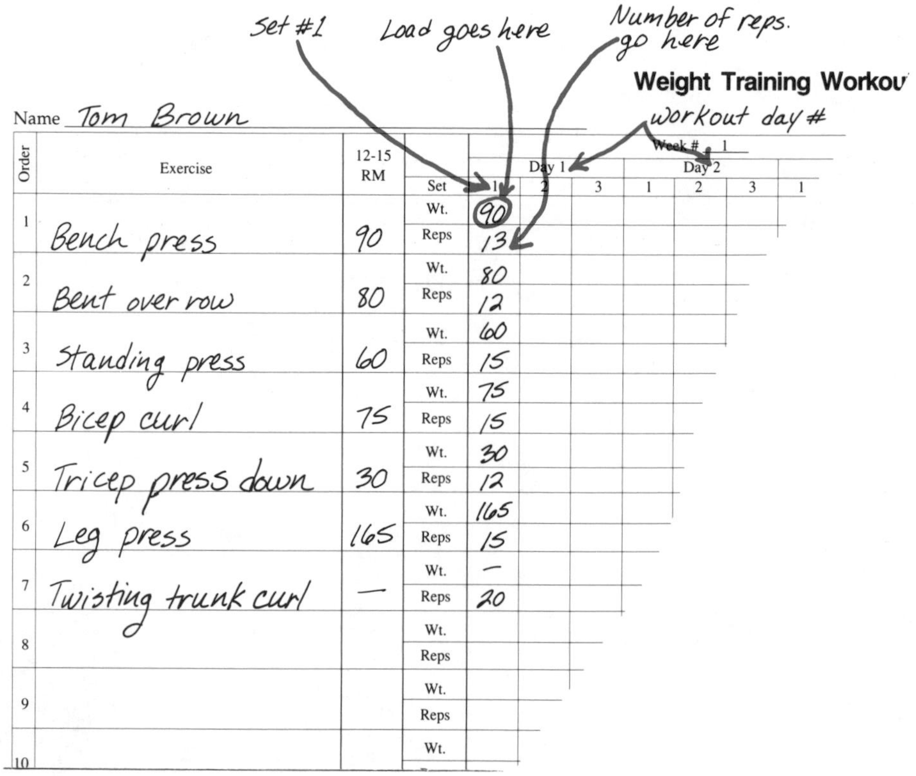

Figure 11.2 Recording loads and reps.

10.____ **Make Appropriate Load Adjustments**
You may want to refer to practice procedure 7 (described in Step 3) for an explanation.

11.____ **Cool Down**
Before leaving the weight room, spend about 5 minutes in some of the stretching activities you used when warming up.

Success Goal = 10 out of 11 tasks are checked off

Your Score =   (#) _____ of tasks checked off

2. *Proper Exercise and Spotting Technique Checkpoints*

In the previous steps (4-10) you learned about the proper execution of exercises and spotting techniques. Go back to Step 4 ("Selecting a Chest Exercise") and have your training partner or a qualified person refer to the Keys to Success and check off each technique you have completed correctly. Do this for the exercises you have selected in Steps 5 through 10, too. If you are free weight training, have a qualified person also observe your spotting technique, and request that she or he check off the techniques you have performed correctly. If you are training by yourself, try using a mirror to observe your technique. If a mirror is not available or appropriate to use with the exercise, visually track the movement patterns and critique them based on what you remember to be correct. Before your next workout, work on the exercise and spotting techniques that are not yet mastered (checked off).

Success Goal = 7 out of 7 exercise and spotting technique (free weight) explanations/illustrations (Keys to Success) presented in Steps 4 through 10 have been reviewed and demonstrated/checked off

Your Score = (check off as performed correctly)
   a. _____ Step 4 (chest exercise)
   b. _____ Step 5 (back exercise)
   c. _____ Step 6 (shoulder exercise)
   d. _____ Step 7 (bicep exercise)
   e. _____ Step 8 (tricep exercise)
   f. _____ Step 9 (leg exercise)
   g. _____ Step 10 (abdomen exercise)

Step 12 Making Needed Workout Changes

Now that the first workout is behind you, have you thought about when you should train again? Do you know when or if loads, reps, and sets should be increased? This step gives you specific instructions on when and how to make needed changes in your workouts. Notice that instructions for workouts 2 through 4 are similar. However, these instructions are different from those for workouts 5 through 15 (Days 2, 3, and 4 and Days 5 through 15, respectively) on the workout chart. Workouts #2 through #4 are less strenuous and provide the stimulation for your body to prepare itself for the more strenuous workouts #5 through #15.

TRAIN THREE TIMES A WEEK

Make a commitment to *train three times a week*, and allow yourself 1 day of rest between workouts (e.g., work out on M-W-F or T-TH-S). If you can train only twice a week, allow no more than 3 days between training sessions (e.g., M-TH, T-SAT, W-SUN). The best improvements will be made when training three times, instead of twice, a week, so make an extra effort to train a 3rd day.

MAKING NEEDED LOAD CHANGES TO KEEP REPS AT 12 TO 15

The challenge is to identify the load that will keep the number of reps at 12 to 15.

As you become more comfortable with the exercise techniques involved and stronger in response to training, you will probably realize that current training loads are no longer heavy enough to limit you to 15 reps. Maintain a high level of enthusiasm and commitment to perform all exercises with excellent technique. A consistent approach will make it easier to identify when your body is adapting, as evidenced by a greater number of reps completed in an exercise.

When you are able to perform 2 or more reps above the intended number (i.e., 17 or more reps) on 2 consecutive training days (the 2-for-2 rule), refer to the Load Adjustment Chart in practice procedure 7 of the exercise being performed, and make appropriate increases to the training load.

Using this **2-for-2** rule makes it easy to remember when to increase training loads. If for some reason the load is too heavy to perform 12 reps in two consecutive training sessions, refer to the Load Adjustment Chart and make appropriate reductions to the load.

ADD SETS

Performing only 1 set the 1st day enables you to concentrate on completing the workout correctly and should not be too physically taxing. However, after the first day you should add an additional set of each exercise, and another set (= 3 sets) after the fourth workout. If you are training with a partner, arrange your training so that you alternate turns performing an exercise until you have completed the desired number of sets.

CONSIDER SHORTENING YOUR REST PERIODS

As your muscular endurance improves in response to training, your ability to recover from the fatigue of each set will also improve. If you feel that your ability to recover between sets is good, consider shortening the rest period from 1 minute to 45 or 30 seconds. Rest periods shorter than 30 seconds do not provide sufficient time to recover. The *advantage* of shortening the rest period is that you reduce the amount of time needed to complete a training session. The *disadvantage* is that if you do not give yourself adequate rest, the number of reps completed will be fewer. This means you are not accomplishing what you set out to do (i.e., performing more reps in each exercise). Pay attention to the length of the rest periods, and try to be consistent between sets and workouts.

Drills for Making Needed Workout Changes

1. Workout #2

With the previous information in mind, complete the second workout. Record the loads and reps on your Workout Chart as is illustrated in Figure 12.1. After doing so, check off all tasks completed.

Weight Training Workout Chart

Name *Tom Brown*   Year *1991*

Order	Exercise	12-15 RM	Set	Week # 1 Day 1 1	2	3	Day 2 1	2	3	Day 3 1	2	3	Week # 2 Day 1 1	2	3	Day 2 1	2	3
1	Bench press	90	Wt.	90			90	90		90	90		90	90		90	90	90
			Reps	13			12	12		14	12		15	14		16	15	12
2	Bent over row	80	Wt.	80			80	80		80	80		80	80		80	80	80
			Reps	12			13	12		14	13		14	14		15	14	12
3	Standing press	60	Wt.	60			60	60		60	60		60	60		65	65	65
			Reps	15			15	13		16	15		17	17		15	12	12
4	Bicep curl	75	Wt.	75			75	75		75	75		75	75		75	75	75
			Reps	15			14	14		15	14		16	15		17	16	15
5	Tricep press down	30	Wt.	30			30	30		30	30		30	30		30	30	30
			Reps	12			12	11		14	12		15	15		17	15	13
6	Leg press	165	Wt.	165			165	165		170	170		170	170		170	170	170
			Reps	15			17	17		14	13		16	15		18	16	15
7	Twisting trunk curl	—	Wt.	—														
			Reps	20			25	20		25	23		30	25		30	30	25
8			Wt.															
			Reps															
9			Wt.															
			Reps															
10			Wt.															
			Reps															
11			Wt.															
			Reps															
12			Wt.															
			Reps															
	Body weight			140			141			140			142			141		
	Date			9/23			9/25			9/27			9/30			10/2		
	Comments			one set first workout, 2 sets in workouts 2, 3, + 4									3 sets starting in workout 5					

(handwritten notes:) 2 sets in workouts #2,3,4   start 3 sets in workout #5

Figure 12.1 Sample record of workouts #2 through #5.

Success Goal = 6 out of 6 checklist tasks completed after the second workout

Workout #2 Checklist

1. ____ 3 training days are scheduled into every week.
2. ____ 2 sets of each exercise are performed.
3. ____ 12 to 15 reps in each set are performed.
4. ____ 30- to 60-second rest periods are used.
5. ____ Needed load changes are made using Load Adjustment Chart.
6. ____ Loads and reps are recorded in the first column under ''Day 2'' as shown in Figure 12.1.

Your Score =   (#) ____ of checklist tasks completed (workout #2)

2. Workouts #3 and #4

Continue performing 2 sets of each exercise in workouts #3 and #4. Keep in mind two very important thoughts while training. First, all reps should be performed with excellent technique—don't sacrifice technique for additional reps. The quality (technique used) of the reps is more important than the number performed. Give each set your best effort, and apply the 2-for-2 rule to keep the number of reps between 12 and 15 in each set.

You may find helpful the guidelines presented in Table 12.1 for making needed changes in workouts #2 through #4 and #5 through #15.

Table 12.1 Making Workout Changes Summary

Variable	Workouts #2-#4	Workouts #5-#15
Loads	Continue to make changes in the loads so that they are heavy/light enough to produce 12 to 15 reps	
Reps	12 to 15	12 to 15
Sets	2 sets	3 sets
Rest period	1 minute	30 seconds to 1 minute

Success Goals = 5 out of 5 checklist tasks completed after both the third and the fourth workouts

Workouts #3 and #4 Checklist

1. ____ 2 sets of each exercise are performed.
2. ____ 12 to 15 reps in each set are performed.
3. ____ Loads and reps are recorded correctly on your Workout Chart (see Figure 12.1).
4. ____ 30- to 60-second rest periods are used.
5. ____ Needed load changes are made using the Load Adjustment Chart.

Your Scores =

   a. (#) ____ of checklist tasks completed (workout #3)

   b. (#) ____ of checklist tasks completed (workout #4)

3. *Workout #5*

In workout #5, perform 3 (instead of 2) sets of each exercise. The challenge again is to keep the loads heavy or light enough that you are performing 12 to 15 reps—with good technique! Record all 3 sets as illustrated in Figure 12.1. After doing so, check off all tasks completed.

Success Goal = 5 out of 5 checklist tasks are completed after the fifth workout

Workout #5 Checklist

1. ____ 3 sets of each exercise are performed.
2. ____ 12 to 15 reps in each set are performed.
3. ____ Loads and reps are recorded correctly in the column on your Workout Chart (see Figure 12.1).
4. ____ 30- to 60-second rest periods are used.
5. ____ Needed load changes are made using Load Adjustment Chart.

Your Score =   (#) ____ of checklist tasks completed (workout #5)

4. *Workouts #6 Through #15*

Continue performing 3 sets of each exercise in workouts #6 through #15. Refer to Table 12.1 for a summary of how to make needed changes during workouts.

Looking Ahead

When workout #15 has been completed (in 5 weeks in a 3-days-a-week program), you should begin a new training approach. In preparation for this, you should now begin to read and complete the tasks described in Steps 13, 14, 15, and 16.

Success Goals = 6 out of 6 checklist tasks are completed after the 6th through the 15th workouts

Workouts #6 Through #15 Checklist

1. ____ 3 training days are scheduled into every week.
2. ____ 12 to 15 reps in each set are performed.
3. ____ 3 sets of each exercise are performed.
4. ____ Loads and reps are recorded correctly on your Workout Chart (see Figure 12.1).

5. ____ 30- to 60-second rest periods are used.

6. ____ Needed load changes are made using the Load Adjustment Chart.

Your Scores =

   a. (#) ____ checklist tasks completed (workout #6)

   b. (#) ____ checklist tasks completed (workout #7)

   c. (#) ____ checklist tasks completed (workout #8)

   d. (#) ____ checklist tasks completed (workout #9)

   e. (#) ____ checklist tasks completed (workout #10)

   f. (#) ____ checklist tasks completed (workout #11)

   g. (#) ____ checklist tasks completed (workout #12)

   h. (#) ____ checklist tasks completed (workout #13)

   i. (#) ____ checklist tasks completed (workout #14)

   j. (#) ____ checklist tasks completed (workout #15)

Step 13   # How to Select and Arrange Exercises

Up until now you have been following a program designed by others. Steps 13 through 15 present information that will enable you to design your own program in Step 16. The factors you need to know and understand before you begin designing a program are referred to as *program design variables*. Each of these is presented in the order in which they will be discussed in the next three steps.

- *Step 13*   Selecting Exercises
  Arranging Exercises in the Workout
- *Step 14*   Determining the Loads to Use
  Determining How Many Reps to Perform
  Determining How Many Sets of an Exercise to Complete
  Determining the Length of Rest Between Sets
- *Step 15*   Determining the Frequency of Training
  Determining How to Vary the Program

WHY IS IT IMPORTANT TO KNOW HOW TO SELECT EXERCISES?

The exercises you select will determine which of your muscles become stronger, more enduring, and thicker. Your selection will also dictate whether you will acquire a symmetrical (balanced development) musculature—one in which muscle groups are proportional and strength on both sides of a joint is somewhat equal. The former is important for fitness and appearance, and the latter is important in reducing muscle and joint injuries.

HOW TO SELECT EXERCISES

An advanced program may include as many as 20 exercises. However, a beginning or basic program (which is what you are following)

needs only to include one exercise for each of the large muscle areas. The muscle areas of particular importance here are the chest, arms (biceps and triceps), shoulders, back (latissimus dorsi, trapezius, rhomboids), thighs (quadriceps and hamstrings), and abdomen.

In Steps 4 through 10 you selected one exercise for each of these muscle areas. You will want to add exercises for the forearm, lower back, and calves because doing so will give you a well-rounded program that includes the major, and most of the "minor," muscle groups. Athletes in wrestling and football should also add one or more exercises for the neck. You may also want to emphasize one or two other muscle areas, such as the chest and back, if you feel that these areas are especially weak or that you would like more muscle tone or size in them. Appendix A, "Alternate Exercises," includes exercises that you can add to your present program. You might also consider exchanging one exercise for another that you believe is more enjoyable or more effective. In Appendix A, exercises are categorized by the muscle area they work, in an effort to assist you in your selection process. You will need to read about all of these exercises to complete this step. Look at Appendix B, "Muscles of the Body," and decide which muscles you want to begin training or to emphasize. Then refer to Appendix A and consider which exercise(s) may be suitable. Before making a final decision on which exercises to select, you should understand the concepts and principles that follow.

Apply the Specificity Concept

Your task is to determine the muscle groups (from Appendix B) you really want to develop, then determine which exercises will recruit those muscles. This involves application of a very important concept, the *specificity* concept.

This concept refers to training in a specific manner to produce outcomes that are specific (to that method of training). For example, developing the chest requires exercises that recruit chest muscles, and developing the thigh requires exercises that recruit thigh muscles.

Even the specific angle at which a muscle is called into action determines whether and to what extent a muscle or muscles will be stimulated. For example, Figure 13.1 illustrates how a change in body position changes the specific angle at which the barbell is lowered and pushed upward from chest. The angle at which the bar is moved dictates whether the top, middle, or lower portion of the chest muscles become more or less involved in the exercise.

The type and width of the grip are equally important, because they also change the angle and thus the specific effect on the muscles. That's why it is so important to perform exercises exactly as they are described in this text.

Consider the Need for Balance

Select exercises that help to balance muscle size and strength of opposing muscle groups. This will help you develop a proportional physique and good posture.

Pair up opposing muscle group exercises like this:

a Incline position
Upper chest and shoulders become more involved

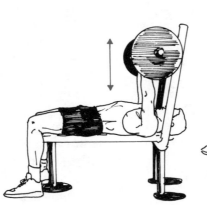

b Horizontal position
Middle section of chest becomes more involved

c Decline position
Lower section of chest becomes more involved

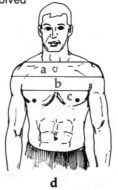

d

Figure 13.1 Changes in body position (a, b, and c) affect the angle at which the barbell is lowered and raised from the chest, thus influencing muscle involvement (d).

Chest with an upper back

Front of upper arm with back of upper arm

Front (palm side) of forearm with back (knuckle side) of forearm

Abdominal with lower back

*Front of thigh with back of thigh

*Front of ankle with back of ankle

Consider Equipment Needs

Consider what equipment is needed. Determine the equipment needs for each exercise before making a final decision. You may not have the equipment needed.

Consider the Need for a Spotter

Determine whether a spotter is needed in the exercises you are considering. If one is needed, and there is not a qualified spotter available, choose a different exercise to work the same muscle group.

Consider the Time Required

Be aware that the more exercises you decide to include in your program, the longer the workout will take. It is a common mistake to include too many! Figure approximately 1-1/2 minutes per exercise, and do not forget to consider the number of sets in determining the total workout time required. This is discussed in greater detail in Step 14.

HOW TO ARRANGE EXERCISES

There are almost as many ways to arrange exercises in a workout as there are exercises from which to select. The following list presents three common arrangements that you might use when designing your own program (Step 16).

- Large muscle group exercises first
- Alternate push with pull exercises
- Alternate upper body with lower body exercises

WHY IS THE ARRANGEMENT OF EXERCISES IMPORTANT?

The order of exercises affects the intensity of training. For instance, alternating upper and lower body exercises does not produce as high an intensity level as performing all lower body exercises first. Performing exercises that involve a lot of joints and muscles are more intense than those that involve only one joint and less muscle.

Exercise Large Muscle Groups First (L/S)

Exercising the large (L) muscle groups before smaller (S) groups is an approach that is accepted by many. For example, rather than exercising the calf (a smaller muscle group) followed by exercising the thigh (a larger muscle group), thigh exercises would be performed first. Note that although the muscle area of the upper arms is considered a large muscle group, the front and back are viewed individually and are referred to as small muscle groups. An example of the method of arranging exercises with the large muscle group first is shown in Table 13.1.

Table 13.1   Exercise Arrangement: Large Muscle Groups First

Exercise	Type (L/S)	Muscle group
Lunge	Large	Thigh and hip
Heel raises	Small	Calf
Bench press	Large	Chest
Tricep extension	Small	Arm (posterior)
Lat pull-down	Large	Upper back
Bicep curl	Small	Arm (anterior)

Alternate Push With Pull Exercises (PS/PL)

You may also arrange exercises so that those that result in extension of joints are alternated with those that result in flexion of joints.

---

*You may also want to pair up muscles that work the inside and outside of the ankle and thigh.

Extension exercises require that you "push," whereas flexion exercises require you to "pull"—thus the name of this arrangement— push (PS) with pull (PL). An example would be the tricep extension (push), followed by the bicep curl (pull). This is a good arrangement to use because the same muscle is not worked back to back; that is, the same muscle group is not worked two or more times in succession. This arrangement should give your muscles sufficient time to recover. An example of this method of arranging exercises is shown in Table 13.2

Table 13.2 Exercise Arrangement: Alternate Push With Pull

Exercise	Type (PS/PL)	Muscle group
Bench press	Push	Chest
Lat pull-down	Pull	Back
Seated press	Push	Shoulder
Bicep curl	Pull	Arm (anterior)
Tricep extension	Push	Arm (posterior)
Leg curl	Pull	Thigh (posterior)
Knee extension	Push	Thigh (anterior)

Alternate Upper Body With Lower Body Exercises (UB/LB)

Another arrangement you might use involves alternating upper body (shoulders to abdomen) with lower body (hips to ankles) exercises. For example, a bicep curl (upper body) exercise is followed by a leg press (lower body) exercise. Two things make this arrangement more exhausting than the two already dis-

Table 13.3 Exercise Arrangement: Alternate Upper Body With Lower Body

Exercise	Type (UB/LB)	Muscle group
Bench press	Upper body	Chest
Lunge	Lower body	Thigh and hip
Bicep curl	Upper body	Arm (anterior)
Knee extension	Lower body	Thigh (anterior)
Standing press	Upper body	Shoulder
Leg curl	Lower body	Thigh (posterior)

cussed: (1) leg exercises are more physically demanding than other exercises, and (2) this arrangement includes more of them. A typical upper body (UB)/lower body (LB) workout might include one or two leg exercises—in this arrangement you will have at least double that number. An example of this method of arranging exercises is shown in Table 13.3.

OTHER ARRANGEMENT CONSIDERATIONS

Sets Performed in Succession Versus Alternating Sets

When more than one set of an exercise is going to be performed, you need to decide whether to perform all sets of an exercise one after another (in succession) or whether to perform them alternated with other exercises. Arrangements of exercises performed for 3 sets in succession and alternated are shown below:

In succession = **shoulder press, shoulder press, shoulder press**

Alternated = **shoulder press**, bicep curl, **shoulder press**, lunge, **shoulder press**, trunk curl

Alternated = **shoulder press**, bicep curl, lunge, sit-ups (repeated three times)

In each of these arrangements, 3 sets of shoulder presses are performed, each with an intervening rest period. The "in succession" arrangement is the approach preferred by most.

Tricep Exercises *After* Upper Body Pressing Exercises

When arranging exercises in your program, be sure that tricep extensions, tricep pushdowns, and other elbow extension exercises are *not* performed before pushing exercises such as the bench/chest press or standing press. These pushing exercises rely on elbow extension strength from the tricep muscles to assist. When tricep exercises precede pushing exercises, they fatigue the triceps, reducing the number of reps and the effect on the muscles the exercise was to develop.

Detecting Selection and Arrangement of Exercises Errors

The errors that you are likely to make when selecting and arranging exercises in your workout are usually associated with balancing the number of exercises for the different body parts so that muscular development is symmetrical. For instance, you will tend to include too many exercises for the chest and arms and not enough for the lower body. This error and others that are commonly made, along with suggestions for corrections, are presented next.

ERROR ⊘

CORRECTION

ERROR	CORRECTION
1. Your musculature is not proportional.	1. There may be too many exercises (and/or sets) for certain muscle groups, and none for the others. Reduce the number of exercises (and/or sets) for the overly developed muscle groups, and/or increase the number of exercises for under developed muscle areas.
2. Large variation occurs in reps completed from workout to workout.	2. Avoid performing exercises out of sequence—perform them in the same order each workout. Keep the length of your rest periods constant.
3. The number of reps declines in upper body exercises.	3. Do not perform tricep exercises immediately before upper body pushing exercises.
4. Your workouts take too long.	4. Reduce the number of exercises and/or sets. Unless your goal is muscular endurance, keep rest periods the same.

Drills for Selecting and Arranging Exercises

1. Specificity Concept Applied to Exercise Selection Drill

This drill requires reviewing the exercises in Steps 4 through 10 and in Appendix A. Demonstrate your understanding of the specificity concept by identifying and circling which of the four muscle areas listed in the left column of the following chart are *not* developed by the exercise listed on the right.

Specificity Concept Applied to Exercise Selection Quiz

Exercise	Muscle area developed
1. Back extension	Lower back
2. Supine tricep extension	Back of upper arm
3. Standing press	Back
4. Heel raises	Calf
5. Lunge	Thigh and hips
6. Bent over row	Upper back
7. Trunk curl	Abdomen
8. Shoulder shrug	Shoulders
9. Upright row	Chest
10. Concentration curl	Front of upper arm
11. Wrist flexion	Palm side of forearm
12. Standing press	Shoulders
13. Lat pull-down	Lower back
14. Bent-leg deadlift	Lower back
15. Dumbbell fly	Shoulders
16. Back squat	Thigh and hips

Success Goal = 4 out of 4 inappropriate muscle areas are identified

Your Score = (#) ____ inappropriate muscle areas correctly identified

Answers to Specificity Concept Applied to Exercise Selection Quiz

The four inappropriate muscle areas follow:

1. **#3 (should be shoulders)**
2. **#9 (should be shoulders)**
3. **#13 (should be upper back)**
4. **#15 (should be chest)**

2. Select Balanced Exercises Drill

Identify which two of the paired exercises in the following quiz are *not* balanced. Mark an X to the left of them.

Paired Exercises Quiz

a. ____ Back extensions—bent-leg deadlift

b. ____ Hamstring curl—knee extension

c. ____ Concentration curl—tricep extension

d. ____ Bent-arm fly—bent-knee sit-ups

Success Goal = 2 out of 2 of the unbalanced pairs of exercises are marked

Your Score = (#) _____ unbalanced pairs marked

Answers to Paired Exercises Quiz

The two incorrect pairs of exercises follow:

1. #a (should be back extensions matched with bent-knee sit-up, trunk curl, or twisting trunk curl exercises)
2. #d (should be dumbbell flys matched with bent over row, lat pull-down, or rowing exercises)

3. Arranging Exercises Drill

Before you are able to really understand how to arrange exercises in a workout, you need to be able to recognize the characteristics displayed by them. Consider the size of the muscles, the push-pull movement patterns, and the body parts involved in each of the following exercises. Then fill in the missing quiz information using the letters L (large muscle exercise) or S (small muscle exercise), PS (pushing exercises) or PL (pulling exercises), and UB (upper body exercise) or LB (lower body exercise).

Recognizing Exercise Characteristics Quiz

Exercise	Type of exercise		
	L/S	PS/PL	UB/LB
1. Dumbbell fly	____	____	____
2. Wrist flexion	____	____	____
3. Supine tricep press	____	____	____
4. Back squat	____	____	____
5. Trunk curl	____	____	____
6. Bicep curl	____	____	____
7. Concentration curl	____	____	____
8. Heel raise	____	____	____
9. Upright row	____	____	____
10. Knee extension	____	____	____

Success Goals =

a. 9 out of 10 answers under the L/S column are correct

b. 9 out of 10 answers under the PS/PL column are correct

c. 9 out of 10 answers under the UB/LB column are correct

Your Scores =

a. (#) _____ of correct answers under L/S column

b. (#) _____ of correct answers under PS/PL column

c. (#) _____ of correct answers under UB/LB column

Answers to Recognizing Exercise Characteristics Quiz

The correct exercise characteristics follow:

Exercise	Type of exercise		
	L/S	PS/PL	UB/LB
1. Dumbbell fly	L	PL	UB
2. Wrist flexion	S	PL	UB
3. Supine tricep press	S	PS	UB
4. Back squat	L	PS	LB
5. Trunk curl	L	PL	UB
6. Bicep curl	S	PL	UB
7. Concentration curl	S	PL	UB
8. Heel raise	S	PS	LB
9. Upright row	L	PL	UB
10. Knee extension	L	PS	LB

Summary

When selecting exercises, keep in mind the specificity concept and the equipment and spotter requirements of each exercise. Also, include at least one exercise for each large muscle area, and remember the need to select balanced pairs of exercises. Select enough exercises to acquire a symmetrical physique, but not so many that workouts take too long. Last, remember that how you arrange exercises and the order in which you actually perform them has a direct impact on your success.

Step 14 How to Manipulate Training Loads, Reps, Sets, and Rest Periods

Now that you have a better understanding of exercise selection and arrangement, the next step leading us to Step 16, where you design your own program, is to gain an understanding of the loads, reps, sets, and rest periods to use. There are many differing opinions on how to manipulate these program design variables, but general consensus is that decisions should be based on the specificity concept (introduced in Step 13), and what is referred to as the *overload principle*. The overload principle asserts that each workout should place a demand on the muscle or muscles that is greater than in the previous workout. Training that incorporates this principle challenges the body to meet and adapt to greater than normal physiological stress. As it does, a new threshold is established that requires an even greater stress to produce an overload. Introducing overloads in a systematic manner like this is referred to as *progressive overload*.

This step provides an explanation of these variables and is followed by guidelines on how to apply the specificity concept and the overload principle when designing your own programs.

AMOUNT OF LOAD TO USE

Determining the amount of the load to use is one of the most confusing, yet probably *the* most important, aspect of designing a program. It is important because the load selected determines the number of repetitions you will be able to perform and the amount of rest you need between sets and exercises. It also influences your decisions concerning the number of sets and the frequency at which you should train.

METHODS FOR DETERMINING LOADS

Described next are two approaches that can be taken when deciding on the amount of load to use in training.

12-15RM Method

In Steps 4 through 10 your body weight was used to determine initial training loads. The calculations were designed to produce light loads so that you could concentrate on developing correct technique and avoid undue stress on bones and joint structures. Your goal was to identify a load that resulted in 12 to 15 reps. This method of determining a load that will produce muscular failure at 12 to 15 reps is referred to as a 12-15RM method (for assigning loads). The letter R is an abbreviation for *repetition* and the M is for *maximum*, meaning the maximum amount of load that you succeeded with for 12 to 15 reps.

1RM Method

Another method that could have been used is the 1RM method—a single (*1*) repetition (*R*) maximum (*M*) effort. Or said another way, this is the maximum amount of load that you can succeed with for 1 repetition in an exercise. Although this is not a perfect method to use, it is more accurate than using body weight, especially when you have developed good exercise techniques and are conditioned to safely handle heavier loads. This is *not* an appropriate method for a beginner, however, because it requires skills and a level of conditioning developed only through training. Furthermore, this method is not appropriate for all exercises.

This method of determining loads should be used only with exercises that involve more than one joint and recruit large muscle groups that can withstand heavy training loads. Exercises with these characteristics are sometimes referred to as *core exercises*. The term *core* also indicates that these exercises are focal points of your training (that is, you are building the program around them). Examples of core exercises in your workout include those presented for the chest, shoulders, and legs (Steps 4, 6, and 9). The exception here concerns the leg exercises. Because of the stress placed on the knees in the lunge and leg press (Step 9) exercises, these are not good ones in which to perform a 1RM. The back squat (Appendix A), on the other hand, with the use of proper technique, is an excellent one to use.

Soon you will be instructed to determine the 1RM for several core exercises. But first, realize that you should keep the number of sets to 3 and the number of reps at 12 to 15 in other exercises. Gradually increase the number of reps to 15 to 30 reps per set in the abdominal exercises performed without weights. The rationale for the greater number of reps suggested here for the abdominal exercises is that you are using a light load (your upper body weight), which should make it easier to perform a greater number.

Caution: Before undertaking an effort to predict a 1RM, be sure you have perfected your exercise technique and have 5 weeks of training "under your belt."

Procedures for Predicting the 1RM

To give you experience at using the 1RM method, you are given eight procedures for determining the 1RM for the chest and shoulder exercises you selected in Steps 4 and 6. Begin with the chest exercise. Fill in the requested information as you read through procedures 1 through 8 here:

1. The exercise you have selected is _____ .

2. Warm up by performing one set of 10 reps with your current 12-15RM load. Your current 12-15RM load is _____ pounds.

3. Add 10 pounds, or a weight-stack plate that is closest to equaling 10 pounds, and perform 3 reps. Your 12-15-pound load + 10 pounds = _____ . Perform 3 reps.

4. Add 10 more pounds, or the next heaviest weight-stack plate, and, after resting 2-5 minutes, perform *as many reps as possible*. Give this your best effort! The load in procedure 3 = _____ + 10 pounds = _____ . Perform as many reps as possible with this load.

5. Locate Table 14.1a, and fill in the name of the exercise involved, the load used, and the reps made.

6. Refer to Table 14.2, "Prediction of 1RM." Obtain and circle the "rep factor" associated with the number of repetitions you completed with that load in the chest exercise.

   Figure 14.1 (p. 144) illustrates how Tables 14.1a (chest) and 14.1b (shoulders) can be used with Table 14.2 to predict a 1RM in the next three procedures. In the example, 6 reps are performed with the 120 pounds in the bench press exercise. The rep factor to the right of 6 reps is 1.20, which when multiplied by 120 equals 144 pounds, or 145 pounds (rounded off to the nearest 5 pounds or weight-stack plate).

7. Record the circled rep factor for your chest exercise in Table 14.1a.

8. Multiply the rep factor by the load in this table to obtain the predicted 1RM for this exercise.

Repeat these same procedures to acquire the 1RM for your shoulder exercise (see Table 14.1b).

USING THE 1RM TO DETERMINE TRAINING LOADS

To use the 1RM to determine a training load, multiply the 1RM by a percentage. For example, if your 1RM in the standing press is 100 pounds, and you decide to use a 75 per-

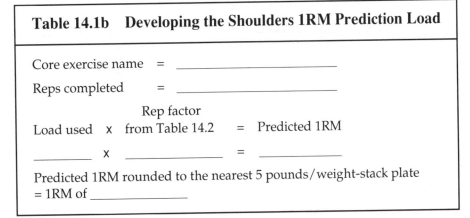

Table 14.1a   Developing the Chest 1RM Prediction Load

Core exercise name   = _____

Reps completed   = _____

Load used   x   Rep factor from Table 14.2   =   Predicted 1RM

_____   x   _____   =   _____

Predicted 1RM rounded to the nearest 5 pounds/weight-stack plate

= 1RM of _____

Table 14.1b   Developing the Shoulders 1RM Prediction Load

Core exercise name   = _____

Reps completed   = _____

Load used   x   Rep factor from Table 14.2   =   Predicted 1RM

_____   x   _____   =   _____

Predicted 1RM rounded to the nearest 5 pounds/weight-stack plate
= 1RM of _____

Table 14.2   Prediction of 1RM

Reps completed	Rep factor
1	1.00
2	1.07
3	1.10
4	1.13
5	1.16
6	1.20
7	1.23
8	1.27
9	1.32
10	1.36

Note. From *Beginning Weight Training: The Safe and Effective Way* (p. 201) by V.P. Lombardi, 1989, Dubuque, IA: Brown. Copyright 1989 by William C. Brown. Adapted by permission.

cent load, the training load would equal 1RM × 0.75 or 100 × 0.75 = 75 pounds. This will be discussed further in this step.

1RM Load Questions

Answer the following questions by checking off (✔) the correct answer:

1. The load selected influences the [____ number, ____ kind of reps] that are possible.
2. The load you select should also influence the [____ number of, ____ length of] the rest period between sets.
3. 1RM refers to [____ 1-repetition maximum, ____ one real mean dude].

Answers to Using the 1RM Method to Determine Training Loads Questions

1. **number**
2. **length of**
3. **1-repetition maximum**

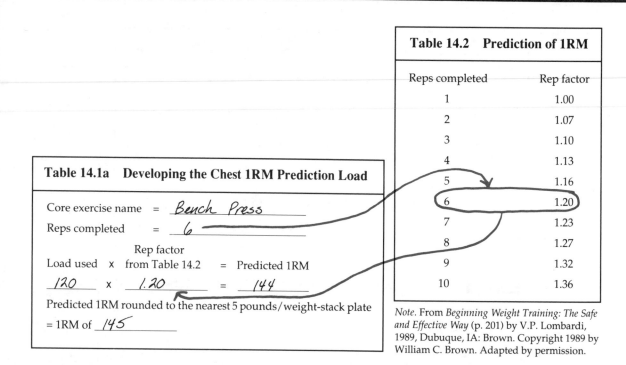

Figure 14.1 Predicting a 1RM.

WHEN AND HOW MUCH TO INCREASE LOADS

It is important that you assume heavier loads as soon as you are able to complete the required number of reps. However, changes should not be made too soon. Wait until you can complete 2 or more reps above the intended number in two consecutive workouts (the 2-for-2 rule, Step 12). When you have met the 2-for-2 rule, instead of referring to the Load Adjustment Charts in Steps 3 through 10, simply increase loads by 5 pounds. The Load Adjustment Charts were used initially to assist primarily with large fluctuations in the number of reps performed. However, you will now find that fluctuations are much smaller, and that using the 2-for-2 criterion with a 5-pound increase works well. There are two exceptions. In exercises involving large muscle (e.g., legs, shoulders, chest), you may need to make heavier increases. However, it is always better to underestimate than to overestimate the increase needed. The other exception concerns the use of smaller increments (2-1/2 pound) in arm (bicep, tricep, forearm) and neck exercises (provided 1-1/4 pound plates are available). It is appropriate to use smaller load increments in exercises that involve smaller muscles. As training progresses, you may choose to vary the loads used in a different manner (and/or reps and sets performed).

When and How Much to Increase Loads Questions

Answer the following questions by checking off (✔) the correct answer:

1. The 2-for-2 rule concerns [___ resting 2 minutes after every two exercises, ___ completing 2 or more reps in two consecutive workouts before increasing the training load].
2. Load increases for leg press exercises are more likely to be [___ heavier, ___ lighter] than those for arm exercises.

Answers to When and How Much to Increase Loads Questions

1. completing 2 or more reps for two consecutive workouts before increasing the training load
2. heavier

NUMBER OF REPS

The number of reps you will be able to perform is directly related to the load you select.

As the loads become heavier, the number of reps possible becomes fewer, and as the loads become lighter, the number of reps possible becomes greater. Assuming that a good effort is given in each set of exercises, the factor that dictates the number of reps is the load selected.

Number of Reps Questions

Answer the following questions by checking off (✔) the correct answer:

1. Heavier loads are associated with a [____ greater, ____ fewer] number of reps.
2. The factor that dictates the number of reps completed is the [____ load, ____ exercise] selected.

Answers to Number of Reps Questions

1. fewer
2. load

NUMBER OF SETS

Although some controversy exists as to whether multiple (2 or more) sets are better than single sets for developing strength, hypertrophy, and/or muscular endurance, research is more supportive of multiple sets. It seems reasonable to expect that the multiple-set approach to training would provide a better stimulus for development. The rationale is that a single set of an exercise does not recruit all the fibers in a muscle. A 2nd set will recruit additional fibers because some that were involved in the 1st set will not be sufficiently recovered and, therefore, will rely on "fresh" fibers (not previously stimulated) for assistance. This is especially evident if an additional load is added to the 2nd or 3rd set.

When 3 or more sets are performed, the likelihood of recruiting additional fibers becomes even greater. Further support for multiple sets comes from observations of the programs followed by successful competitive weight lifters, power lifters, and bodybuilders. It is well known that these competitors rely on multiple sets for achieving high degrees of development. As you will see later, your goals for training should influence the number of sets you perform.

There is one more thing to consider. How much *time* do you have for training? For instance, if you choose to rest for 1 minute between exercises in your program, you should figure a minimum of 1-1/2 minutes per exercise (30 seconds to perform the exercise, 60 seconds rest). Thus, your program of 7 exercises, in which you perform 1 set of each, should take 10-1/2 minutes. If you increase the number of sets to 2, and then to 3, your workout time will increase to 21 and 31-1/2 minutes, respectively. This assumes a 60-second rest period after each set. The actual time for rest between sets, as you will read soon, may vary between 30 seconds and 5 minutes.

Number of Sets Questions

Answer the following questions by checking off (✔) the correct answer:

1. The fewest number of sets being recommended is [____ 1, ____ 2].
2. The basis for multiple-set training is that the additional sets are thought to [____ recruit, ____ relax] a greater number of muscle fibers.

Answers to Number of Sets Questions

1. 2
2. recruit

LENGTH OF THE REST PERIOD

The impact of the rest period between sets on the intensity of training is not usually recognized, but should be. Longer rest periods provide time for the "energizers" (phosphagens) of muscle contraction to rebuild, enabling muscles to exert greater force. If the amount of work is the same and the rest periods are shorter, the intensity of training increases. As you will see later, the length of time between exercises or sets has a direct impact on the outcomes of training. A word of caution, however: Moving too rapidly from one exercise or set to another often reduces the number of reps you are able to perform and may cause you to become dizzy and nauseated.

Length of the Rest Period Questions

Answer the following questions by checking off (✔) the correct answer:

1. Longer rest periods enable you to exert [____ greater, ____ lesser] force.
2. The length of the rest period has [____ an effect, ____ no effect] on the outcome of training.

Answers to Length of the Rest Periods Questions

1. greater
2. an effect

APPLY THE SPECIFICITY CONCEPT

The discussion of the specificity concept in Step 13 addressed only the issue of exercise selection, but this concept is broader in scope as it relates to program design. Table 14.3 shows how loads, reps, sets, and rest periods are manipulated using the specificity concept in designing three different programs: muscular endurance, hypertrophy, and strength. This table illustrates a continuum where the variable for the percentage of 1RM, number of reps and sets, and length of the rest period are presented. It reveals that *muscular endurance* programs (as compared to other programs) should include lighter loads (<70 percent of 1RM), permitting 12 to 20 reps, fewer sets (2 or 3), and shorter rest periods (20 to 30 seconds). In contrast, programs designed to develop *strength* should include heavier loads (80 to 100 percent of 1RM) with fewer reps (1 to 8), more sets (3 to 5 or more), and longer rest periods between sets (2 to 5 minutes). Programs designed to develop *hypertrophy* (muscle size increases) should include reps, sets, and resting time variables that fall within the two extremes of muscle endurance and strength.

An example of how these guidelines may be used in designing programs specifically for developing muscular endurance, strength, and hypertrophy outcomes are discussed and illustrated in the following pages. They are basic introductory programs that you will probably want to refer to when completing Step 16.

Muscular Endurance Program

The program you are presently following is designed to develop muscular endurance. In Table 14.3 you will notice some similarities between your program and the program for muscular endurance. The loads you are using now may permit you to perform 15, but not quite the suggested 20, reps. Also, your rest periods are close to the suggested 20 to 30 seconds if you have made an effort to shorten your rest period, and the number of sets are the same. If you choose in Step 16 to continue with your muscular endurance program, do not increase the load until you are able to perform 22 reps in two consecutive workouts, and reduce the rest periods to no less than 30 seconds. Rest periods shorter than 30 seconds are grueling. Except for specific situations, such as training for competitive endurance events, rest periods less than 30 seconds are not recommended.

Table 14.3 Specificity Concept Applied to Program Design Variables

Relative loading	Outcome of training	% 1RM	Rep range	# of sets	Rest between sets
Light	Muscular endurance	<70	12-20	2-3	20-30 seconds
Moderate	Hypertrophy	70-80	8-12	3-6	30-90 seconds
Heavy	Strength	80-100	1-8	3-5+	2-5 minutes

Muscular Endurance Program Questions

Answer the following questions:

1. The guidelines to use when designing your program for muscular endurance are as follows:
   a. Relative loading = _____
   b. Percentage of 1RM load = _____
   c. Repetition range = _____
   d. Number of sets = _____
2. Unless there is a specific reason, the appropriate amount of rest between sets and exercises in a muscular endurance program is [____ 30 seconds, ____ 20 seconds].

Answers to Muscular Endurance Program Questions

1. a. light b. <70 percent c. 12 to 20 d. 2 or 3
2. 30 seconds

Hypertrophy Programs

If you decide in Step 16 to emphasize hypertrophy, review the guidelines in Table 14.3, and consider the example in Table 14.4 where 1RM = 100 pounds when modifying your program.

The keys of a successful hypertrophy program appear to be associated with the use of (a) moderate loads—70 to 80% 1RM, (b) a medium number of reps per set, (c) a good number of sets (3-6), and (d) moderate rest periods between exercises and sets. You will observe that successful bodybuilders usually do not rest long between sets and that they perform a lot of sets. Thus, they combine the multiple-set program (same load in each set of an exercise) described earlier in this step, with the rest period and load guidelines presented in Table 14.3, to promote improvements in hypertrophy.

Two unique methods implemented in hypertrophy programs are the super set and the compound set. A *super set* occurs when the individual performs two exercises that train opposing muscle groups without rest between the two exercises—for example, 1 set of bicep curls followed immediately by 1 set of tricep extensions. Consecutively completing two exercises that train the same muscle group without rest between them is termed a *compound set*. An example of this is to perform 1 set of barbell bicep curls followed immediately by dumbbell bicep curls. The fact that these approaches deviate from the rest periods shown in Table 14.3 certainly does not mean that such approaches are ineffective. The time frames indicated are only guidelines. There are many ways to manipulate program design variables to produce positive outcomes.

Hypertrophy Program Questions

Answer the following questions:

1. The guidelines to use when designing your program so that hypertrophy is the outcome are as follows:
   a. Relative loading = _____
   b. Percentage of 1RM load = _____

Table 14.4 Example: Hypertrophy Program Multiple Set–Same Load Training (1RM = 100 pounds)

Set	% 1RM	Weight/resistance pounds	Reps
1	75	75	8-12
2	Use same % load		8-12
3	Use same % load		8-12
Length of rest between sets = 30-90 seconds			

c. Repetition range = _____
d. Number of sets = _____
e. Rest period = _____
2. Given a 1RM of 100 pounds, a 75-pound load is associated with achieving the goals of a [___ strength, ___ hypertrophy, ___ muscular endurance] program.
3. When opposing muscle groups are exercised without rest, this arrangement is referred to as a [___ super set, ___ compound set].

Answers to Hypertrophy Program Questions

1. a. moderate b. 70 to 80 percent c. 8 to 12 d. 3 to 6 e. 30 to 90 seconds
2. hypertrophy
3. super set

Strength Programs

There are many ways to approach programs designed to produce significant strength gains. The two presented here are commonly used by successful power lifters and weight lifters, and apply best to large muscle (core) exercises.

Pyramid Training

If you decide in Step 16 to change your program to emphasize strength development, one method of applying the guidelines presented in Table 14.3 can be seen in Table 14.5. The example uses a predicted 1RM of 150 pounds in the bench press exercise. To bring about the proper loading to produce the goal of 6 to 8 reps in the 1st set, use 80 percent of the 1RM. This percentage will equal 120 pounds (150 × 0.80 = 120). Now, to incorporate the concept of progressive overload, you can use what is referred to as (light to heavy) *pyramid training*, where each succeeding set becomes heavier. Increase the load to equal approximately 85 percent of the 1RM, or 130 pounds, in the 2nd set, and to 90 percent of the 1RM, or 135 pounds, in the 3rd set. Note that sometimes you will need to round off loads to the nearest 5 pounds/weight stack-plate, as has been done with the 85 percent load in set 2. If 5 sets are to be performed, increase the load to equal 95 percent of the 1RM for the 4th and 5th sets. Between each set, rest 2 or more minutes. Do not be surprised when the number of reps decreases as you continue from set 1 to 2, set 2 to 3, and so on. In fact, the load increases are designed to decrease the number of reps: 6 to 8 in set 1, 4 to 7 in set 2, 1 to 3 in set 3

Table 14.5 Example: Strength Program Pyramid Training and Use of the 1RM (1RM in bench press = 150 pounds)

Set	1RM x % 1RM = Load	Goal reps
Warm-up	Use present training load	10
1	150 x 0.80 = 120 Training load = 120 pounds	6-8
2	150 x 0.85 = 130 Training load = 130 pounds	4-7
3	150 x 0.90 = 135 Training load = 135 pounds	1-3

Length of rest between sets = 2-5 minutes

(and 1 or 2 in sets 4 and 5 in more advanced training programs). Use this approach with large muscle (core) exercises while performing 3 sets of 8-12 reps in other exercises. Heavy loads tend to produce too much stress on the smaller muscle and joints.

Forcing yourself to train to the point of muscular failure while using progressively heavier poundages from set to set (progressive overload principle) will provide the stimulus for dramatic strength gains. As training sessions continue, the need to add weight to 1 or more successive sets will be a natural outcome. As training continues and the intensity of workouts increases, there will be a time when training to muscular failure is appropriate only in certain exercises and on designated days. This is discussed in Step 15.

Multiple Sets–Same Load Training

Another popular approach used to develop strength is to perform 3 to 5 sets of 2 to 8 reps with the same load in the core exercises and 3 sets of 8 to 12 reps in other exercises, as shown in Table 14.6. The program can be made more aggressive by decreasing the goal reps—which means you must use heavier loads: 6 reps = 85 percent; 4 = 90 percent; 2 = 95 percent of the 1RM. Notice how the percentage of the 1RM is associated with the goal reps of 6, 4, and 2 at the bottom of this table. You will find that completing the specified number of reps in set 1 is usually easy, set 2 is more difficult, and set 3 is very difficult, if not impossible. With continued training, sets 2 and 3 will become easier, and eventually you will need to increase loads. As already mentioned, keeping the loads the same in several sets of the same exercise is also a popular training approach among bodybuilders. The difference here is that the loads used for developing strength are heavier.

Strength Program Questions

Answer the following questions (check off two answers for question 4):

1. The guidelines to use when designing your program so that strength is the outcome are as follows:
   a. Relative loading = _____
   b. Percentage of 1RM load = _____
   c. Repetition range = _____
   d. Number of sets = _____
   e. Rest period = _____
2. Given a 1RM of 200 pounds and a goal of strength development, the lightest load for a first set should be [_____ 160 pounds, _____ 140 pounds].

Table 14.6   Example: Strength Program Multiple Sets–Same Load Training (1RM in bench press = 150 pounds)

			Core exercises			
Set	1RM	x	% 1RM	=	Load	Goal reps
1	150	x	0.80	=	120	8
2	150	x	0.80	=	120	8
3	150	x	0.80	=	120	8

Use % 1RM of 0.85 for goal reps of 6
Use % 1RM of 0.90 for goal reps of 4
Use % 1RM of 0.95 for goal reps of 2
(Other exercises: 3 sets of 8-12 reps)

3. The use of progressively heavier poundages in each set of the pyramid training approach demonstrates the use of the [___ specificity concept, ___ overload principle].
4. The two strength development programs described here have been referred to as [___ 1RM, ___ pyramid, ___ multiple set–same load, ___ overload].
5. Heavier loads are not used with [___, smaller, ___ larger] muscle groups because that method of training imposes too much stress on the involved muscle and joint structures.

Answers to Strength Program Questions

1. a. heavy b. 80 to 100 percent c. 1 to 8 d. 3 to 5 e. 2 to 5 minutes
2. 160
3. overload
4. pyramid, multiple set–same load
5. smaller

Manipulating Program Design Variables Drills

1. Loads, Reps, Sets, and Rest Period Drill

You have had an opportunity to learn about how the specificity concept and overload principle are used in determining loads, the implications of these loads on the number of reps and sets, and the length of the rest periods between exercises and sets. As a review, fill in the missing information in Table 14.7.

Success Goal = Correctly fill in 7 of the 9 empty blanks in Table 14.7

Your Score = (#) ___ of blanks filled in correctly [compare your answers with those in Table 14.3]

Table 14.7 Loads, Reps, Sets, and Rest Period Drill

Relative loading	Outcome of training	% 1RM	Rep range	# of sets	Rest between sets
_____	Strength	_____	1-8	_____	2-5 minutes
Moderate	_____	70-80	_____	3-6	_____
_____	Muscular endurance	_____	12-20	_____	20-30 seconds

2. Determining Load Ranges

This drill will give you experience in determining training loads using the predicted 1RM, and in applying the knowledge you have gained concerning training load *ranges*. Using the previously predicted 1RM in your *shoulder* (core) exercise, multiply the 1RM by the appropriate percentages to determine load ranges for strength, hypertrophy, and muscular endurance programs.

Here is an example. Let's say your 1RM for the shoulder press exercise equals 80 pounds. Depending on your goal for training, this is how to determine load ranges. Remember to round off numbers to the nearest 5 pounds or closest weight-stack plate.

Goal	1RM	×	Training Load (%)	=	Training Load Ranges*
Strength	80		80 to 100%		
example:	80	×	.80 to 1.00	=	65 to 80 pounds
Hypertrophy	80		70 to 80%		
example:	80	×	.70 to .80	=	60 to 70 pounds
Muscular endurance	80		50 to 60%		
example:	80	×	.50 to .60	=	40 to 50 pounds

*Rounded off to the nearest 5 pounds or weight-stack plate.

Success Goal = 3 out of 3 load ranges for the training outcomes listed are accurately determined

Your Score =   (#) _____ training load ranges accurately determined

The predicted 1RM for your shoulder exercise = _____.

For the shoulder exercise selected, the appropriate load ranges are

a. =   _____   to   _____   pounds for strength development;
b. =   _____   to   _____   pounds for hypertrophy; and
c. =   _____   to   _____   pounds for muscular endurance development.

Summary

The importance of applying the specificity concept and the overload principle when making load, reps, set, and rest period training decisions should now be apparent. Equally apparent should be the realization that you can dictate the outcomes of training (muscular endurance, hypertrophy, strength) by the manner in which you manipulate program design variables.

Step 15 How to Determine Training Frequency and Program Variation

Training frequency and program variation are the last program design variables to be covered before you are challenged to design your own program. Essentially, the questions answered in this step are (a) How often should you train? and (b) How should you change the program so improvement continues?

WHY IS UNDERSTANDING TRAINING FREQUENCY AND PROGRAM VARIATION IMPORTANT?

If you perform the same number of sets and reps, with the same loads week after week, a plateau in strength will occur. Remember your body will adapt after a period of time and will need to be subjected to a greater number of reps, sets, and/or loads if improvement is to continue. On the other hand, programs with too many exercises performed too many times, with inadequate rest periods and/or excessive loads, can result in injury, extended muscle soreness, and can aggravate existing joint problems. The effects of over training are described in greater detail in the "Physiological Considerations" section. The goal, therefore, is to design programs that vary the overall intensity of training, providing the needed overload as well as rest to bring about maximum gains without injury.

FREQUENCY OF TRAINING

The overload principle and frequency of training are essential elements in establishing the proper intensity in successful programs. To be effective, training *must* occur on a regular basis. Sporadic training short-circuits your body's ability to adapt. But also realize that rest between training days is just as important as the actual training! Your body needs time

to recover: to remove the waste products of exercise from muscle, and to move in nutrients that are essential to muscle's continued growth. Often individuals who are new to weight training become so excited with the changes in their strength and appearance that they come in to train on the scheduled rest days. More is not always better, especially during the beginning stages of your program! Allow at least 48 hours before you train the same muscle again, which usually means training 3 days a week as recommended in Step 12. Typically, this means training on Monday, Wednesday, and Friday; Tuesday, Thursday, and Saturday; or Sunday, Tuesday, and Thursday. In a 3-days-a-week program, all exercises are performed each day.

A *split program* is a more advanced method of training that typically involves splitting a program of exercises in half and performing one half of them 2 days a week (e.g., Monday and Thursday) and the other half on 2 different days (e.g., Tuesday and Friday). A split program typically involves more exercises and sets, and 4 training days scheduled as shown in Table 15.1. In the top half of this table (option A) are exercises split into *upper body* and *lower body*, with abdominal exercises on all training days. Option B in the lower half of this table illustrates another common option, dividing exercises on all training days. Notice that an effort has been made in both options to arrange exercises so that pushing and pulling exercises are alternated and so that tricep exercises are located after upper body pressing movements (as suggested in Step 13).

The split program offers several advantages. It spreads the exercises in your workout over 4 instead of 3 days, thereby usually reducing the amount of time required to complete each

Table 15.1   4-Days-a-Week Split Training Program

Option A		Option B	
Exercise	Type	Exercise	Type
Monday and Thursday, upper body		**Monday and Thursday, chest, shoulders, and arms**	
Bench press	Push	Bench press	Push
Lat pull-down	Pull	Bicep curl	Pull
Dumbbell flys	Push	Standing press	Push
Bicep curl	Pull	Abdominal crunch	Pull
Standing press	Push	Tricep extension	Push
Abdominal crunch	Pull		
Tricep extension	Push		
Tuesday and Friday, lower body		**Tuesday and Friday, legs and back**	
Lunge	Push	Leg press	Push
Leg curl	Pull	Leg curl	Pull
Leg extension	Push	Leg extension	Push
Bent-knee sit-up	Pull	Bent-knee sit-up	Pull
Seated toe raise	Push		

workout. This offers the opportunity to add more exercises and sets while keeping workout time reasonable. Because you can add more exercises, you are able to emphasize muscular development in specific muscle groups, should you decide to do so. Its disadvantage is that you must train 4 instead of 3 days a week.

Frequency of Training Questions

Answer the following questions by checking off (✔) the correct answer:

1. Establishing the proper stimulus for improvements is dependent upon use of the overload principle and training [___ on a regular basis, ___ in a sporadic manner].

2. Compared to a split program, the 3-days-a-week program typically includes a [___ greater, ___ fewer] number of exercises.

3. Compared to the 3-days-a-week program, the split program usually takes [___ less, ___ more] time to complete.

4. The [___ split, ___ 3-days-a-week program] offers the best opportunity for emphasizing development in specific muscle areas.

Answers to Frequency of Training Questions

1. on a regular basis
2. fewer
3. less
4. split

TRAINING VARIATION

Training variation involves systematically manipulating the variables of

- training frequency,
- exercises selected,
- arrangement of exercises,
- number of reps per set,
- number of sets,
- length of the rest periods between workout sessions.

Program approaches designed to vary the intensity of training pay special attention to the loads assumed by large muscle groups (leg, shoulder, chest). It is believed that the larger muscle mass and the joint structures of the larger muscle groups are better suited to withstand the rigors of training (compared to the smaller groups). You may recall (Step 14) that the large muscle groups were identified as being appropriate for the heavier loads assumed in the pyramid (strength development) program, for the same reason.

Some of the common approaches used to vary the intensity of workouts are to

1. use heavy, light, and medium-heavy loads on different days of the week;
2. increase loads from week to week; or
3. change loads in a cyclical manner every 2 or more weeks.

The approaches here concern only the core exercises and are most applicable to programs designed for strength development and hypertrophy involving 3 or more sets. The loads used in the noncore exercises should permit 8 to 12 reps, and these loads should be gradually increased following the 2-for-2 rule. Although the discussion here focuses on the loads used, you should realize that the number of reps and sets may also be manipulated (and usually are) to vary training intensities.

Within the Week Variations

Three different ways to increase loads within a week follow.

3 Days a Week–Same Load in Sets Approach

Table 15.2 shows you an example of a 3-days-a-week workout program where heavy (H), light (L), and medium-heavy (MH) loads are varied *within the week*. The loads used *in a particular day's workout* stay the same (they are not increased, thus the "same load in sets approach" name). The 2 × 8-12 means 2 sets (X)

Table 15.2   Within-Week Training Load Variation (3-Days-a-Week, Same Load in Sets Approach)

Exercise	Monday	Wednesday	Friday
**Chest press	H 3 x 3-8	L 3 x 10	MH 3 x 6-8
Bent over row	2 x 8-12	2 x 8-12	2 x 8-12
**Standing press	H 3 x 3-8	L 3 x 10	MH 3 x 6-8
Bicep curl	2 x 8-12	2 x 8-12	2 x 8-12
Tricep extension	2 x 8-12	2 x 8-12	2 x 8-12
**Back squat	H 3 x 3-8	L 3 x 10	MH 3 x 6-8
Abdominal crunch or sit-up	2 x 15 – 30 reps each day		

Explanation of loads: H (Heavy) = 85, L (Light) = 70, MH (Medium-Heavy) = 80 % 1RM
**Core exercises, 3-5 sets

of 8 to 12 reps; 3 sets of 8 to 10 reps would be written 3 × 8-10. If you perform 3 sets of 8-10 reps with 120 pounds, you would write it like this: 120 × 3 × 8-10.

Notice that in these tables only exercises for the larger muscles are associated with the letters H, MH, or L, designating the use of heavy (80 to 90 percent of 1RM), medium-heavy (80 percent of 1RM), and light (60 to 70 percent of 1RM) loads, respectively. Other exercises involve loads permitting 8 to 12 reps. Even though you may be able to, do not perform more than 10 reps on your light (L) day (Wednesday) and 8 reps on your medium-heavy day (Friday). Notice that Monday, the more intense training day, is followed by the least intense training day, which is then followed by a medium-intensity day, so that your body has a chance to recover. You will see this pattern repeat itself in all the training program examples provided in this step.

3-Days-a-Week, Pyramid Approach

In Step 14 you learned about the use of the pyramid approach, where progressive load increases occur from one set to another until all sets for a specific exercise are completed. In Table 15.3 you will recognize these progressive increases, but also realize that the loads used vary from 80 to 90 percent of 1RM on Monday (H), from 70 to 80 percent on Wednesday (L), and from 75 to 85 percent on Friday (MH). The example uses a 1RM of 150 pounds.

4-Days-a-Week Heavy-Light Split Program Approach

Tables 15.4, a and b, show how a 4-days-a-week (split) program might be organized to vary heavy and light loads *within the week*. Table 15.4a shows the assignment of loads on Monday and Thursday for the chest, shoulder, and arm exercises. Table 15.4b shows load assignments on Tuesday and Friday for the back and leg exercises.

Week-to-Week Variations

Two ways to increase loads on a weekly basis are shown in Table 15.5 (p. 157). Option A involves simply scheduling a 3 percent increase *each* week. Option B also shows a 3 percent increase (Monday) each week, followed by the use of light and medium-heavy loads on Wednesday and Friday, respectively.

Cyclical Training Variations

The previously explained approaches provide variations in the intensity of training. If, however, you were to continue following such programs for an extended period of time, a plateau or an overtraining injury would most likely be the outcome. You will recall the earlier emphasis on the need for proper rest. Programs that continue to increase loads (and reps or sets) without scheduling rest time will not produce optimal gains. The term *cycling* here refers to the scheduling of cycles of high intensity with low-intensity training periods.

Table 15.3 3-Days-a-Week Pyramid Approach Within-Week Methods of Varying Loads (Current predicted 1RM = 150 pounds)

Monday-heavy (H)				Wednesday-light (L)				Friday-medium-heavy (MH)			
% Load				% Load				% Load			
1RM	lb	# Sets	Reps	1RM	lb	# Sets	Reps	1RM	lb	# Sets	Reps
80	120	x 1	x 6-8	70	105	x 1	x 10	75	115	x 1	x 8
85	130	x 1	x 4-7	75	115	x 1	x 8	80	125	x 1	x 6
90	135	x 1	x 1-3	80	120	x 1	x 6	85	130	x 1	x 4

Table 15.4a   Monday-Thursday Split Program
(Chest, Shoulders, and Arms)

Exercise	Monday	Thursday
**Chest press	H	L
Bicep curl	4 x 8-12	4 x 8-12
**Standing press	H	L
Tricep extension	4 x 8-12	4 x 8-12
Abdominal crunch	2 x 15 – 30 reps each day	

H = 80-90% 1RM, L = 60-70% 1RM, MH = 70-80% 1RM
** = Core exercises

Table 15.4b   Tuesday-Friday Split Program
(Back and Legs)

Exercise	Tuesday	Friday
**Back squat	H	L
Bent over row	4 x 8-12	4 x 8-12
Abdominal crunch	2 x 15 – 30 reps each day	

H = 80-90% 1RM, L = 60-70% 1RM, MH = 70-80% 1RM
** = Core exercises

Table 15.6 represents a 7-week cycle that includes load variations within the week, and load and set increases every 3 weeks of training. Following Table 15.6 is an explanation of the 7-week cycle. Notice that the 7th week involves lighter loads and fewer sets (less intensive workouts), providing an opportunity for the body to recover as well as to make jumps over previous strength levels in succeeding weeks. Load increases that occur after the 3rd and 6th weeks are determined by the number of reps completed during the Friday workouts of the 3rd and 6th weeks. The number of sets may also be increased after each 3-week period. A 4-days-a-week program could be cycled in a similar way. The decision to increase the number of sets to 5 or 6 after a 7-week cycle should be based upon how well you are able to recover from your program and how much time you have for training.

7-Week Training Cycle Explained

Weeks 1 and 2
Core exercises:

- Monday workouts—perform as many reps as possible.
- Wednesday and Friday workouts—reps stay within recommended ranges.

Other exercises:

- Perform as many reps as possible, and increase loads using the 2-for-2 rule.
- Abdominal exercises—perform 15 to 30 reps per workout.

Table 15.5   Within- and Between-Weeks Load Variations

Option A   Same loads within the week, increases between weeks

Week	Monday % 1RM	Wednesday % 1RM	Friday % 1RM
1	80	80	80
2	83	83	83
3	86	86	86

Option B   Within- and between-week load variations

Week	Monday % 1RM	Wednesday % 1RM	Friday % 1RM
1	80	70	75
2	83	73	78
3	86	76	81

Table 15.6   7-Week Training Cycle

Week	Sets	Monday	Wednesday	Friday
1	3	*H	L	MH
2	3	H	L	MH
3	3	M	L	Test
4	4	*H	L	MH
5	4	H	L	MH
6	4	M	L	Test
7	2	L	L	L
8	Repeat 7-week cycle with new training loads			

H = 80% 1RM, L = 70% 1RM, MH = 75% 1RM
* Indicates that new loads are used

Week 3

Core exercises:

- Monday workout—use medium-heavy loads.
- Wednesday—use light loads.
- Friday—test on your 3rd set, and calculate your new training load.

Other exercises:

- Perform as many reps as possible, and increase loads using the 2-for-2 rule.

- Abdominal exercises—perform 15 to 30 reps per workout.

Weeks 4 and 5

- Starts as the first week, but with new training loads.

Week 6

- Test again and calculate new training loads.

Week 7

- Use light (new) loads for 2 sets in *all* exercises this week.

Week 8

- Repeat 7-week cycle with new training loads.

Procedures for Testing on the 3rd and 6th Weeks of the 7-Week Cycle

Use the following procedures on the Friday of each 3rd week of the training period to determine new training loads. Notice that a shortcut for identifying training loads is also explained.

1. Warm up as usual, then use Friday's loads in sets 1 and 2, but perform only 5 and 3 reps, respectively.

2a. If you are using the pyramid method, perform as many reps as possible with the *heaviest load used thus far in this cycle.*

2b. If you are using the "same load in each set" method, *increase the load by 10 pounds* and perform as many reps as possible.

3. Predict the 1RM using the procedures you learned in Step 14.

Shortcut for Determining Training Loads

Instead of multiplying the predicted 1RM by the desired training percentage, as you did in Step 14, to determine training loads, refer to Table 15.7 and follow these procedures:

1. Refer to Table 15.7 and locate and circle where your predicted 1RM value is located in the far left-hand 1RM column.

2. Identify the desired training percentage (50 to 90 percent) column.

3. Follow the percentage column down until it parallels the location of your predicted 1RM value.

4. Circle where these two points converge. The number you circle is your training load.

The example in Figure 15.1 (p. 160) is of someone who completed 7 reps with 90 pounds and wants a training load that represents 85 percent of 1RM. Performing 7 reps with 90 pounds equals a 1RM of 110 pounds using the "Prediction of 1RM" (Table 14.2) from Step 14. Notice that in Table 15.7 under the column heading "1RM" that 110 pounds is found on line 9. Where line 9 and the 85 percent column converge is the load you should use. The number 94 is rounded to the nearest 5 pounds or weight-stack plate, which is 95 pounds in this example.

Whatever method is chosen to create variations in intensity, you should perform as many reps as possible on the heavy day of your workout in the core exercises, but keep the reps within the designated ranges during the Wednesday and Friday workouts. This means that even though you are capable of performing more reps with the lighter Wednesday and Friday loads—*don't!* In the other (noncore) exercises, perform as many reps as possible in all workouts, and use the 2-for-2 rule for increasing loads.

Program Variation Questions

Answer the following questions by checking off (✔) the correct answer:

1. The reps performed on light and medium-heavy training days provide the opportunity for you to [____ apply the overload principle, ____ recover from the overloading].

2. You should perform [____ the designated number of reps, ____ as many reps as possible] on heavy training days.

3. The two variables that have been manipulated in the 7-week cycle program in Table 15.6 are [____ reps and sets, ____ loads and sets].

Table 15.7 Training Load Determination

1RM	50%	60%	70%	75%	80%	85%	90%	95%
1. 30	15	18	21	23	24	26	27	29
2. 40	20	24	28	30	32	34	36	38
3. 50	25	30	35	38	40	43	45	48
4. 60	30	36	42	45	48	51	54	57
5. 70	35	42	49	52	56	60	63	67
6. 80	40	48	56	60	64	68	72	76
7. 90	45	54	63	68	72	77	81	86
8. 100	50	60	70	75	80	85	90	95
9. 110	55	66	77	83	88	94	99	105
10. 120	60	72	84	90	96	102	108	114
11. 130	65	78	91	98	104	111	117	124
12. 140	70	84	98	105	112	119	125	133
13. 150	75	90	105	113	120	128	135	143
14. 160	80	96	112	120	128	136	144	152
15. 170	85	102	119	128	136	145	153	162
16. 180	90	108	126	135	144	153	162	171
17. 190	95	114	133	143	152	162	171	181
18. 200	100	120	140	150	160	170	180	190
19. 210	105	126	147	158	168	179	189	200
20. 220	110	132	154	165	176	187	198	209
21. 230	115	138	161	173	184	196	207	219
22. 240	120	144	168	180	192	204	216	228
23. 250	125	150	175	188	200	213	225	238
24. 260	130	156	182	195	208	221	234	247
25. 270	135	162	189	203	216	230	243	257
26. 280	140	168	196	210	224	238	252	266
27. 290	145	174	203	218	232	247	261	276
28. 300	150	180	210	225	240	255	270	285
29. 310	155	186	217	233	248	264	279	295
30. 320	160	192	224	240	256	272	288	304
31. 330	165	198	231	248	264	281	297	314
32. 340	170	204	238	255	272	289	306	323
33. 350	175	210	245	263	280	298	316	333
34. 360	180	216	252	278	288	306	324	342
35. 370	185	222	259	280	296	315	333	352
36. 380	190	228	266	285	304	323	342	361
37. 390	195	234	273	293	312	332	351	371
38. 400	200	240	280	300	320	340	360	380

Answers to Program Variation Questions

1. recover from the overloading
2. as many reps as possible
3. loads and sets

Table 14.2 Prediction of 1RM

Reps completed	Rep factor
1	1.00
2	1.07
3	1.10
4	1.13
5	1.16
6	1.20
(7)	1.23
8	1.27
9	1.32
10	1.36

Note. From *Beginning Weight Training: The Safe and Effective Way* (p. 201) by V.P. Lombardi, 1989, Dubuque, IA: Brown. Copyright 1989 by William C. Brown. Adapted by permission.

(handwritten) → x 90 = (110 pounds) (rounded)

(handwritten) 94 rounded to the nearest 5 pounds = 95 pound training load

Table 15.7 Training Load Determination

1RM	50%	60%	70%	75%	80%	85%	90%	95%
1. 30	15	18	21	23	24	26	27	29
2. 40	20	24	28	30	32	34	36	38
3. 50	25	30	35	38	40	43	45	48
4. 60	30	36	42	45	48	51	54	57
5. 70	35	42	49	52	56	60	63	67
6. 80	40	48	56	60	64	68	72	76
7. 90	45	54	63	68	72	77	81	86
8. 100	50	60	70	75	80	85	90	95
9. 110	55	66	77	83	88	94	99	105
10. 120	60	72	84	90	96	102	108	114
11. 130	65	78	91	98	104	111	117	124
12. 140	70	84	98	105	112	119	125	133
13. 150	75	90	105	113	120	128	135	143
14. 160	80	96	112	120	128	136	144	152
15. 170	85	102	119	128	136	145	153	162
16. 180	90	108	126	135	144	153	162	171
17. 190	95	114	133	143	152	162	171	181
18. 200	100	120	140	150	160	170	180	190
19. 210	105	126	147	158	168	179	189	200
20. 220	110	132	154	165	176	187	198	209
21. 230	115	138	161	173	184	196	207	219
22. 240	120	144	168	180	192	204	216	228
23. 250	125	150	175	188	200	213	225	238
24. 260	130	156	182	195	208	221	234	247
25. 270	135	162	189	203	216	230	243	257
26. 280	140	168	196	210	224	238	252	266
27. 290	145	174	203	218	232	247	261	276
28. 300	150	180	210	225	240	255	270	285
29. 310	155	186	217	233	248	264	279	295
30. 320	160	192	224	240	256	272	288	304
31. 330	165	198	231	248	264	281	297	314
32. 340	170	204	238	255	272	289	306	323
33. 350	175	210	245	263	280	298	316	333
34. 360	180	216	252	278	288	306	324	342
35. 370	185	222	259	280	296	315	333	352
36. 380	190	228	266	285	304	323	342	361
37. 390	195	234	273	293	312	332	351	371
38. 400	200	240	280	300	320	340	360	380

Figure 15.1 A shortcut for determining training loads.

Training Load Drills

1. Shortcut Method

This drill is designed to give you experience in the shortcut method of determining training loads using Table 15.7. Assume that you performed 8 reps with 150 pounds and want to identify a training load that represents 75 percent of 1RM. What is the correct load? Remember to use the "Prediction of 1RM" Table (14.2) first, then use this 1RM value and the 75% 1RM column to locate the correct training load. Round off this value to the nearest 5-pound increment or weight-stack plate.

Success Goal = "Yes"—the calculated training load equals 145 pounds

Your Score = ( ) Yes

( ) No

Answer to Calculating Training Load Question

Training load = 145 pounds. The rep factor from Table 14.2 for 8 reps = 1.27. 150 pounds × 1.27 = 190.5 pounds. 190 pounds is located on line 17 in Table 15.7. Where line 17 intersects with the 75% column is the number 143. Rounded off, this number equals the training load of 145 pounds.

2. Determining Training Loads in a Program

To give you another opportunity to determine training loads using Table 15.7 and the prediction of the 1RM table, fill in training loads for the program in Table 15.8a. In this drill assume that *5 reps* have been performed with *100 pounds*. Refer back to the previous drill if you are not sure how to determine training loads. After you have completed this drill, refer to Table 15.8b to check your answers.

Table 15.8a Determining Loads in a Program

Week	Monday % 1RM	# Sets	Wednesday % 1RM	# Sets	Friday % 1RM	# Sets
1	80 = _____	5	70 = _____	3	75 = _____	4
2	80 = _____	5	70 = _____	3	75 = _____	4
3	80 = _____	5	70 = _____	3	75 = _____	4

Success Goal = 9 out of 9 load assignments are correct

Your Score = (#) _____ load assignments correct

Table 15.8b   Answers to Determining Loads in a Program

Week	Monday % 1RM	# Sets	Wednesday % 1RM	# Sets	Friday % 1RM	# Sets
1	80 = _95_	5	70 = _85_	3	75 = _90_	4
2	80 = _95_	5	70 = _85_	3	75 = _90_	4
3	80 = _95_	5	70 = _85_	3	75 = _90_	4

Note that load used = 100 x rep factor of 1.16 (for 5 reps) = 116.
116 rounded = 120 pounds for the predicted 1RM, which is line 10 in Table 15.7.
120 x .80 = 96 pounds (round to 95), 120 x .70 = 84 pounds (round to 85),
and 120 x .75 = 90 pounds.

Summary

There are many ways to vary the intensity of training, the most common of which involves manipulating the amount of the load, the number of sets and reps, and the number of training days. The use of cycling programs that include aggressive training weeks, followed by a week (or weeks) of less aggressive training, provides an appropriate overload and an opportunity for the body to recover and make significant gains. As you become more experienced, you will want to learn more about the cycling concept. Excellent discussions of this approach are presented by Fleck and Kraemer (1987), Garhammer (1986), Lombardi (1989), and Stone and O'Bryant (1987).

Step 16 How to Tailor a Program to Your Needs

Now you will have a chance to apply all that you have learned in this text and develop your own weight training program. You will be prompted to use the knowledge you acquired concerning the program design variables (Steps 13 to 15) and to apply the overload and specificity concepts in designing a program that meets your specific needs. To simplify this task, the program design variables, which were grouped together in Steps 13 to 15, are now separated, and in one instance (training frequency) the order of coverage has been changed. Follow the order of the tasks presented below. When finished, you will have developed a well-conceived weight training program that meets your specific needs. You may also use these tasks as a self-assessment of the knowledge you have acquired from this text on how to design a weight training program.

Follow this order when tailoring your program:

1. Determine your goals.
2. Select exercises.
3. Decide on frequency of training.
4. Arrange exercises in the workout.
5. Decide which loads to use.
6. Decide how many reps to perform.
7. Decide how many sets of an exercise to complete.
8. Decide on length of rest periods.
9. Decide how to vary the program.

1. DETERMINE YOUR GOALS FOR TRAINING

Decide on and check (✔) one or more of the following goals that apply. Then read the section that follows, which briefly explains how to accomplish each goal. My goal(s) for training:

( ) Strength
( ) Hypertrophy
( ) Muscular endurance
( ) Strength and hypertrophy
( ) General muscle toning
( ) Body composition (reproportioning)
( ) Other (list) _____

Goal Is Muscular Endurance

As you have learned (Step 14), your present program is designed to improve muscular endurance. If this is the outcome you want from training, you will not need to change what you are doing to any great extent. Simply try to increase the number of reps to 20 in each set and perhaps shorten the rest periods gradually (to not less than 20 seconds). More changes, however, are indicated if strength or hypertrophy are the desired outcomes.

Goal Is Hypertrophy

To produce hypertrophy, you need to use loads that will keep your reps between 8 to 12, and you probably will need to include a good number of exercises and sets. You may want to initially focus on chest and arm development. Avoid the common tendency to spend too much time on these body parts at the exclusion of your legs. Also realize the greater number of exercises and the recommended number of sets (3 to 6) means a substantial time commitment (1-1/2 to 2-1/2 hours, three or four times a week).

Goal Is Strength

An important thing to remember, when your goal is strength development, is that to safely and effectively handle the heavier loads used to develop strength, you must have fairly long rest periods (2 to 5 minutes) between sets. A common mistake is to rush through sets, which compromises your body's ability to recover enough to exert maximum effort.

Goal Is a Combination of Strength and Hypertrophy

If strength and hypertrophy are your goals, design your program using loads that produce 6 to 12 reps (approximately 85 to 70 percent of 1RM) for the core exercises, and 8 to 12 reps in other exercises. Perform 3 to 6 sets in the core exercises and 3 sets in noncore exercises. Rest approximately 1 to 2 minutes between sets.

Goal Is General Muscle Toning

Follow the guidelines presented for muscular endurance programs to accomplish general muscular toning.

Goal Is Body Composition (Reproportioning)

If reproportioning your body is your goal, it is likely that you believe you are carrying too much fat, not enough muscle, or both. Consider doing three things: (a) Use a hypertrophy program to increase muscle mass, (b) select your foods more carefully, and (c) begin an aerobic program to increase the number of calories you burn. The texts by Corbin and Lindsey (1988), Getchell (1983), and Hoeger (1989) provide good direction on how to design aerobic training programs. For the hypertrophy program, simply follow the guidelines presented in this text. When selecting foods, make sure that you eat a balanced diet, increase your intake of complex carbohydrates, and decrease your intake of fats. Also realize that a normal diet will supply the amount of protein typically needed. For more information on nutrition, see the ''Nutritional Considerations'' section.

Goal Is Other

If you have special needs (e.g., improving athletic performance; competitive bodybuild-ing, weight lifting, power lifting) refer to the texts by Fleck and Kraemer (1987), Garhammer (1986), Lombardi (1989), O'Shea (1976), Pauletto (1991), and Stone and O'Bryant (1987).

2. SELECT EXERCISES

The exercises included in your present program are few in number, but they work most of the major muscle areas of the body. It is a basic program that will benefit from the addition of exercises for the lower back, forearm, and calf muscle areas. If your goal is to increase your muscular endurance, muscle size, or strength in a particular body part, it is a good idea to add another exercise designed to work that body part. If you decide to add exercises, do not select more than 2 per muscle area at this time, and try to not include more than 12 exercises if you are following a 3-days-a-week program. As you will remember from Step 15, the 4-days-a-week program provides the opportunity to add more exercises. Thus, you may choose to include 3 exercises for a particular body part if you decide to follow a 4-days-a-week program. Keep in mind the amount of time you have for training and the number of days in a week you plan to train, when selecting exercises.

In Table 16.1, decide which of the following muscle areas you want exercises for or want to emphasize (meaning you already have one exercise for this muscle area, and you want to add more). Before completing this task, you may want to refer back to Steps 4 through 10 and Appendix A to review explanations for the various free weight and machine exercises. Remember to consider equipment and spotter requirements. After considering your goals, write in the name of the exercise(s) selected to the right of the appropriate muscle areas in Table 16.1.

3. DECIDE ON FREQUENCY OF TRAINING

Decide whether you are going to use a 3-days-a-week or 4-days-a-week (split) program now. If your choice is to use a split program, determine how you will split the exercises among

Table 16.1   Exercise Selection

Days	Muscle area	Exercises	
( )	Chest	_____	_____
( )	Back (upper)	_____	_____
( )	Back (lower)	_____	_____
( )	Shoulders	_____	_____
( )	Arms (back of)	_____	_____
( )	Arms (front of)	_____	_____
( )	Forearm (palm side)	_____	_____
( )	Forearm (knuckle side)	_____	_____
( )	Legs (upper)	_____	_____
( )	Calves	_____	_____
( )	Abdomen	_____	_____

the 4 days. Your decision here may require you to reconsider the number of exercises you have selected. Remember, you can include more exercises in split programs than in a 3-days-a-week program.

Decide and check (✔) which schedule of training you will follow.

( ) 3 days a week—if you checked this option, skip to task #4 and check (✔) which approach you will use

( ) 4 days a week (split program)

If you plan to follow a split program, decide which of the following you will use:

( ) Chest, shoulders, and arms 2 days; legs and back the other 2 days

( ) Upper body 2 days; lower body 2 days

Once you've made these decisions, write in the brackets to the left of each muscle area (under the "Days" column) in Table 16.1 which days you plan to perform the exercises. Use the letters M, T, Th, and F (as shown in Figure 16.1) to do this.

4. ARRANGE EXERCISES

Next decide on how you will arrange these exercises within a workout. As you recall from Step 13, there are several options. Check (✔) which of these arrangements you plan to use:

( )   Larger muscle group exercises first
( )   Alternate push with pull exercises
( )   Alternate upper body with lower body exercises

Now look again (see Table 16.1) at the exercises that you decided to include in your program. Decide how you will arrange the order in which you will perform them. List your order on Table 16.2, using the left-hand column if you plan to follow a 3-days-a-week program and the right-hand column for a 4-day (split) program.

Now, record the exercises and their order from Table 16.2 onto either Table 16.3, if you checked (✔) 3-days-a-week program, or on Table 16.4, if you checked (✔) 4-days-a-week program. The 4-days-a-week chart assumes

Table 16.1 Exercise Selection

Days	Muscle area	Exercises	
(M, Th)	Chest	Bench press	Dumbbell flys
(T, F)	Back (upper)	Bent over row	
(T, F)	Back (lower)	Back extension	
(M, Th)	Shoulders	Upright row	Seated press
(M, Th)	Arms (back of)	Tricep extension	
(M, Th)	Arms (front of)	Bicep curl	Concentration curl
(M, Th)	Forearm (palm side)	Wrist curl	
(M, Th)	Forearm (knuckle side)	Wrist extension	
(T, F)	Legs (upper)	Back squat	
(T, F)	Calves	Heel raise	
(all)	Abdomen	Bent-knee sit-up	

Figure 16.1 This is an example of a split program where chest, shoulder, and arm exercises are worked on Mondays and Thursdays, back and legs on Tuesdays and Fridays, and abdominal exercises on all workout days.

that you are training Monday/Thursday and Tuesday/Friday.

5. DECIDE WHICH LOADS TO USE

Consider the overload principle and specificity concept in making decisions for assigning the loads needed to achieve the previously stated goals for training.

Approach
Decide and check (✓) which approach to the assignment of loads you will use.

( ) Pyramid
( ) Same load

Determine Starting Loads
Using the guidelines given in Steps 14 and 15 for core and noncore exercises, record loads for the exercises selected onto your workout chart (either Table 16.3 or 16.4). To save time, remember you can use the Determining Training Loads—Shortcut, explained in Figure 15.1 of Step 15. Do this now.

6. DECIDE HOW MANY REPS TO PERFORM

Decide and check (✓) the number of reps you intend to perform in each set.

( ) 12 to 20
( ) 8 to 12
( ) 1 to 8 core, 8 to 12 noncore
( ) Other (describe) _____

7. DECIDE HOW MANY SETS TO PERFORM

Decide on the number of sets you plan to perform in the exercises listed on your workout chart. Under the heading "Exercise" and just below the name of each exercise, record the sets and reps (indicated previously) you plan to perform (see Figure 16.2, p. 170). Do this now.

If the number of *sets* in the core exercises and other exercises are to increase, decide when and in which exercises. Do this now if this is what you plan to do.

Table 16.2   Exercise Arrangement

3 Days/week program		4 Days/week split program	
Order	Exercise	Order	Exercise
1.	_____	1.	_____
2.	_____	2.	_____
3.	_____	3.	_____
4.	_____	4.	_____
5.	_____	5.	_____
6.	_____	6.	_____
7.	_____	7.	_____
8.	_____	8.	_____
9.	_____	9.	_____
10.	_____	10.	_____
11.	_____	11.	_____
12.	_____	12.	_____
		13.	_____
		14.	_____

Core Exercises

The number of *sets* will increase to ____ after ____ weeks of training in the following core exercises:

_____

_____

_____

Other Exercises (Noncore)

The number of sets will increase to ____ after ____ weeks of training in the following noncore exercises described as:

Exercise name	Number of sets
_____	_____
_____	_____
_____	_____
_____	_____

8. DECIDE ON THE LENGTH OF REST PERIODS

Based upon your goals for training, decide on and check (✔) which rest period you will use.

( ) 20 to 30 seconds

( ) 30 to 90 seconds

( ) 2 minutes or longer

9. DECIDE ON HOW TO VARY THE PROGRAM

Decide and check (✔) which method of varying load intensities you will use.

( ) Within week (e.g., H, L, MH)

( ) Between weeks

( ) Both

Decide and check (✔) which method of scheduling *load* increases you will use.

Table 16.3   Weight Training Workout Chart (3-Days-a-Week Program)

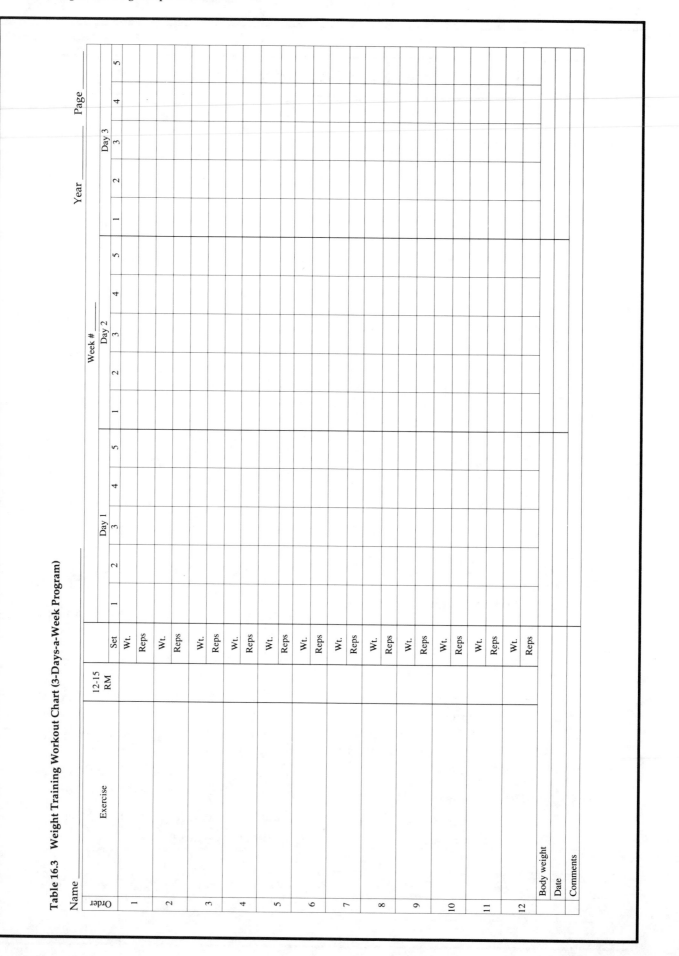

Table 16.4 Weight Training Workout Chart (4-Days-a-Week Program)

Name _____

Week # _____   Year _____   Page _____

Order	Monday/Thursday Exercises	12-15 RM	Set	Day 1—Monday					Day 2—Tuesday					Day 3—Thursday					Day 4—Friday				
				1	2	3	4	5	1	2	3	4	5	1	2	3	4	5	1	2	3	4	5
1			Wt. Reps																				
2			Wt. Reps																				
3			Wt. Reps																				
4			Wt. Reps																				
5			Wt. Reps																				
6			Wt. Reps																				
7			Wt. Reps																				
	Tuesday/Friday Exercises																						
8			Wt. Reps																				
9			Wt. Reps																				
10			Wt. Reps																				
11			Wt. Reps																				
12			Wt. Reps																				
13			Wt. Reps																				
14			Wt. Reps																				
Body weight																							
Date																							
Comments																							

Weight Train

Name _John Brown_

5 sets of 8-12 reps. →

Order	Exercise	12-15 RM		Week # 1				
				Day 1			Day 2	
			Set	1	2	3	1	2
1	Dumbbell flys 5×8-12		Wt.					
			Reps					
2	Bicep curl 3×12		Wt.					
			Reps					
3	Standing press 5×8-12		Wt.					
			Reps					
4	Bent over row 3×12		Wt.					
			Reps					
5	Tricep extension 3×12		Wt.					
			Reps					
6	Wrist curl 2×12		Wt.					
			Reps					
7	Wrist extension 2×12		Wt.					
			Reps					
8	Back squat 5×8-12		Wt.					
			Reps					
9	Trunk curl 3×20		Wt.					
			Reps					
10			Wt.					
			Reps					
11			Wt.					
			Reps					
12			Wt.					
			Reps					
	Body weight							
	Date							
	Comments							

Figure 16.2 Workout chart with numbers of sets and reps filled in.

( ) Weekly

( ) Every 2 weeks

( ) Other (describe) _____

Determine and check (✔) the basis for the scheduled *load* increases you plan to use.

( ) Increase loads by a specified percentage. How much? ____ %

( ) Base decisions on testing, as described in Step 14.

Decide and check (✔) the number of training weeks that you will follow before a week of low-intensity training is scheduled.

( ) 5 weeks

( ) 6 weeks

( ) 7 weeks

( ) 8 weeks

Depending on which method of program variation you plan to follow, fill in the loads, reps, and sets for all exercises for a 7-week period. Refer back to Step 15 if you need help. Remember to be consistent with the length of the rest periods.

LOOKING AHEAD

You have already decided how you plan to vary the intensity of training. You may now want to consider looking ahead to consider how to modify or manipulate the program design variables during the next year. Individuals in serious training usually develop short training cycles that are a part of larger cycles, which in turn are a part of even larger yearly cycles. It is probably too early for you to be concerned about such detailed planning. In the future, however, you should review the available information (cited in Step 14) and consider using such approaches. Also consider adding more advanced multijoint exercises (involving three or more joints and large muscle groups) illustrated and explained in texts by Baechle and Earle (1989), Fleck and Kraemer (1987), Garhammer (1986), Lombardi (1989), O'Shea (1976), and Stone and O'Bryant (1987).

Summary

The activities included in this step required an application of all that you have learned concerning how to design a weight training program. You are now capable of designing not only a program that meets your needs, but also one for others. In the process of learning about equipment, exercise techniques, and program design variables, you have probably gained a better appreciation of the expertise required to design programs for athletes in various sports, and programs for special populations (prepubescents, cardiacs, arthritics, those with osteoporosis, hypertension, injuries being rehabilitated). It is again appropriate to emphasize here that no program will amount to much unless it is approached with a positive attitude. If you train hard, train smart, and eat sensibly, you are virtually guaranteed success and the opportunity to enjoy "wearing your workout" proudly.

Rating Your Total Progress

Each exercise you completed in this book had a success goal, which prompted you to develop your physical skills and knowledge. The following inventory allows you to rate the overall progress you have made. Read the items carefully and respond to them thoughtfully.

TECHNIQUES AND SKILLS

How would you rate your success level in performing exercises for the following muscle groups?

	Very good	Good	Okay	Poor
Chest	_____	_____	_____	_____
Back	_____	_____	_____	_____
Shoulder	_____	_____	_____	_____
Arms	_____	_____	_____	_____
Legs	_____	_____	_____	_____
Abdomen	_____	_____	_____	_____

ANATOMICAL KNOWLEDGE

How would you rate your knowledge of the names of specific muscles in each of the following muscle groups?

	Very good	Good	Okay	Poor
Chest	_____	_____	_____	_____
Back	_____	_____	_____	_____
Shoulders	_____	_____	_____	_____
Arms	_____	_____	_____	_____
Legs	_____	_____	_____	_____
Abdomen	_____	_____	_____	_____

PROGRAM DESIGN CONCEPTS

How would you rate your level of knowledge and understanding of the following program design variables?

	Very good	Good	Okay	Poor
Selection of exercises	_____	_____	_____	_____
Training frequency	_____	_____	_____	_____
Arrangement of exercises	_____	_____	_____	_____
Loads to use	_____	_____	_____	_____
Number of reps to perform	_____	_____	_____	_____

	Very good	Good	Okay	Poor
Number of sets to perform	_____	_____	_____	_____
Length of rest periods to use	_____	_____	_____	_____
How to vary the program	_____	_____	_____	_____

How would you rate your ability to design a program?

Very good	Good	Okay	Poor
_____	_____	_____	_____

OUTCOMES OF TRAINING

How would you rate the progress you have made in the following areas?

	Very good	Good	Okay	Poor	Does not apply
Strength level	_____	_____	_____	_____	_____
Muscular size	_____	_____	_____	_____	_____
Muscular endurance	_____	_____	_____	_____	_____
Flexibility	_____	_____	_____	_____	_____
Body composition	_____	_____	_____	_____	_____

How would you rate the impact of training on your attitudes in the following areas?

	Very pleased	Pleased	Not pleased
Your appearance	_____	_____	_____
General attitude	_____	_____	_____
General self-concept	_____	_____	_____

Appendix A Alternate Exercises

This section includes one or more exercises for each muscle group presented in the basic program, *plus* exercises for the forearm, calf, and lower back. These exercises can be used to complement or replace exercises currently included in your program. A priority should be given to adding exercises for the forearm, calf, and lower back because they are needed to provide a balanced program. Each of the exercises in this section is identified as a "push" or "pull" exercise, to assist you in arranging them in your workout. Also note that in Steps 4 through 10 you were referred to the anatomical drawings in Appendix B along with the Keys to Success. This made it easy for you to associate exercises with the muscles they work. Try to also remember the locations of the specific muscles mentioned in each of the following exercise descriptions.

If you need help you can refer to Appendix B for the names and locations of various muscles.

Exercises in this section are grouped and organized in the following order:

1. Chest
2. Upper back
3. Lower back
4. Shoulders
5. Upper arms
6. Forearms
7. Upper legs
8. Lower legs (calves)
9. Abdominals

DETERMINING LOADS FOR NEWLY ADDED EXERCISES

Now that you have gained some experience in selecting and using loads, follow these procedures for establishing loads for these new exercises:

1. Begin learning new exercises using an empty bar or the lightest weight plate possible, and perform 15 reps.
2. Next make a guess at the poundage that will allow you to perform 12 to 15 reps, and perform only 6 reps with it.
3. After approximately 2 minutes, increase the load by 10 pounds and perform as many reps as possible.
4. Next refer to Step 15 for the shortcut for determining training loads.
5. If after using the training load you find the reps performed are not in accord with your goals for training, use one of the Load Adjustment Charts in Steps 4 through 10 (see practice procedure 7).

CONCENTRATE ON AND USE PROPER TECHNIQUE

During your warm-up and training sets, concentrate on and use the proper grip, body position, movement pattern, breathing, range of motion, controlled speed, and smooth execution. Ask a partner to check off the Keys to Success items as you demonstrate them.

Alternative Exercise for Developing the Chest

The dumbbell fly exercise (see Figure A.1) is frequently used as a supplement or alternate exercise for the chest exercises presented in Step 4. The major area involved is the same (pectoralis major). This is a pushing exercise.

Figure A.1 Keys to Success: *Dumbbell Flys*

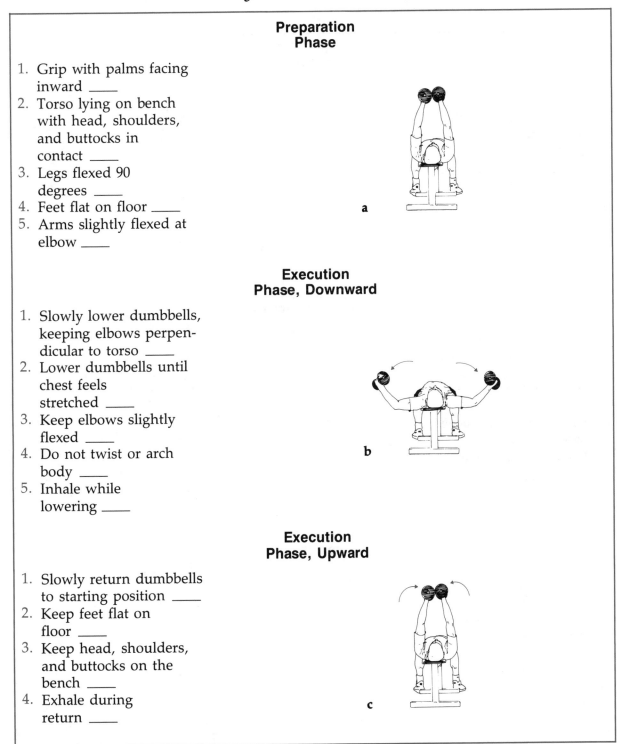

Preparation Phase

1. Grip with palms facing inward ____
2. Torso lying on bench with head, shoulders, and buttocks in contact ____
3. Legs flexed 90 degrees ____
4. Feet flat on floor ____
5. Arms slightly flexed at elbow ____

a

Execution Phase, Downward

1. Slowly lower dumbbells, keeping elbows perpendicular to torso ____
2. Lower dumbbells until chest feels stretched ____
3. Keep elbows slightly flexed ____
4. Do not twist or arch body ____
5. Inhale while lowering ____

b

Execution Phase, Upward

1. Slowly return dumbbells to starting position ____
2. Keep feet flat on floor ____
3. Keep head, shoulders, and buttocks on the bench ____
4. Exhale during return ____

c

Alternative Exercise for Developing the Upper Back

The lat pull-down (see Figure A.2) develops the upper back (latissimus dorsi, rhomboids, trapezius) and involves some chest (pectorals), and anterior upper arm (bicep) muscles. This exercise is considered to be an alternate exercise for the back exercises presented in Step 5 and is a pulling exercise.

Figure A.2 Keys to Success: Lat Pull-Down

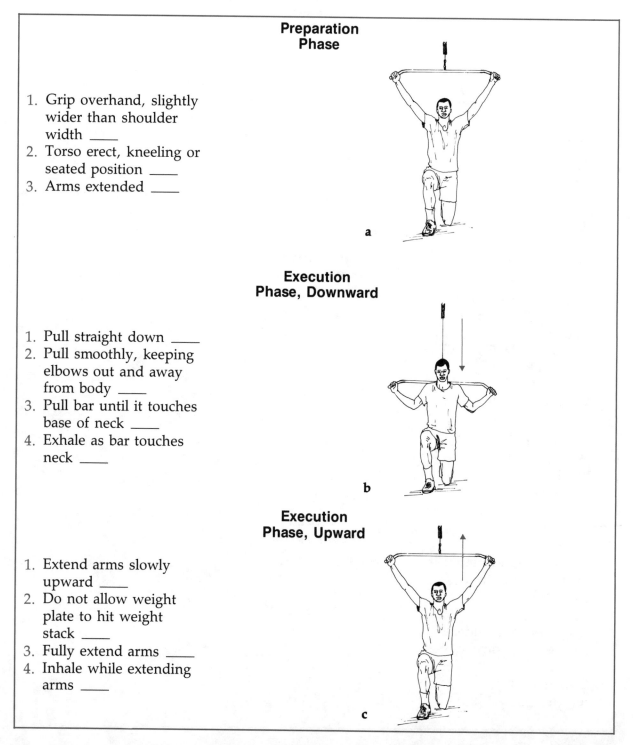

Preparation Phase

1. Grip overhand, slightly wider than shoulder width ____
2. Torso erect, kneeling or seated position ____
3. Arms extended ____

a

Execution Phase, Downward

1. Pull straight down ____
2. Pull smoothly, keeping elbows out and away from body ____
3. Pull bar until it touches base of neck ____
4. Exhale as bar touches neck ____

b

Execution Phase, Upward

1. Extend arms slowly upward ____
2. Do not allow weight plate to hit weight stack ____
3. Fully extend arms ____
4. Inhale while extending arms ____

c

Alternative Exercises for Developing the Lower Back

The bent-leg dead lift and back extension exercises are used to strengthen the muscles of the lower back (erector spinae and quadratus lumborum). The bent-leg dead lift, somewhat described in Step 2, involves pulling the bar from the floor to hip level. The only change involves using an alternate grip (see Figure 2.3). The back extension exercise (see Figure A.3) is performed on the back extension station of a multi- or single-unit machine.

Figure A.3 Keys to Success: Back Extension Exercise

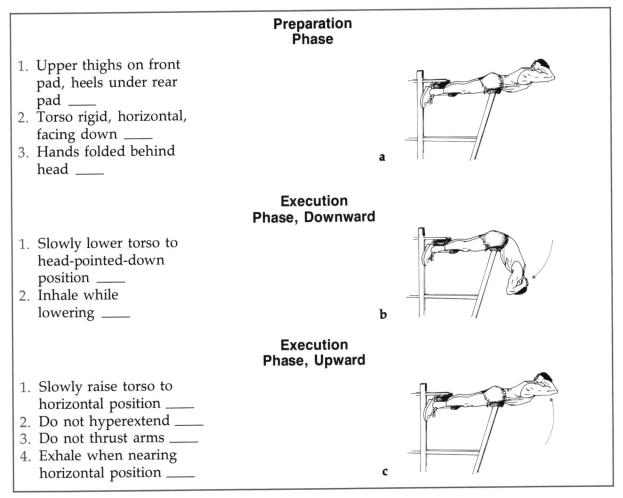

Preparation Phase

1. Upper thighs on front pad, heels under rear pad ____
2. Torso rigid, horizontal, facing down ____
3. Hands folded behind head ____

a

Execution Phase, Downward

1. Slowly lower torso to head-pointed-down position ____
2. Inhale while lowering ____

b

Execution Phase, Upward

1. Slowly raise torso to horizontal position ____
2. Do not hyperextend ____
3. Do not thrust arms ____
4. Exhale when nearing horizontal position ____

c

Alternative Exercise for Developing the Shoulders

The upright row (see Figure A.4) develops the shoulders (deltoids) and is considered to be an alternate exercise for the overhead pressing exercises presented in Step 6. This exercise can be performed using a barbell, or dumbbells, or the low pulley station on a multi- or single-unit machine. This is a pulling exercise.

Figure A.4   Keys to Success:
Upright Row

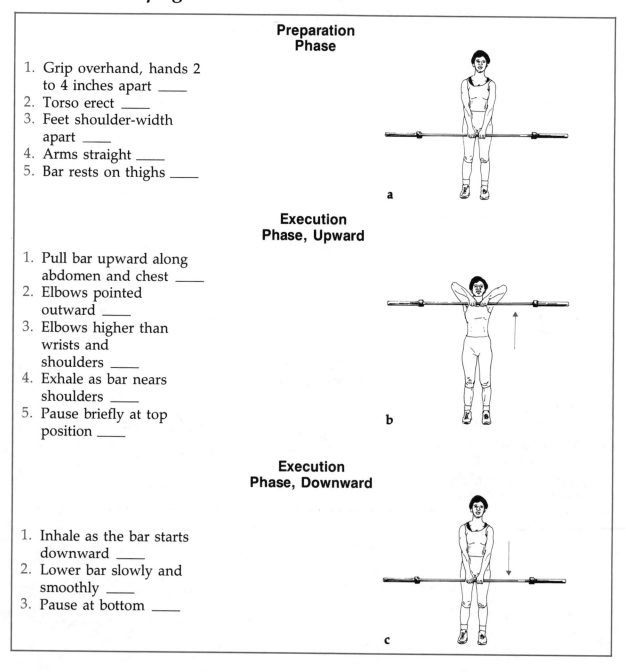

Preparation Phase

1. Grip overhand, hands 2 to 4 inches apart ____
2. Torso erect ____
3. Feet shoulder-width apart ____
4. Arms straight ____
5. Bar rests on thighs ____

a

Execution Phase, Upward

1. Pull bar upward along abdomen and chest ____
2. Elbows pointed outward ____
3. Elbows higher than wrists and shoulders ____
4. Exhale as bar nears shoulders ____
5. Pause briefly at top position ____

b

Execution Phase, Downward

1. Inhale as the bar starts downward ____
2. Lower bar slowly and smoothly ____
3. Pause at bottom ____

c

Alternative Exercise for Developing the Anterior Upper Arm

The concentration curl (see Figure A.5) is frequently used as a supplement to other bicep exercises presented in Step 7, often to add definition to, or to "peak out," the bicep. This pulling exercise is performed using a dumbbell.

Figure A.5 Keys to Success:
Concentration Curl

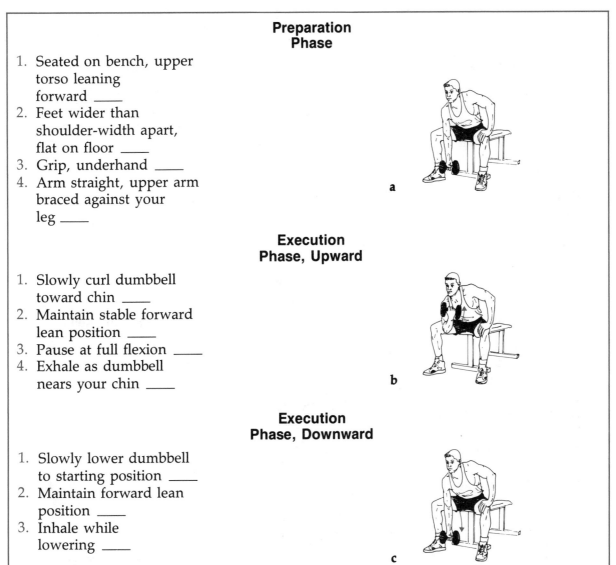

Preparation Phase

1. Seated on bench, upper torso leaning forward ____
2. Feet wider than shoulder-width apart, flat on floor ____
3. Grip, underhand ____
4. Arm straight, upper arm braced against your leg ____

a

Execution Phase, Upward

1. Slowly curl dumbbell toward chin ____
2. Maintain stable forward lean position ____
3. Pause at full flexion ____
4. Exhale as dumbbell nears your chin ____

b

Execution Phase, Downward

1. Slowly lower dumbbell to starting position ____
2. Maintain forward lean position ____
3. Inhale while lowering ____

c

Alternative Exercise for Developing the Posterior Upper Arm

The supine tricep extension (see Figure A.6) can be used as an alternative to the tricep (posterior upper arm) exercises presented in

Step 8. This pushing exercise is performed lying on a bench using a barbell or dumbbell.

Figure A.6 Keys to Success: Supine Tricep Extension

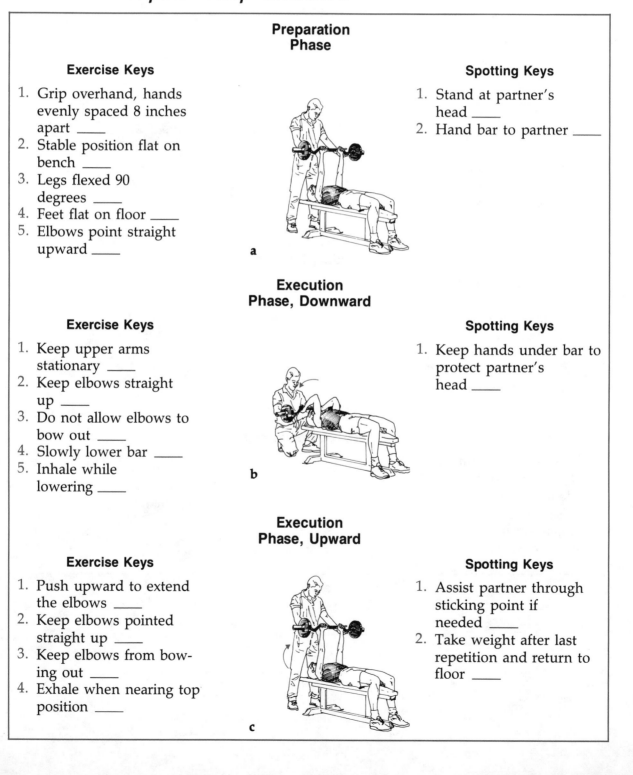

Preparation Phase

Exercise Keys

1. Grip overhand, hands evenly spaced 8 inches apart ____
2. Stable position flat on bench ____
3. Legs flexed 90 degrees ____
4. Feet flat on floor ____
5. Elbows point straight upward ____

Spotting Keys

1. Stand at partner's head ____
2. Hand bar to partner ____

a

Execution Phase, Downward

Exercise Keys

1. Keep upper arms stationary ____
2. Keep elbows straight up ____
3. Do not allow elbows to bow out ____
4. Slowly lower bar ____
5. Inhale while lowering ____

Spotting Keys

1. Keep hands under bar to protect partner's head ____

b

Execution Phase, Upward

Exercise Keys

1. Push upward to extend the elbows ____
2. Keep elbows pointed straight up ____
3. Keep elbows from bowing out ____
4. Exhale when nearing top position ____

Spotting Keys

1. Assist partner through sticking point if needed ____
2. Take weight after last repetition and return to floor ____

c

Alternative Exercise for Developing the Forearm

Wrist flexion (palms up) and wrist extension (palms down) exercises performed on a bench are common exercises for developing the lower arm (forearm). These exercises can be performed using a barbell (see Figure A.7), dumbbells, or the low pulley station on a multi- or single-unit machine.

Figure A.7 Keys to Success: Wrist Flexion and Extension

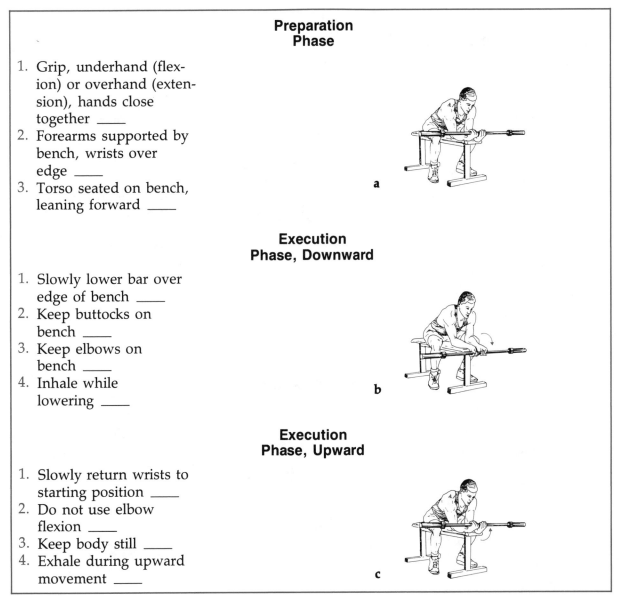

Preparation Phase

1. Grip, underhand (flexion) or overhand (extension), hands close together ____
2. Forearms supported by bench, wrists over edge ____
3. Torso seated on bench, leaning forward ____

a

Execution Phase, Downward

1. Slowly lower bar over edge of bench ____
2. Keep buttocks on bench ____
3. Keep elbows on bench ____
4. Inhale while lowering ____

b

Execution Phase, Upward

1. Slowly return wrists to starting position ____
2. Do not use elbow flexion ____
3. Keep body still ____
4. Exhale during upward movement ____

c

Alternative Exercises for Developing the Upper Legs

The back squat (see Figure A.8) develops the lower back (erector spinae), hips (gluteal muscle), front of upper leg (quadriceps), and back of the upper leg (hamstrings). The knee extension (see Figure A.9) and knee flexion (see Figure A.10) exercises develop the quadriceps and hamstrings, respectively. These exercises can be used as alternates for the lunge and leg press exercises presented in Step 9.

Caution: The back squat exercise should never be performed without a spotter. When only one spotter is available, this exercise should be performed in a rack similar to that shown in Figure A.8

Figure A.8   Keys to Success: Back Squat

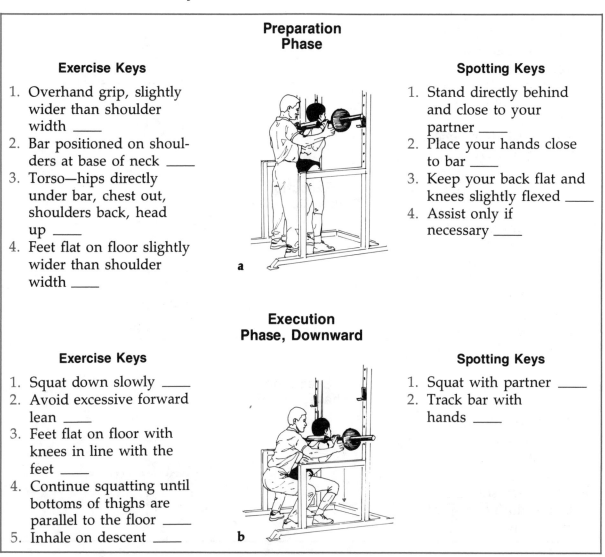

Preparation Phase

Exercise Keys

1. Overhand grip, slightly wider than shoulder width ____
2. Bar positioned on shoulders at base of neck ____
3. Torso—hips directly under bar, chest out, shoulders back, head up ____
4. Feet flat on floor slightly wider than shoulder width ____

Spotting Keys

1. Stand directly behind and close to your partner ____
2. Place your hands close to bar ____
3. Keep your back flat and knees slightly flexed ____
4. Assist only if necessary ____

a

Execution Phase, Downward

Exercise Keys

1. Squat down slowly ____
2. Avoid excessive forward lean ____
3. Feet flat on floor with knees in line with the feet ____
4. Continue squatting until bottoms of thighs are parallel to the floor ____
5. Inhale on descent ____

Spotting Keys

1. Squat with partner ____
2. Track bar with hands ____

b

Execution
Phase, Upward

Exercise Keys

1. Begin movement with legs first ____
2. Keep head up and chest out ____
3. Straighten hips and knees ____
4. Exhale during sticking point ____

Spotting Keys

1. Ascend with partner ____
2. Keep hands close to bar ____
3. Assist only when necessary ____

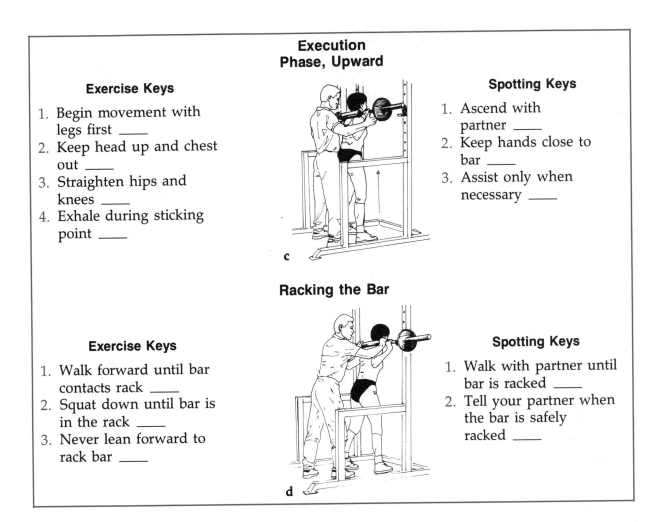

c

Racking the Bar

Exercise Keys

1. Walk forward until bar contacts rack ____
2. Squat down until bar is in the rack ____
3. Never lean forward to rack bar ____

Spotting Keys

1. Walk with partner until bar is racked ____
2. Tell your partner when the bar is safely racked ____

d

Figure A.9 Keys to Success: Knee Extension

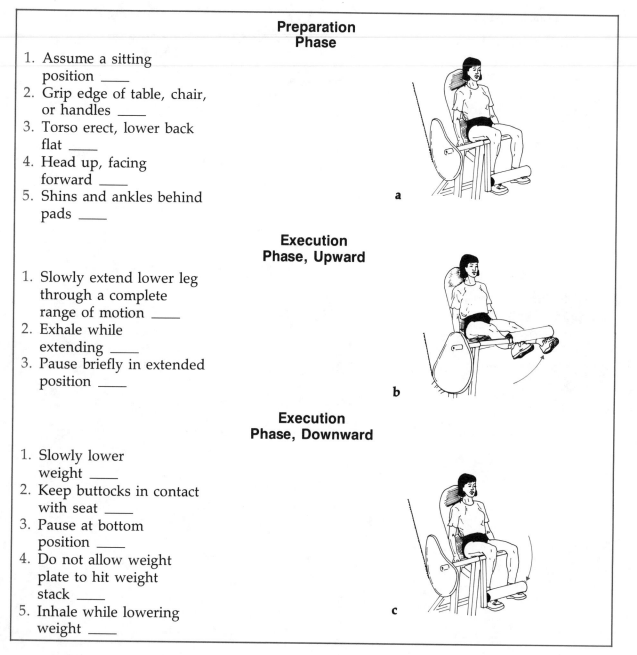

Preparation Phase

1. Assume a sitting position ____
2. Grip edge of table, chair, or handles ____
3. Torso erect, lower back flat ____
4. Head up, facing forward ____
5. Shins and ankles behind pads ____

a

Execution Phase, Upward

1. Slowly extend lower leg through a complete range of motion ____
2. Exhale while extending ____
3. Pause briefly in extended position ____

b

Execution Phase, Downward

1. Slowly lower weight ____
2. Keep buttocks in contact with seat ____
3. Pause at bottom position ____
4. Do not allow weight plate to hit weight stack ____
5. Inhale while lowering weight ____

c

Figure A.10 Keys to Success:
          Knee Flexion

Preparation Phase

1. Assume a prone position ____
2. Grip handles or edge of bench ____
3. Hips flat, chest on bench ____
4. Kneecaps below edge of bench, ankles under pads ____

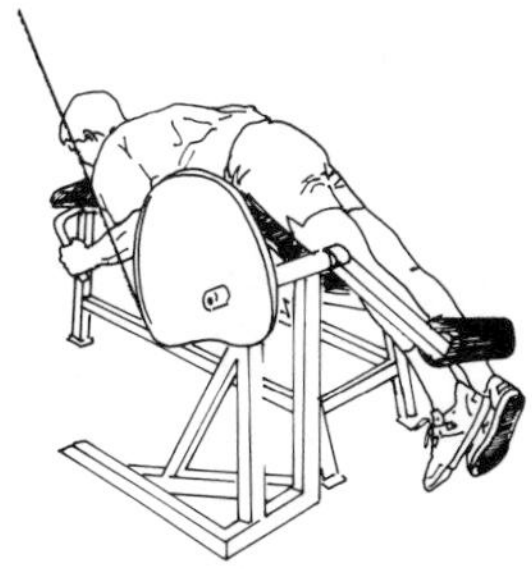

a

Execution Phase, Upward

1. Flex heels as far as possible toward buttocks ____
2. Exhale during upward movement ____
3. Pause briefly in fully flexed position ____

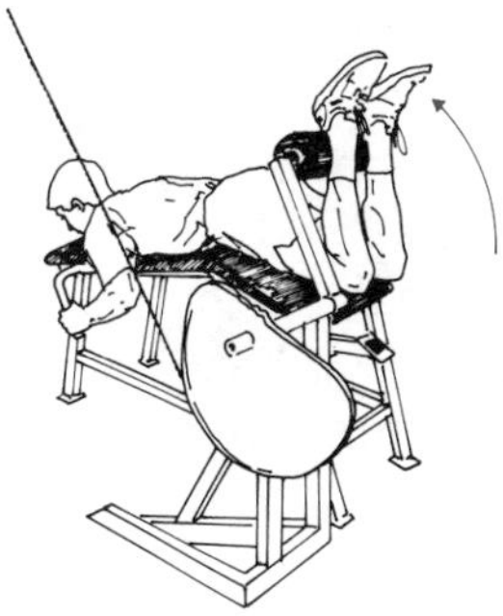

b

Execution Phase, Downward

1. Lower weight slowly ____
2. Do not allow hips to rise off bench ____
3. Keep chest on bench ____
4. Inhale during downward movement ____

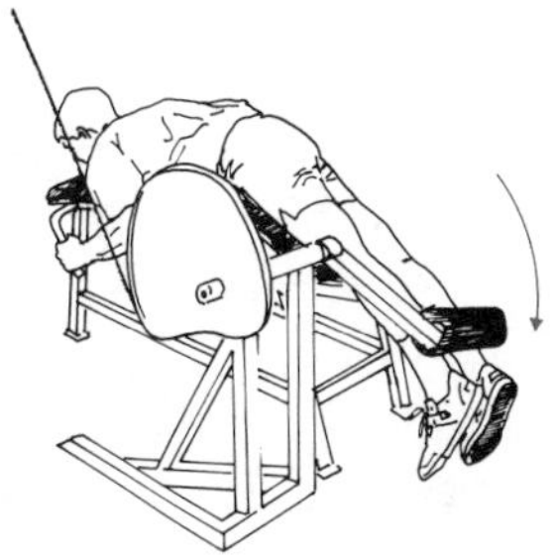

c

Alternative Exercise for Developing the Lower Leg (Calves)

Heel raises, or plantar flexion at the ankle joint, exercise the calf muscles (soleus, gastrocnemius). This exercise can be performed using a barbell across the shoulders, holding dumbbells (see Figure A.11), or using the overhead press station on a single- or multi-unit machine. Be sure that the board being used is stable.

Figure A.11 Keys to Success: Heel Raises

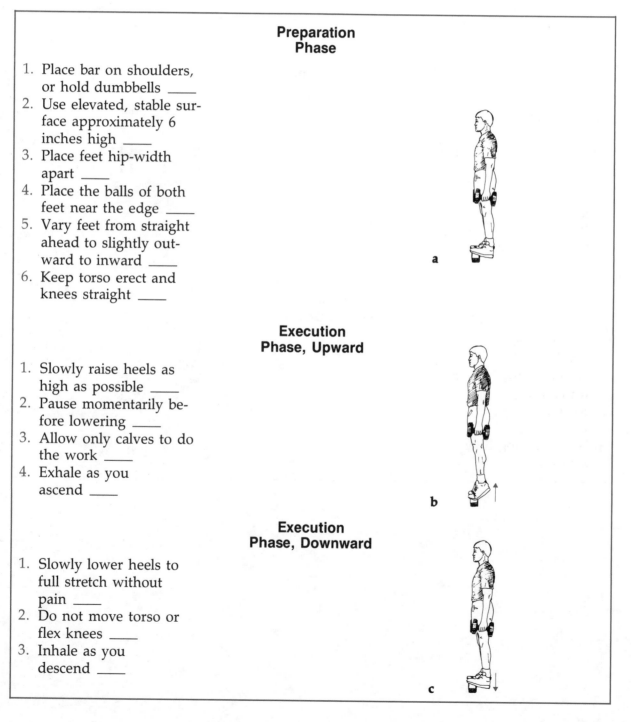

Preparation Phase

1. Place bar on shoulders, or hold dumbbells ____
2. Use elevated, stable surface approximately 6 inches high ____
3. Place feet hip-width apart ____
4. Place the balls of both feet near the edge ____
5. Vary feet from straight ahead to slightly outward to inward ____
6. Keep torso erect and knees straight ____

a

Execution Phase, Upward

1. Slowly raise heels as high as possible ____
2. Pause momentarily before lowering ____
3. Allow only calves to do the work ____
4. Exhale as you ascend ____

b

Execution Phase, Downward

1. Slowly lower heels to full stretch without pain ____
2. Do not move torso or flex knees ____
3. Inhale as you descend ____

c

Alternative Exercise for Developing the Abdominals

The bent-knee sit-up (see Figure A.12) can be performed either on a flat surface or on an incline board. Begin performing this exercise on a flat surface. The bent-knee sit-up is completed when the shoulders are elevated 30 to 45 degrees and then returned to the starting position. This exercise is a supplement or an alternative to the Twisting Trunk Curl and the Machine Curl presented in Step 10.

Figure A.12   Keys to Success:
Bent-Knee Sit-Up

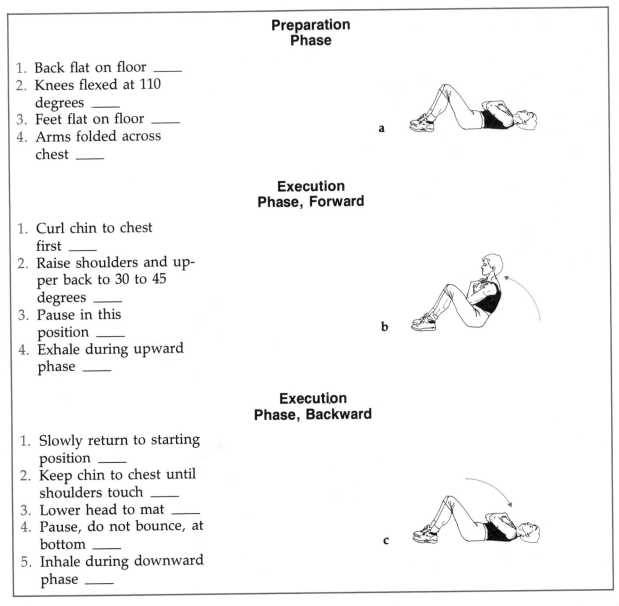

Preparation Phase

1. Back flat on floor ____
2. Knees flexed at 110 degrees ____
3. Feet flat on floor ____
4. Arms folded across chest ____

a

Execution Phase, Forward

1. Curl chin to chest first ____
2. Raise shoulders and upper back to 30 to 45 degrees ____
3. Pause in this position ____
4. Exhale during upward phase ____

b

Execution Phase, Backward

1. Slowly return to starting position ____
2. Keep chin to chest until shoulders touch ____
3. Lower head to mat ____
4. Pause, do not bounce, at bottom ____
5. Inhale during downward phase ____

c

Appendix B Muscles of the Body

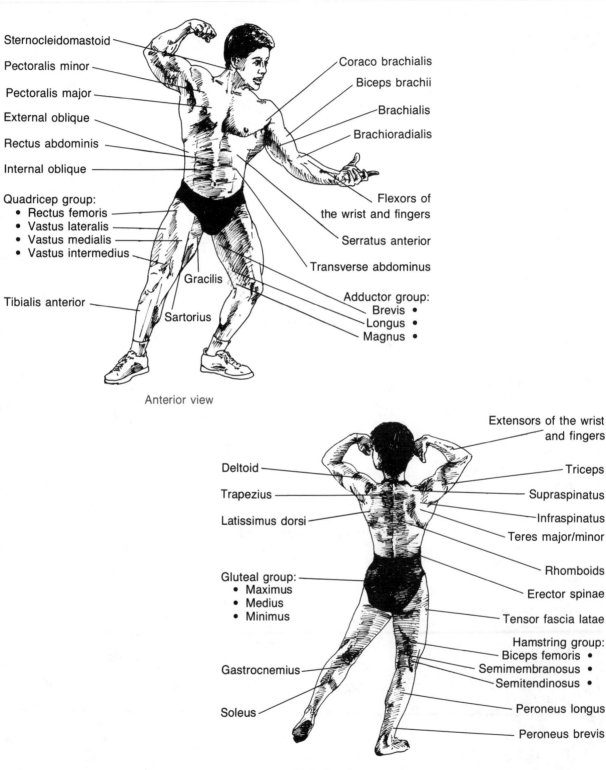

Sternocleidomastoid

Pectoralis minor

Pectoralis major

External oblique

Rectus abdominis

Internal oblique

Quadricep group:
- Rectus femoris
- Vastus lateralis
- Vastus medialis
- Vastus intermedius

Gracilis

Tibialis anterior

Sartorius

Coraco brachialis

Biceps brachii

Brachialis

Brachioradialis

Flexors of the wrist and fingers

Serratus anterior

Transverse abdominus

Adductor group:
- Brevis
- Longus
- Magnus

Anterior view

Deltoid

Trapezius

Latissimus dorsi

Gluteal group:
- Maximus
- Medius
- Minimus

Gastrocnemius

Soleus

Extensors of the wrist and fingers

Triceps

Supraspinatus

Infraspinatus

Teres major/minor

Rhomboids

Erector spinae

Tensor fascia latae

Hamstring group:
- Biceps femoris
- Semimembranosus
- Semitendinosus

Peroneus longus

Peroneus brevis

Posterior view

Appendix C Weight Training Workout Chart

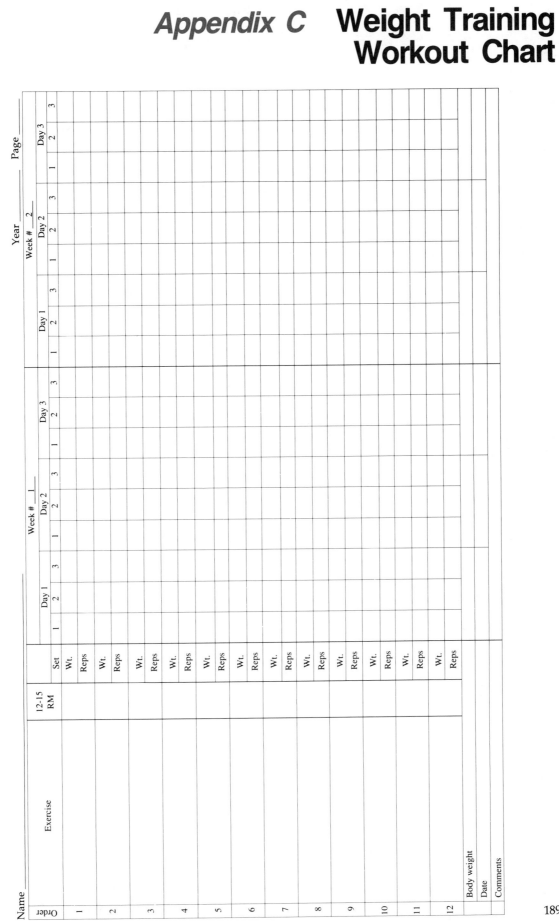

189

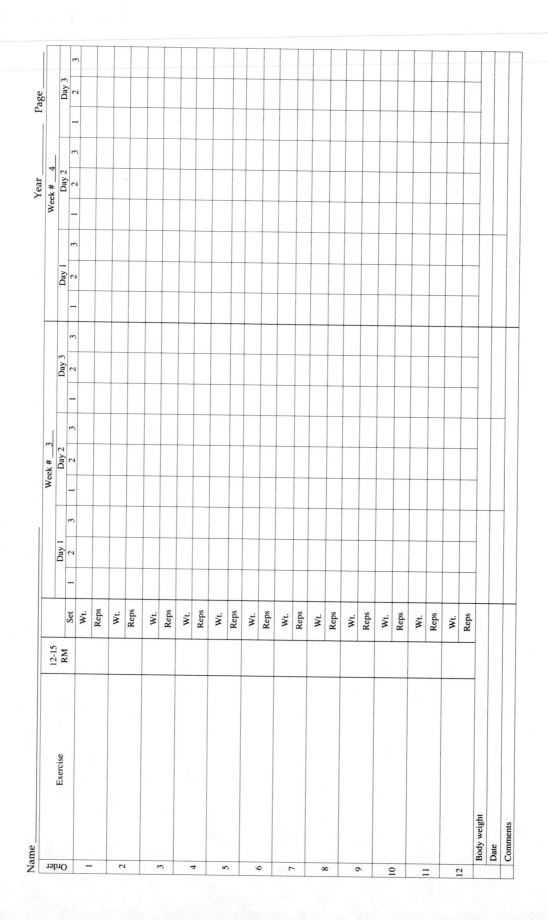

Name _____   Year _____   Page _____

Order	Exercise	12-15 RM	Set	Week # 5 Day 1 1	2	3	Day 2 1	2	3	Day 3 1	2	3	Week # 6 Day 1 1	2	3	Day 2 1	2	3	Day 3 1	2	3
1			Wt.																		
			Reps																		
2			Wt.																		
			Reps																		
3			Wt.																		
			Reps																		
4			Wt.																		
			Reps																		
5			Wt.																		
			Reps																		
6			Wt.																		
			Reps																		
7			Wt.																		
			Reps																		
8			Wt.																		
			Reps																		
9			Wt.																		
			Reps																		
10			Wt.																		
			Reps																		
11			Wt.																		
			Reps																		
12			Wt.																		
			Reps																		

Body weight

Date

Comments

Glossary

absolute strength—A comparative expression of strength based upon actual load lifted.

adipose tissue—Fat tissue.

aerobic—In the presence of oxygen.

aerobic capacity—A measurement of physical fitness based on maximum oxygen uptake.

aerobic energy system—The metabolic pathway that requires oxygen for the production of ATP.

aerobic exercise—When a person is exercising aerobically, the muscle cells are receiving enough oxygen to continue at a steady state. Walking, biking, running, swimming, and cross-country skiing are examples of this type of exercise.

all-or-none law—A muscle cell that is stimulated by the brain will contract maximally or not at all; a stimulus of insufficient intensity will not elicit a contraction.

alternated grip—A grip where one hand is supinated and the other hand is pronated. Also called a reverse grip. It is the grip used in the dead lift exercise and for spotting the bench press. Thumbs point in the same direction.

amino acids—Nitrogen-containing compounds that form the building blocks of protein.

anabolic—Tissue building that is conducive to the constructive process of metabolism.

anabolic steroid—Testosterone, or a steroid resembling testosterone, which stimulates the body anabolically as well as androgenically.

anaerobic—In the absence of oxygen.

anaerobic exercise—Exercise during which the energy needed is provided without the utilization of inspired oxygen. Examples include weight lifting and the 100-meter sprint.

androgen—Any compound that has masculinizing properties.

atrophy—A decrease in the cross-sectional size of the muscle fiber due to a lack of use or disease.

assistance exercises—Exercises that are used as the supplementary exercises to the main or core exercise. For example, knee extensions may be used as a supplement to the squat.

barbell—A piece of free weight equipment that consists of a long bar with weight plates on each end and is to be used in two-arm exercises.

basal metabolic rate (BMR)—The amount of energy, expressed in kilocalories, that the body requires to carry on its normal functions at rest.

bodybuilding—A sport that involves weight training to develop muscle hypertrophy. Bodybuilders are judged on their muscle size, definition, symmetry, and posing skill.

body composition—The quantification of the various components of the body, especially fat and muscle. Various methods exist for its determination: skinfold calipers, girth measurement, impedance methods, and underwater (hydrostatic) weighing are commonly used.

calorie—The measure of the amount of energy released from food or expended in metabolism (exercise). The standard unit is termed a kilocalorie (Kcal or Calorie), or 1,000 calories, but is usually incorrectly expressed by many as simply a "calorie." One kilocalorie is the amount of energy required to raise one kilogram of water one degree centigrade.

carbohydrate (CHO)—A group of chemical compounds composed of carbon, hydrogen, and oxygen. Examples include sugars, starches, and cellulose. It is a basic foodstuff that contains approximately 4 kilocalories per gram.

cardiac muscle—A type of striated involuntary muscle tissue located only in the heart.

cardiorespiratory fitness—(cardio—heart, respiratory—lungs) This category of fitness pertains to the efficiency of the heart and lungs to deliver oxygen to the working muscles.

circuit training—A variation of interval training that uses weights and timed work and rest periods. This type of weight training program is typically designed to increase muscular endurance.

compound set—Performing two exercises consecutively that work the same muscle group, without rest between them. For example, a compound set for the chest would be a set of bench presses followed immediately by a set of dumbbell flys. Often this method of training is misnamed a "super set."

concentric muscular contraction—A type of muscular contraction characterized by tension being developed while the muscle is shortening (e.g., the upward phase of a bicep curl).

conditioning—A process of improving the capacity of the body to produce energy and do work.

cool-down—The period in which an individual performs light or mild exercise immediately following competition or a training session. The primary purpose of a cool-down is to hasten the removal of lactic acid from the muscles and allow the body to gradually return to a resting state.

core exercises—The primary weight training exercises that stress the large muscle groups of the body.

cycles—A specific period of time (weeks, months, or years) over which the volume, intensity, and mode of training are varied to promote continued progress in a systematically organized program.

cycling—Changing the frequency, duration, intensity, and specificity of the training schedule.

dumbbell—A piece of weight training equipment that consists of a short bar with weight plates on each end that is used in single-arm exercises.

dynamic—Moving, or nonstationary.

dynamic contraction—Involves movement and consists of concentric, eccentric, or both types of contraction.

eccentric muscular contraction—A muscular contraction in which the muscle actually lengthens while tension is being developed. An example can be seen in the pull-up exercise when an individual's body gradually gets farther away from the bar instead of closer. Eccentric muscle contractions are associated with the muscle soreness commonly experienced in dynamic weight training.

essential fat—The fat stored in the marrow of the bones as well as in the heart, lungs, liver, spleen, kidneys, muscles, and lipid-rich tissues throughout the central nervous system. A minimum value of 3 percent for males and 12 percent in females is required for normal physiological functioning.

exercise prescription—An exercise program based on present fitness levels and desired goals or outcomes.

extension—A movement occurring at a joint that increases the angle of the joint. The tricep push-down movement is an example of elbow extension.

fast-twitch fiber—A type of skeletal muscle fiber that is highly recruited during explosive muscular activities (e.g., sprinting, shot-putting, and competitive weight lifting). White muscle fiber.

fat—Nonmetabolically active tissue that contains 9 kilocalories per gram and should constitute approximately 25 to 30 percent of the diet.

flexibility—The ability of a joint to move through its range of motion.

flexion—A movement occurring at a joint that decreases the angle of the joint. The bicep curl movement is an example of elbow flexion.

free weight—An object of determined weight used for physical conditioning and competitive lifting. Examples include barbells and dumbbells.

frequency—The number of training sessions in a given time period.

hormone—A chemical substance secreted by an endocrine gland that has a specific effect on activities of other cells, tissues, and organs.

hydrostatic weighing—A method of body-composition determination utilizing underwater weighing and calculation of body volume and density. Generally accepted as the most accurate method of determining body composition.

hyperplasia—An increase in muscle size due to muscle fibers splitting and forming separate fibers. As of yet, hyperplasia has not been scientifically proven to occur in humans.

hypertension—High blood pressure. Systolic BP over 140 mmHg and/or diastolic BP over 90 mmHg.

hypertrophy—A term used to describe an increase in the cross-sectional area of the muscle. More simply stated, an increase in muscle size.

hyperventilation—Excessive ventilation of the lungs, caused by the increased depth and frequency of breathing and usually resulting in the elimination of carbon dioxide. Accompanying symptoms include low blood pressure, dizziness, and rapid breathing.

intensity—The relative stress level that the exercise stimulus places on the appropriate system. In essence, the amount of work completed in a specified period of time.

ischemia—A condition where there is reduced supply of oxygen to working tissues.

isokinetic—A type of muscular activity in which contractions occur at a constant velocity as controlled by an ergometer. The term can only describe a concentric (dynamic) muscle contraction.

isometric (or static) contraction—A type of muscular activity in which the muscle does not shorten, because the bony attachments are fixed or the forces functioning to lengthen the muscle are countered by forces that are equal to or greater than generated by the muscle to shorten.

isotonic—Implies a dynamic event in which the muscle generates the same amount of force throughout the entire movement. Such a condition occurs infrequently, if at all, in human performance. Therefore, it is proposed that the term should not be employed to describe human exercise performance. In loose terms, however, it is used to describe dynamic free weight exercises and some machine exercises.

kilocalorie (Kcal)—A unit of work or energy equal to the amount of heat required to raise the temperature of 1 kilogram of water 1 degree Celsius. A quantity of energy equal to 1,000 calories.

lean body weight—Body weight minus fat weight; nonfat or fat-free weight.

ligament—Dense connective tissue that attaches two articulating surfaces of bone together.

load—Total amount of weight lifted.

locks—On barbells or dumbbells, these are located on the outside of the collars and serve to hold the plates (weights) on the bar.

metabolism—The sum total of the chemical changes or reactions occurring in the body.

motor unit—An individual motor nerve and all the muscle fibers it innervates (stimulates).

movement pattern—The line of travel of the body and the bar or equipment during a repetition.

multipurpose machine—A training apparatus that has several exercise stations.

multiple sets—Performing more than one set of an exercise (after a rest period) before moving to another.

muscle-bound—A term that has been used to link individuals who weight train with limited joint flexibility. This reduced flexibility can be due to a lack of muscle activity or to chronic use of poor lifting and stretching methods. The term is inappropriate for those who practice sound weight training techniques and proper stretching exercises.

muscle contraction—The active state of muscle. The attempt of a muscle cell or muscle tissue to shorten along the longitudinal axis when activated.

muscular endurance—The capacity of a muscle to repeatedly contract over a period of time without undue fatigue. This is a local muscle characteristic.

muscular strength—The capacity of a muscle to contract maximally once. This is a local muscle characteristic.

Nautilus—A brand of dynamic resistance training equipment.

negative exercise—A form of exercise in which the muscle lengthens rather than shortens during muscular tension. Also termed eccentric exercise.

nutrition—The study of food and how the body uses it. The sum total of the processes involved in taking in food and the subsequent metabolic effects.

Olympic bar—It is approximately 7 feet in length and has rotating sleeves on the ends to hold the weights. The diameter of the bar is about 1 inch in the middle and 2 inches at the ends. Its weight is 45 pounds; with locks it weighs 55 pounds.

Olympic weight lifting—Competitive lifting that involves execution of the clean and jerk and the snatch.

one-repetition maximum (1RM)—The resistance (load) at which the individual can perform only one repetition.

overhand grip—The hands grip the bar so that the palms are pronated (face down) toward the legs or away from the body with the thumbs toward the center of the bar.

overload principle—Progressively increasing the intensity or volume of workouts over the course of a training program as exercise tolerance improves.

overtraining—A state of undue mental and/or physical fatigue brought about by excessive physical activity without sufficient rest.

oxygen uptake—The ability of the heart and lungs to take in and utilize oxygen. Commonly expressed in milliliters of oxygen per kilogram of body weight per minute ($ml \cdot kg^{-1} \cdot min^{-1}$).

percent body fat—The percentage of body weight that is comprised of fat. The ratio of fat versus fat-free weight. Recommended ranges are 14 to 18 percent for men and 22 to 26 percent for women.

physical fitness—A product of a high level of cardiorespiratory endurance, muscular strength, muscular endurance, and flexibility and a low ratio of body fat to lean body weight.

power lifting—A sport that involves weight training to develop maximum muscular strength in the back squat, bench press, and dead lift exercises.

progressive resistance—Gradually increasing the load (intensity) over time to induce improvements toward a particular exercise goal.

pronated grip—Grasping the bar so the palm is facing down, and thumbs face each other. Also termed an overhand grip.

protein—A food substance that provides the amino acids essential for the growth and repair of tissue and contains approximately 4 kilocalories per gram.

pyramid training—A method of using progressively heavier or lighter loads within a single training session.

quick-lift exercise—A weight training exercise characterized by explosive movements; examples include the power clean, snatch, and hang clean.

range of motion (ROM)—The entire movement through which a body part rotates around a joint.

recruitment—The activation of motor units by the neuromuscular system during a contraction.

relative strength—A comparative measure of strength based upon some variable such as total body weight or lean body weight.

repetition(s)—A completed execution of an exercise. The number of consecutive contractions performed for a particular set of an exercise. Also known as rep(s).

repetition maximal (RM)—The maximum load that a muscle group can lift over a given number of repetitions before fatiguing. For example, a 10RM load is the *maximal* load that can be lifted for 10 repetitions.

resistance training—Any method or form of exercise requiring one to resist or exert force.

rest interval—A given amount of time for the pause between sets or exercises.

set—In weight training, the number of repetitions performed consecutively without resting.

slow-twitch fiber—A type of skeletal muscle fiber that has the ability to repeatedly contract without undue fatigue. This type of muscle fiber is highly recruited for long-distance running, swimming, and cycling events. Red muscle fiber.

smooth muscle—A type of involuntary muscle tissue located in the eyes, and in the walls of the stomach, intestines, bladder, uterus, and blood vessels.

specificity of training—The idea that one should train in a specific manner for a specific outcome. The specific demands of the sport or the desired goals should be determined before designing a resistance training program.

split system (split routine)—A weight training program that typically includes upper body exercises and lower body exercises on alternate days.

squat rack—Standards used to hold a barbell at shoulder height; typically used in placing the bar on the back for the squat exercise.

standard bar—A bar 1 inch in diameter, used for weight training, that typically weighs approximately 5 pounds per foot.

static stretch—Involves holding a static position, passively placing the muscles and connective tissues on stretch.

sticking point—The point in the range of motion of an exercise that is the most difficult to move the weight through.

strength plateau—A temporary leveling off of progress in a strength-training program.

strength training—The use of resistance methods to increase one's ability to exert or resist force for the purpose of improving performance. The training may utilize free weights, the individual's own body weight, machines, or other devices to attain this goal.

striated muscle—Skeletal muscle possessing alternate light and dark bands, or striations. Except for the cardiac muscle, all striated muscles are voluntary.

super set—Consecutively performing two exercises that train opposing muscle groups, without rest between the two exercises.

supinated grip—Grasping the bar so the palms face upward, and thumbs are in opposite directions. Also termed an underhand grip.

supine—Lying on the back, facing upward; the opposite of prone.

supplemental exercise—Exercises used in addition to main or core exercises to enhance a sport-specific movement or to correct a weakness. Sometimes referred to as assistance or noncore exercises.

tendon—Dense connective tissue that attaches a muscle to a bone.

testosterone—A hormone responsible for male sex characteristics.

underwater weighing—A technique utilized to determine body density. Knowing the density of the body, the percentage of body fat can be calculated. Also termed hydrostatic weighing.

Universal—A brand of dynamic resistance equipment.

variation—Manipulating the frequency, intensity, duration, and/or mode of an exercise program to promote maximal improvements with minimal opportunities for overtraining (both mental and physical).

vitamin—An organic material that acts as a catalyst for vital chemical (metabolic) reactions.

volume—The total work load per exercise, per session, per week, etc. In weight training, the volume is proportional to the total number of repetitions times the total amount of weight. Sometimes volume is defined as sets times the number of reps.

warm-up—The period in which an individual performs light or mild exercise immediately before a competition or training session. The primary purpose of the warm-up is to prepare the body for more intense exercise.

weight training—Exercises performed against resistance to improve the quality of the exercising muscles in individuals who are training for improved fitness.

References

American College of Sports Medicine. (1987). Position stand on the use of anabolic-androgenic steroids in sports. *Medicine and Science in Sports and Exercise*, **10** (19), 534-537.

Corbin, C., & Lindsey, R. (1988). *Concepts of physical fitness with laboratories* (6th ed.) Dubuque, IA: Brown.

Baechle, T.R., & Earle, R. (1989). *Weight training: A text for the college student*. Omaha: Creighton University Publishers.

Fleck, S., & Kraemer, W. (1987). *Designing resistance training*. Champaign, IL: Human Kinetics.

Garhammer, J. (1986). *Sports Illustrated strength training*. New York: Harper & Row.

Getchell, B. (1983). *Physical fitness a way of life* (3rd ed.). New York: Wiley.

Hoeger, W.K. (1989). *Lifetime fitness, physical fitness and wellness* (2nd ed.) Englewood, CO: Morton.

Holloway, J., & Baechle, T.R. (1990). Strength training for female athletes. *Sports medicine*, **9** (4), 216-228.

Kraemer, W., & Baechle, T.R. (1989). Development of a strength training program. In J. Ryan & F.L. Allman, Jr. (Eds)., *Sports medicine* (pp. 113-127) (2nd. ed.) San Diego, CA: Academic Press.

Lombardi, V.P. (1989). *Beginning weight training: The safe and effective way*. Dubuque, IA: Brown.

O'Shea, J.P. (1976). *Scientific principles and methods of strength fitness*. Menlo Park, CA: Addison-Wesley.

Pauletto, B. (1991). *Strength training for coaches*. Champaign, IL: Human Kinetics.

Position paper on strength training for female athletes. (1990). Lincoln, NE: National Strength and Conditioning Association.

Stone, M., & O'Bryant, H. (1987). *Weight training: A scientific approach*. Minneapolis: Burgess.

Vickers, J.N. (1990). *Instructional Design for Teaching Physical Activities*. Champaign, IL: Human Kinetics.

Wright, J.E., & Stone, M.H. (1985). *Position paper on anabolic drug use by athletes*. Lincoln, NE: National Strength and Conditioning Association.

About the Authors

Thomas R. Baechle competed successfully for 16 years in weightlifting and powerlifting, setting various Midwest records. For more than 20 years, he has coached collegiate powerlifting teams and taught weight training classes. He received his doctoral degree in adult and higher education from the University of South Dakota in 1976 and is an associate professor and chair of the Department of Physical Education/Exercise Science at Creighton University, where he also serves as director of strength training and conditioning. In addition to being a past president of the National Strength and Conditioning Association (NSCA), Dr. Baechle is the NSCA Director of Certification and an NSCA-certified Strength and Conditioning Specialist. In 1985 he was named Strength Coach of the Year by NSCA. Dr. Baechle also holds certifications as a Level I weightlifting coach from the United States Weightlifting Federation and as a test technologist and exercise specialist from the American College of Sports Medicine (ACSM). He has held various offices in the American Alliance for Health, Physical Education, Recreation and Dance (AAHPERD).

Barney R. Groves has also taught weight training classes for more than 20 years. He received his doctoral degree in physical education from Florida State University and is associate professor of physical education in the Department of Physical Education at Virginia Commonwealth University, where he also serves as strength and conditioning coach and a weight training instructor. He is certified as a Strength and Conditioning Specialist by the NSCA and as a Health/Fitness Instructor by the ACSM. Dr. Groves is a member of the AAHPERD.